RITUAL AND DEFERENCE

SUNY series in Chinese Philosophy and Culture

Roger T. Ames, editor

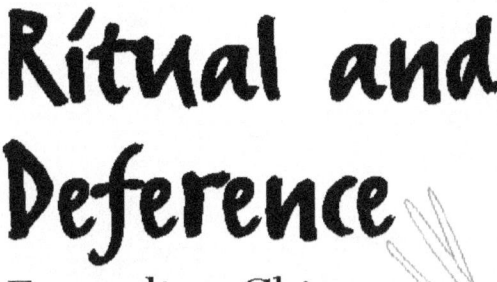

Ritual and Deference

Extending Chinese Philosophy in a Comparative Context

ROBERT CUMMINGS NEVILLE

State University of New York Press

Published by
State University of New York Press, Albany

© 2008 State University of New York

All rights reserved

Printed in the United States of America

No part of this book may be used or reproduced in any manner whatsoever without written permission. No part of this book may be stored in a retrieval system or transmitted in any form or by any means including electronic, electrostatic, magnetic tape, mechanical, photocopying, recording, or otherwise without the prior permission in writing of the publisher.

For information, contact State University of New York Press, Albany, NY
www.sunypress.edu

Production by Marilyn P. Semerad
Marketing by Fran Keneston

Library of Congress Cataloging-in-Publication Data

Neville, Robert C.
   Ritual and deference : extending Chinese philosophy in a comparative context / Robert Cummings Neville.
     p. cm. — (Suny series in chinese philosophy and culture)
   Includes bibliographical references and index.
   ISBN 978-0-7914-7457-0 (alk. paper)
   ISBN 978-0-7914-7458-7 (pbk. : alk. paper)

1. Philosophy, Chinese—To 221 B.C. 2. Philosophy, Comparative. I. Title.
II. Title: Extending Chinese philosophy in a comparative context.

B126.N45 2008
181'.11—dc22

                                                                        2007035300

For John H. Berthrong
Mentor, Colleague, Friend

Contents

PREFACE		xi
ONE	A Confucian Program	1
	Metaphysics	2
	Philosophical Cosmology	5
	Human Nature	7
	Social Theory	10
TWO	The Significance of Confucian Values	15
	Values for the Good Life: Conventional, Yet Normative	15
	A Confucian Solution: Ritual	18
	High Civilizations: Competing Values and Global Rituals	20
	A Homily on Humaneness	23
THREE	Ritual in Xunzi	27
	Initial Considerations of Ritual in Xunzi	27
	Ritual and Semiotics	30
	Ritual and Desire	33
	Ritual, Integration, and Religion	35
FOUR	Daoist Relativism, Ethical Choice, and Normative Measure	41
	A Metaphysical Daoism	43
	Normative Measure	48
	Daoist Ethics	51
	Daoism and Confucianism Compared	54

CONTENTS

FIVE	Chinese Influences in English-Speaking Philosophy	59
	Scholarly Influences	60
	Roger T. Ames and David L. Hall	64
	Tu Weiming and Cheng Chungying	66
	Wu Kuangming	71
SIX	Methodology, Practices, and Disciplines in Chinese and Western Philosophy	75
	The Problem	75
	Methodology as a Concern	77
	Philosophical Practices	80
	Philosophical Discipline	85
SEVEN	Metaphysics for Contemporary Chinese Philosophy	89
	The Need for Metaphysics	90
	Themes of Chinese Philosophy	92
	Metaphysical Directions	95
EIGHT	The Conscious and Unconscious Placing of Ritual and Humanity	101
	The Unconscious as a Problem for Confucian Virtue	101
	Ritual and Humaneness	103
	Deceptions of the Heart: Freud	105
	Deceptions of the Heart: Marx	109
NINE	The Contemporary Mutual Development of Confucianism and Christianity	113
	From Reformation of the Inner Heart to Loving the World	114
	The Location of Ethical Analysis and Rectifying Power	116
	Peace, Action, and Retreat	118
TEN	The Personal and the Impersonal in Conceptions of Divinity	121
	Popular versus Sophisticated Religion Hypothesis	122
	Development Hypothesis: Pre-Axial Age and Axial Age	123
	Semiotic Hypothesis	124
	Ontological-Anthropological Continuum Hypothesis	125

ELEVEN	On Comparison	127
	Models of Comparative Theology	127
	Objectivist Comparison	133
	Normative Comparison	140
	Beyond Comparative to Integrative Philosophy	142
TWELVE	Contributions of Chinese Philosophy: A Summary Discussion	149
	The Happy Portability of Chinese Philosophy	149
	Ritual, Again	153
	Ethics, Again	155
	Orientation and the Self	157
NOTES		163
INDEX		187

Preface

This book is intended for thinkers who have, or ought to have, an interest in comparative philosophy embracing Chinese and Western traditions. My own formal education was strictly in Western philosophy, religion, and culture. Introduced to Chinese philosophy (and Indian philosophy) by Thomas Berry at Fordham University, I could not easily understand my enthusiasm for the Chinese traditions. Indian philosophy was interesting to me, as was a range of other "non-Western" traditions, but none held the degree of fascination China did. Comparative philosophy has helped me see how my particular enthusiasms within Chinese philosophy connect with my enthusiasms in Western thinking.

Unlike most Western thinkers, I have been unable to make any intellectually satisfactory or practically helpful distinction between philosophy and religion. To put the matter more precisely, I have been unable to distinguish between the living practice of philosophy and the practice of religion by intellectually curious people. So I think of myself as a philosopher, or theologian, or philosophical theologian, or philosopher of religion, or religious philosopher, who draws constructively from Chinese as well as Western sources, and from others.

Primarily what I do with these sources is to construct a philosophy with which to engage the issues of our time, including the perennial ones. This philosophy is a complex hypothesis, or a set of hypotheses, or a bunch of hypotheses, that are tested for coherence and consistency, applicability to our world, adequacy in representing the things of importance within it, and fruitfulness in advancing the global conversation about what to be and do. The cases to be made for the various points in my philosophy are of many different sorts, but rarely of the sort that says my hypothesis is strictly true and everyone else's is mistaken. Rather, I usually want to call attention to points that other philosophies neglect, and to criticize that neglect while making my own hypotheses vulnerable to correction. The chapters in this book collectively represent a partial reading of Chinese philosophy, often in explicit comparison with philosophies from other traditions, and as making a contribution to the larger world philosophic dialogue.

I write as a constructive and systematic philosopher (although my own system is not much expressed directly in this volume), not as a Sinologist. Most English-speakers writing about Chinese philosophy are Sinologists, and will immediately see the failures in these chapters to exhibit the discipline and perspective of Sinology. The virtues I hope they see instead are the particular insights that come from engaging the Chinese tradition as a living philosophy. The reception of my *Boston Confucianism: Portable Tradition in the Late-Modern World* encourages me to stake out a place as a Confucian philosopher and practitioner.[1] I hope readers will overlook the hubris involved in suggesting that one of the many interesting ways in which Confucianism is being developed in our time is the way my philosophy does so. Although I share the Confucian tradition's emphasis on ethics, self-cultivation, and social philosophy, I also have devoted much time to metaphysical issues. The metaphysical system I have been developing derives many of its terms and issues from Western philosophy. Nevertheless, it gives contemporary representation to fundamental Confucian metaphysical themes such as process, organic connection, the pervasiveness of value, a continuum of immanent and relatively transcendent principles, and the conviction that metaphysics is pragmatically necessary for living well. Systematic thinking is for the sake of deepening practice to make it more attentive to the truly important things in the world. All these themes are Platonic as well as Confucian, and all comport with certain traditions within Christian theology. So I admit to being a Platonist and Christian, as well as a Confucian. In modern terms, I am an heir and extender of pragmatism as well.

Some thinkers are deeply concerned with "membership," that is, with whether one is truly and wholehearted committed to one's tradition. In Chinese philosophy this concern manifests itself in disputes about the "true lineage" of Confucianism. For instance, Zhu Xi read Xunzi out of the lineage when he edited the classics, and, more recently, Mou Zhongsan suggested that Wang Yangming rather than Zhu Xi is the authentic transmitter of the Mencian tradition. Western philosophy has had a myriad of schools of Platonism, not only Ancient, Middle, and Neo. Christianity, of course, is rife with divisions. Many Christians believe that salvation depends on whether one belongs to their particular sect, and not to the others, surely not to a non-Christian group. For thinkers concerned with membership, it often seems impossible to be a Confucian, Platonist, and Christian at once.

I do not share this deep concern for membership. In each of the sources commended for contemporary life, we should emphasize some strains and not others. Given the contradictions, even violent contradictions, between kinds of Christianity, only some can be affirmed. I have a particular reading of Platonism quite different from the readings popularized by Aristotelians (who tend to treat him as a dualist who believed in independent existence for separate forms). In contrast to several of my close Confucian colleagues, for instance, Tu Weiming, Cheng Chungying, and Liu Shu-hsien, all of whom take their agenda from an extension of Neo-Confucianism, I take mine from ancient Confucianism, particularly from Xunzi's reading of Confucius. In this I join with Roger Ames and David Hall, although we differ on other issues. The point is, a constructive philosophy draws affirmatively from a highly select reading of its sources. The corollary is that a large part of the defense of a philosophy comes from dialogue about why these strains are the ones to affirm and others to suppress.

The chapters in this volume all originated as invited lectures or essays solicited for particular occasions or projects. Although they have been edited to cohere in this book, with cross-references and the elimination of some repetition, their different tones reflect the differences in their origins. Originally stand-alone presentations, they have accessibility rare in my usually oh-so-serious, turgid, monographic prose. The first two chapters express my most general assessment of what is valuable in Confucianism for the contemporary age and articulate the development of these themes as projects. Chapter 1 began as the Daxia Lecture for 2005, delivered at the East China Normal University in Shanghai, under the original title "The Expanding Family of Contemporary Confucian Thought." It was translated into Chinese and I understand has circulated widely over the internet in China. The chapter, as an introduction to this volume, claims that the Confucian tradition has worthy themes to develop in metaphysics, cosmology, the understanding of human nature and experience, and in social theory. But those themes need to be restated in ways that connect with the larger philosophical discussion for Confucianism to be a vital participant in the dialogue.

Chapter 2 originated as "The Contemporary Significance of Confucian Values," a lecture at a conference in Seoul, Korea, honoring Yulgok on the general theme "From Chaos to Order," in February 2005; it was published in English, Korean, and Chinese, in the *Journal of Yulgok Studies* 1:1 (Fall 2005). A briefer version of the lecture was delivered at the 2004 meeting of the American Philosophical Association. Its principal thesis is that Confucian values can be rearticulated to express a conception of the "good life" in a global, multicultural context in which basic values in life are disputed; the chief Confucian contribution is its theory of ritual for how one can negotiate fundamental differences about the good life.

Chapter 3 is an analysis of ritual and desire in Xunzi, the great ancient theoretician of Confucian ritual themes. It expands on the remarks about Xunzi's ritual theory in chapter 2 and argues that Charles Peirce's pragmatic semiotic theory is well suited to bring ritual theory into the present discussion. Then it analyzes the role of ritual in the formation of desire, according to Xunzi, and the role of desire in forming great civilizational values such as the "good life." The competition among desires, and the martial and psychic forces required for their integration in ritual, together constitute a conception of the inner self as filled with explosive contradictions, under pressure, that relates far more closely to post-Freudian and Nietzschean thinking than to the relatively simpler idealism of Mencius. An earlier version of this chapter is forthcoming in a volume of essays on Xunzi edited by T. C. Kline III.

Chapter 4 continues the exploration of the ancient Chinese tradition with a focus on Daoist ethics, and some comparisons with the Confucian. Whereas metaphysics has often been an assumed subtheme in Confucianism, in philosophical Daoism the vision of nature and its fundamental characters is an immediate and important source for ethics. The chapter explores Daoist metaphysics in the *Daodejing* and in Wangbi. A critical difference between Daoist and Confucian approaches to ethics derives from their different senses of timing. Whereas for the classical philosophical Daoists the continuities and spontaneous changes in nature set the time, for the Confucians time is kept by the scale of human projects, administering the yearly changes, raising a family, getting through the semester. The first three sections of this chapter began with a version published with the same title in the *Journal of Chinese Philosophy* 29:1 (March 2002), pp. 5–20.

Chapters 5 and 6 deal with the reception and use of Chinese philosophy in the contemporary situation. Chapter 5 classifies and surveys influences of Chinese philosophy in the English-speaking world, from translations to working philosophers. Several of our contemporary thinkers, in English, about Chinese philosophy are discussed at length. The chapter began as an article called "Chinese Philosophy in English-Speaking Countries," published in Chinese in a volume entitled *The Map of Contemporary British and American Philosophy*, edited by Kang Ouyang and Steve Fuller (Beijing: People's Press, 2005); more material from that article is in chapter 12. Chapter 6, which in an early draft was published with the title "Methodology, Practices, and Discipline in Chinese and Western Philosophy" in *Two Roads to Wisdom?*, edited by Bo Mou (LaSalle, IL: Open Court, 2001), discusses at length what the practice of philosophy means when based on Chinese models.

Chapter 7 expands the discussion of metaphysics broached in chapter 1 by arguing, first, that there is a legitimate need for metaphysics, Kantian refutations notwithstanding, and, second, that China as well as the West need to adapt their metaphysical ideas to the new world of science. Some of these ideas are spelled out, and directions for their development are indicated. This chapter began as a contribution for the special thirtieth anniversary edition of the *Journal of Chinese Philosophy* 30:3, 4 (September/December 2003), pp. 313–326.

Herbert Fingarette was one of the first Western trained philosophers to take Confucianism seriously, and his *Confucius: The Secular as Sacred* made the classic argument that the twin themes of humaneness (*ren*) and ritual propriety (*li*) get to the heart of Confucianism as a contemporary viable philosophy. His thesis is discussed at several places in this volume. Chapter 8 asks a Western question about humaneness and ritual propriety. How do they stand with respect to unconscious motivation and value? A Freudian reading and a Marxist reading are developed. The overall point of the argument is that those Confucian values (and much else in Chinese thought) need to lose the "first naiveté" of mere cultural transmission and be rethought through the masters of suspicion. This chapter continues the development of a modern Confucian theory of interiority. One early version of this chapter was presented as part of a Festschrift to Mikhail L. Titarenko in *China in the Dialogue of Civilizations: For the 70-Year Jubilee of Academician Mikhail L. Titarenko* (Moscow: Russian Academy of Sciences/Institute of Far Eastern Studies/Pamyatniki Istoricheskoy Mysli, 2004), pp. 653–660. Another early version was published in *Confucianism in Dialogue Today: West, Christianity, and Judaism*, edited by Liu Shu-hsien, John H. Berthrong, and Leonard Swidler (Philadelphia, PA: Ecumenical Press, 2004), pp. 48–58.

Chapter 9 is the first of three that focus explicitly on comparative issues. It takes up the question of the relation between Confucianism and Christianity and originated as a keynote address for a conference honoring the late Julia Ching. Professor Ching was probably our greatest student of the ongoing historical connections between those two religious traditions and collaborated in several works with the Roman Catholic theologian Hans Kung, who also delivered a keynote address. The focus of the chapter is on how the two traditions contribute to one another now, a topic of obvious importance to people who admit to be practicing both. The argument is about practical politics, putting forward a Confucian/Christian alternative to the preemptive war practice of the American government and Al Qaeda. The original lecture was published in *Wisdom in China and the West: Chinese Philosophical Studies XXII*, edited by Vincent Shen and Willard Oxtoby, Cultural Heritage and Contemporary Change Series III, Asia, Volume 22, 2004, general editor George F. McLean.

Chapter 10 deals with the question of whether the ultimate is to be conceived in personal or impersonal terms, according to Chinese and Western traditions, and I argue that every tradition has a spectrum of issues that cause it to deal with both personal and impersonal representations. An early draft was presented at a session on Field-Being at the American Academy of Religion in 1999.

Chapter 11 is devoted to issues of comparison per se. It first discusses issues in comparative theology, where concerns for the ultimate are uppermost and the nagging meta-issue is whether a thinker needs to belong to several traditions in order to compare them; what is the relation of comparative theology to religious practice? Then it distinguishes two forms of comparative philosophy (and the forms apply as well to comparative theology), namely, descriptive or objective comparison and normative comparison that attempts to say what is true and valuable in the traditions compared. Finally it defends a move beyond comparison, even normative comparison, to integrative philosophy. Integrative philosophy is constructive, and so this argument is crucial for my own project, and that of those contemporary thinkers whom I hope to inspire to take Chinese philosophy as a major resource. Part of this chapter appeared in the inaugural edition of *Dao: A Journal of Comparative Philosophy* 1:1 (Winter 2001), pp. 1–13; other parts were published in the American Philosophical Association special newsletter on comparative philosophy, edited by Chenyang Li, in 2001–2002.

Chapter 12 summarizes the main themes of the previous chapters, presenting them as tasks for future work developing the Confucian tradition in its relations with others.

Transliterating Chinese names and words into English is impossible to make consistent, especially when quoting someone else. Generally I have followed the pinyin system but sometimes have quoted the Wade-Giles. I tend to use the names of contemporary authors in the form in which they publish, although many of these authors have moved from Wade-Giles to pinyin, and there is little consistency. I tend to conflate the double given names of authors into one, even when I use the Wade-Giles transliteration system. We all need a sense of humor about this, and I need forgiveness from my friends who might not like the way I spell their names.

The debts of a thinker such as I who has gone far beyond the boundaries of the disciplines of formal education are enormous and innumerable. I thank all my teachers and my students, the close friends whose work is discussed here, and those authors whom I do not know but whose direct work in Sinology has made mine possible. I salute the younger generation of scholars who have been preparing for comparative work throughout their education, a near impossibility for a philosopher of my generation. Most of all I thank my colleague at Boston University, John H. Berthrong. We were colleagues in the administration of that university's School of Theology for fifteen years. But more, we have been and still are colleagues in the development of an intellectual life that learns from both China and the West. Together we have worked on the development of the South-of-the-Charles School of Boston Confucianism (Tu Weiming leads the North-of-the-Charles School, which emphasizes Mencius over against Xunzi). Many years ago, when he was the interfaith officer for the United Church of Canada, John taught me that it is possible to be a person of integrity and an institutional bureaucrat at once. This possibility, of course, is a necessity if one is to be a Confucian scholar-official, something to which we both aspire. I gratefully dedicate this book to him.

1
A Confucian Program

CONFUCIANISM IS A LIVING tradition that contributes to contemporary global philosophical inquiry and religious culture formation. The effectiveness with which Confucianism does this, however, is proportional to the extent to which it engages the realities of contemporary life. For this reason, the cultural expressions of the ancient Confucianism of Confucius, Mencius, and Xunzi, and the Neo-Confucianism of Zhou Dunyi, Zhu Xi, and Wang Yangming, are inadequate by themselves for the tradition's contemporary life. We need to understand the Confucianism of the past in historical perspective, and the Confucianism of the present in the perspective of thought-forms that address contemporary problems and discussions.

Contemporary Confucianism therefore cannot limit itself to critical studies of the great thinkers of the past. Of course it is imperative for a tradition continually to examine and reinterpret its past, and so historical studies are always necessary. Nevertheless, this cannot be the whole of contemporary Confucian philosophical practice. I shall argue here that Confucianism needs to expand its family of discourses in four related areas. It needs a contemporary metaphysical discourse, a contemporary discourse in philosophical cosmology in connection with science, a contemporary discourse about human nature and experience, and a contemporary discourse of social theory. In each of these four discourses, classical themes of Confucianism indicate what the interests and positions of Confucianism ought to be. The discourses themselves arise not only from East Asian thought but also from South Asian and Western traditions, and they need to have forms that reflect the best of the current discussions. Soon the Muslim tradition will enter the conversation. As a living tradition, Confucianism can contribute to the current discussions. Nevertheless, Confucianism also will be changed by engaging those discussions: this is what it means to be a living tradition.

In what follows, I shall say first, regarding each topic, a bit about what I mean by metaphysics, philosophical cosmology, human nature, and social theory. Then I shall indicate the classic Confucian motifs and themes that are at stake in each. Briefly I shall suggest what I believe the shape of each new Confucian discourse should be. And finally I shall indicate how Confucianism itself is changed by the new discourse.

METAPHYSICS

Metaphysics is the Western term indicating the philosophical problems having to do with being and nonbeing, what it means to exist, what kinds of things there are, and why there is something rather than nothing. The word comes from the title of Aristotle's book dealing with these issues. Metaphysics has been a central philosophical discipline in the West, and also in South Asia. Its importance lies not only in the intrinsic interest of its topic but in the fact that it defines what is ultimately real and therefore sets the patterns for what is ultimately important in life. One's metaphysics determines the shape of one's ultimate orientations.

I need to say a word in defense of metaphysics as an important discourse, for two reasons. The first reason is that in the West many people since Kant have argued that metaphysics is impossible, a vain form of inquiry. But what they had in mind as metaphysics was the foundationalist project of establishing cognitively certain and a priori metaphysical knowledge as a base on which all other knowledge can be built. By contrast, I understand metaphysics to be the generation and defense of good hypotheses about the problems of being, and so forth. Hypotheses are always fallible, though not always wrong. Metaphysical hypotheses reflect a particular history and language and are subject to correction. This surely was what Plato and Aristotle thought they were doing when they dealt with the problems of being—developing the best hypotheses or theories. Spinoza and Leibniz did believe that they were establishing certain and a priori metaphysical theories, and they were wrong about that. Nevertheless, their theories can be understood to be hypotheses and judged according to how good the cases are for them. Dialectic is the kind of argument in Western philosophy by which metaphysical theories are compared and judged relative to one another. The metaphysics of Alfred North Whitehead in the twentieth century is a magnificent recent example of a grand set of hypotheses about the most basic categories of being.

The second objection to metaphysics as a discourse for Confucians is the claim that the Confucian tradition has no metaphysics, only ethics. True, Confucianism does not have a densely elaborated history of metaphysical discussions, as the Western and South Asian traditions have. Confucius himself sometimes turned aside metaphysical questions. It will be necessary for contemporary Confucianism to borrow much of the language and history of Western and South Asian metaphysics if it is to develop its own metaphysical discourse for the contemporary conversation. Nevertheless, Confucianism does have deep metaphysical motifs from which it derives orientation toward what is ultimate in reality. One of the classic discussions is in Zhou Dunyi's *Explanation of the Diagram of the Great Ultimate*, and it is worth quoting at length because it will be useful in discussing philosophical cosmology too.

> The Ultimate of Non-being and also the Great Ultimate! The Great Ultimate through movement generates yang. When its activity reaches its limit, it becomes tranquil. Through tranquility the Great Ultimate generates yin. When tranquility reaches its limit, activity begins again. So movement and tranquility alternate and become the root of each other, giving rise to the distinction of yin and yang, and the two modes are thus established. By the transformation of yang and its union with yin, the Five Agents of Water, Fire, Wood, Metal, and Earth arise. When these five material forces are distributed in harmonious order, the four seasons run their course. The Five Agents constitute one system of yin and yang, and yin and yang constitute one Great Ultimate. The Great Ultimate is fundamentally the Non-ultimate.[1]

This is a complicated passage about which there has been much contentious discussion. Nevertheless it has been very important in the development of the Confucian tradition, summing up not only ancient themes but also motifs of thought in Daoism and Buddhism. I venture to say that the metaphysical motifs of Confucianism that should be embodied in contemporary Confucian metaphysics are these, stated as theses:

1. That to be is to have features, and this is significantly different from non-being, which has no features.
2. Nonbeing is more fundamental than being and gives rise to being.
3. That to be a thing is to be a harmony, at least of yin and yang elements.
4. That to be a harmony is to have value.
5. That there is no "reason" for being or the Great Ultimate to emerge from non-being: it just does.

The importance of these metaphysical motifs for Confucianism can be seen from their negations.

1. If there were no difference between being with features and nonbeing without features, and nonbeing were denied, there would be no subtlety to being, nor mystery, only positivistic presence, contrary to the Confucian sensibility.
2. If nonbeing were not the source of being, then the contingency of being would fail to be registered.
3. If having features in harmony were not the nature of things, things could be conceived as not related to one another, though in Confucian thought all things are related.
4. If harmonies were not valuable, then the aesthetic character of existence would be impossible and the aesthetic perceptiveness of humanity, righteousness, propriety, and wisdom would be false.
5. If there were a reason why being emerges from nonbeing, then nonbeing would have the determinate features necessary for having a motive or goal, and Confucians would ask whence such a "god" arises. The contingency of features is explained only by what can have no features. Nonbeing is simply fecund from the perspective of being.

Now a contemporary metaphysics for Confucianism might take the following form, I suggest. Let it begin with an hypothesis about determinate being as consisting of harmonies with features of two kinds. One kind of feature in a harmony derives from other harmonies to which the first harmony is determinately related. This kind of feature can be called "conditional" because it is how those other harmonies condition the harmony at hand. The other kind of feature can be called "essential" because those features are how the harmony integrates its conditional features to attain its own singular space-time existence. Because of the conditional features, all things are determinately related to some other things, not mere isolated atoms; because of the essential features, each thing has its own being and is not reducible to its relations. A harmony is the fitting together of all its features, a balance, and harmonies constantly shift with time, although that shifting is a topic for philosophical cosmology.

Harmonies relate to one another within space-time by virtue of their various conditional features. But for one harmony to relate to another, its essential features also must be together with the essential features of the other because neither would exist at all without the integration of both essential and conditional features. The mutual relation of essential features of different harmonies cannot be in space-time, for that consists of only conditional relations. It needs rather to derive from or consist in a nontemporal ground that itself has no features, that is, featureless nonbeing or the Ultimate of Nonbeing. If the ground of the relation between essential features of different things were itself to have features, then a deeper ground would have to be found to relate the ground to the harmonies, and an infinite regress would ensue. Therefore, the featureless nonbeing must give rise to being with features. In the West, this has often been explained in the language of divine creation. But if God is conceived to have features that allow for creation, then a deeper ground behind God and created harmonies would be needed. If God is conceived to have no features, then God is indistinguishable from nonbeing. A Confucian metaphysics needs language that says that nonbeing gives rise to determinate being as harmonies, without suggesting that nonbeing itself has a nature that would need further explanation. Determinateness or order needs explanation; complete indeterminateness does not.[2]

Another level of metaphysical hypothesis is needed to understand the hypothesis about harmonies. A harmony can be understood in terms of four elements: (1) the harmony's pattern or form; (2) its components, each of which might have an independent career outside the harmony; (3) the harmony's existential location in space-time; and (4) the value achieved by getting the components together in the particular pattern the harmony has, in the place and time of the harmony. The analysis of pattern or form in harmony is the occasion for developing the Confucian theme of Heaven, or Principle (li). The analysis of the components of a harmony, each of which is itself a harmony of course, is the occasion for developing the Confucian theme of Earth or material force (qi). The analysis of the existential location of a harmony is the occasion for developing the Confucian themes of spontaneity and change, and the multiple locations of patterns as microcosms and macrocosms. The analysis of value in harmony is the occasion for the development of the Confucian sense that harmony is normative and disharmony is the root of evil.[3]

How would Confucianism be changed by committing itself to metaphysical hypotheses such as these? First, it would enter in to a more abstract discourse than has been customary in Confucianism. Second, it would find ways of expressing its main metaphysical themes and motifs in language that also has been used to debate the metaphysical points of Western philosophy, allowing for clearer comparisons as well as dialectical arguments. Third, it would have found a way to express its deep commitment that the universe and human life have real value over against claims in other metaphysical views that reality is value free and that all values are mere human projections. All of these changes would be positive gains, I believe.

PHILOSOPHICAL COSMOLOGY

Philosophical cosmology differs from metaphysics in being more specific to the traits of our world and in being especially sensitive to the findings and speculations of natural science. Frequently, philosophical cosmology is taken to be continuous with metaphysics, and some thinkers use the terms interchangeably. Philosophical cosmology needs to be able to register all the scientific theories that have plausibility as ways of making the cosmology specific. The cosmology should not dictate to science, but must be able to register and reflect science.

The Confucian tradition has a grand set of cosmological commitments. The hypothesis that to be a thing is to be a change stems from the roots of the *Yijing* and dominates the Song Neo-Confucian debates about material force and principle. Along with Daoists, Confucians conceive a harmony to be an event of change, a harmony's pattern to be a pattern of change (as in the *Yijing* hexagrams), a harmony's components to be various processes, a harmony's existential location to be connection, endurance and/or motion, and a harmony's value to be the value of an event, a happening. The Confucian cosmology also regards Heaven as the source of order or pattern that allows various processes to come together as harmonizing. Heaven or principle is not so much itself a pattern as that which makes diverse things fit together in formal patterns. Because harmony is good, always achieving the value of combining the components with a particular pattern in a particular place and time, Heaven or principle is the source of goodness, and is what we look to as normative for human affairs in which we have some control over processes.

Another cosmological theme important to Confucianism (and Daoism) is spontaneity. For all its emphasis on change and process, Confucianism has never held to a strict determinism of the sort that intrigued Western scientists for the last several centuries. Spontaneity not only allows human beings to insert their intentions into process, it also allows for the deepest realm of the relation between nonbeing and being to express itself in process. In a spontaneous act, a person reaches down and inside to the fecundity of nonbeing and places it in a particular circumstance. Spontaneity is a function of essential features bringing something new to the conditions within which a harmony happens.

The obvious Western language for Confucianism to develop for its cosmological discourse is process philosophy. Much work has already been done to develop Confucianism in the philosophical categories of Whitehead, the founder of process philosophy.[4] I believe myself that Whitehead's philosophy needs to be considerably modified by eliminating its conception of God, developing a notion of enduring though always changing entities, and by introducing a notion of eternity against which to make sense of process and change.[5] But these disagreements are internal to debates within process philosophy in general. Confucianism would be well served to enter these debates in order to find contemporary expressions for its commitment to change, to normative patterns, and to spontaneity.

The most important reason for contemporary Confucianism to engage the current debates in philosophical cosmology is so that, in turn, it can engage modern science. Contemporary Confucians of course can be natural scientists. But how do they connect their science with the themes of their Confucian heritage? A customary Marxist criticism of Confucianism is that it is nonscientific. Indeed, the classic texts of Confucianism are truly incommensurate with modern science. Developing a Confucian philosophical cosmology that faithfully represents Confucian cosmological themes and motifs and that also is designed to represent the plausible scientific theories can make Confucianism commensurate with science.

Traditional Confucianism surely would be changed if it were able to take scientific discussions into its own discourse by extending its discourse to philosophical cosmology. This would tone down the humanistic elitism that some Confucians have had in antipathy to the modern world. It would also allow Confucians to take scientific literacy to be a crucial part of humane education. These changes are for the better.

HUMAN NATURE

Human nature is a profound theme in classical Confucianism; some would say it is the principal theme, to the exclusion of metaphysics and philosophical cosmology, although I have argued that this is a false exclusion. The Western term *nature* suggests a static pattern that does not fit well with the process or change-oriented philosophy of East Asia. *Experience* is the Western term better able to convey the Confucian sense of human dynamism.

The Confucian theme of human nature emphasizes a kind of primordial responsiveness to the values of things, the "center" in the *Zhongyong*. Confucius's conception of humaneness (*ren*) had to do with deferring to people according to their real natures, acknowledging the various particularities of value in their character and station. To do so, the sage needs to perceive accurately, and education is required for accurate perception. The sagely response to things is illustrated in Mencius's "Four Beginnings," in which the elemental instincts of the heart are to do the right thing. Of course, selfishness can get in the way, as well as incompetence, and so education and character development are needed for the inner good heart of human nature to express itself in complicated overt action. For a sage to be "sincere," to be "one body with the world," requires that all the avenues of perception and learning, on the one hand, and of action close at hand and at a distance, on the other, need to be brought into harmony. This might take a lifetime of devotion to the path of the sage: Confucius claimed to have attained it only when he was seventy years old. (It also requires a community of good ritual, which I shall discuss shortly.)

Our contemporary conceptions of human nature derive in large part from the natural and social sciences and do not connect easily with the Confucian classic motifs. Contemporary Confucianism therefore needs to develop a discourse about human nature that can relate to science at the same time that it expresses the classic motifs. I suggest, therefore, that Confucianism engage the philosophical discourse of the American pragmatists, beginning with Charles S. Peirce, which develops the hypothesis that human beings are fundamentally interpreters.[6] Human experience is always a matter of interpretation. Interpretation requires accurate input from the things interpreted. Interpretation also requires accurate response to the things interpreted. People interpret well or poorly, and as the Confucian tradition has always said, proper education is required for interpretations to register and respond accurately to the things in the world that are to be interpreted. Specifically, I believe the Confucian discourse on human experience as interpretive should focus on four ways of engaging the values of things with proper comportment toward them: (1) imagination, (2) judgment, (3) theorizing, and (4) the pursuit of responsibility.

A pragmatic theory of imagination says that the signs we develop in our cultural semiotic systems are structured so as to register what it is important for us to register in our environment. In simple cultures these can be very practical indeed, such as signs to distinguish predators from prey, good food from poison, things that might be helpful for shelter and safety, things that are immediately beautiful or repulsive. We register the values of such things in our discriminating signs because they are good or bad for us, in a narrow sense of self-interest. As cultures become more sophisticated, however, we ask more about the values things have in themselves and construe our own interests more broadly so as to be able to relate to what is important in the environment. Imagination supplies the ideas, the symbols, the signs, by which we can make discriminations concerning what is valuable. This is part of the Confucian theme of being able to grasp things according to the character of their value. Imagination by itself merely supplies the signs by which we take in the world: it does not make explicit judgments about whether it is true that the value of a thing we engage is as our signs say it is.

Judgment says that signs interpret things truly or falsely. With judgments go the arguments and cases that are to be made for them. A judgment is true, according to my hypothesis, when it carries across into the experience of the interpreter the value that characterizes the object interpreted, in the respect in which the interpreting signs stand for the object. That is a complicated formula, but its significance for my point is that truth involves the carrying of value over from the object interpreted into the interpreter. The judgment says that the object is a thing with the particular character of value indicated in the sign. Knowing whether that judgment is true depends on independent confirmation of the fact that it carries over the character of its object's value into the interpreter. Of course, most of our judgments are made with the confidence that our personal and social habits of confirmation act automatically and with authority. One special Confucian advantage of this theory of truth and judgment is that it expresses truth as a matter of a causal connection between interpreters and their objects. This means that it has no room for a Cartesian dualism of body and mind. Like Confucianism's view of mind, mental judgment, according to this hypothesis, is a kind of subtle action that is part of nature.[7]

Judgments are rarely made by themselves in isolation. Rather they are set within systems of other judgments that are theories. A theory is a set of judgments or hypotheses that gives something of a synoptic view of its subject matter. Charles Peirce said that theorizing has several important elements. One is the imaginative act of guessing at the integrating idea; a second is the analytic act of translating that integrating idea into formal consistent terms from which logical deductions can be made; a third is the inferential act of deducing what ought to appear in experience if the theory is true, or what would refute the theory if it did appear in experience; a fourth is the testing of the terms of the theory to see whether they distort experience; and a fifth is the cumulative assessment of whether the experiential evidence adds up to confirm, disconfirm, or suggest modifications to the theory.

The most common objection to theorizing in contemporary thought comes from postmodern thinkers who point out that every set of theoretical categories determines what registers as important. Most theories, especially of human culture, marginalize or completely ignore the existence of people who lack the power to control the theories. For instance, the experience of women and ethnic minorities often has been screened out because the dominant theoretical categories recognize only men and the cultural elite, or so postmodernists argue. The answer to this powerful criticism is that the fourth step of theorizing needs to be taken scrupulously. That is, the theory needs to include within its own development and defense a careful survey to make sure that nothing is being left out because it fails to register in the theoretical terms. All theories are fallible and thus subject to this and other kinds of corrections. The Confucian investment in theorizing is to make sure that theories do not distort the values of the things, particularly the persons, that the theories are about.[8]

The fourth kind of interpretation by which we should conceive human experience is the pursuit of responsibility. Pursuit of responsibility, of course, requires the other three ways of engaging the values of things: imagination to have the terms to recognize things' worth, judgment to ascertain the truth of particular interpretations, and theories to provide orientation and a field of vision. Interpretation, as I have argued, changes interpreters so that they experience the world differently and act in accord with that. Not only does interpretation change the way people experience the world, it changes the purposes and valuational drives by which they engage and act. Some actions are better than others, and so people are under obligation to do the better insofar as they can be known. Personal responsibility is the subjective form by which obligations are faced. We are each responsible for doing what ought to be done, when different possible actions lead to different values in the results.

Now actions are rarely done by isolated individuals. Nearly everything we do, even such simple things as listening to a lecture, are conjoint actions, in this case requiring the speaking and the hearing, and the thinking together on a topic expressed in one language system and interpreted in another. How do we act responsibly together? By jointly playing rituals, with many different roles coordinated as in a dance. Language itself is a paradigmatic ritual. But language-speaking always rests within a larger ritual context, such as the ritual character of lectures in academic settings with translators, and so forth. International lectures are sometimes difficult because we do not have clear and easy rituals for working around language barriers. Rituals make possible conjoint actions that would not be possible without them. This appreciation of ritual is Confucianism's most important direct contribution to contemporary philosophy, in my opinion.[9]

I strongly recommend this complex hypothesis about interpretation relative to the values of things as a contemporary discourse within which Confucianism can invest itself. It would bring Confucianism into play with semiotic theory and ally it with the rich tradition of pragmatism. Moreover, it would allow Confucianism to contribute its most original motif: the necessity of ritual for human formation.

How would Confucianism be changed by developing itself in this discourse about human nature and experience? First of all, the emphasis on ritual would bring Xunzi back into favor as one of the most original minds of the tradition, after long having been subordinated to Mencius. Second, Confucianism would internalize a rich discussion within pragmatism, which several important thinkers have advocated.[10] Third, it would give Confucianism a philosophical language for contemporary epistemology that expresses its basic motifs about human nature, especially the valuational element. These are all changes for the better.

SOCIAL THEORY

My discussion so far has been strangely neglectful of something that Confucianism has known since its beginning, namely, the social character of human reality. We become persons in families and fulfill highest virtue through generalized forms of filial piety. Confucians have known the importance of ritual for defining character and better than most other traditions of philosophy have understood the political roles of individuals and groups. Now let me correct this neglect in my argument.

The problem for contemporary Confucianism in China is that it has been under attack by Marxist philosophers for decades as being mired in a feudal social theory. To be sure, there are complicated problems defining feudalism, in Europe or in China, and Marxism might not have the last word on the topic. Nevertheless, its attack is quite correct if Confucianism is to be limited to the social theory it developed in the Zhou, Song, or Ming dynasties. As a Western philosophy, Marxism is not limited to the feudal social theories of Thomas Aquinas and other Western thinkers who lived in feudal Europe. On the contrary, it arose out of nineteenth-century social science. To answer the Marxist criticism, Confucianism needs to develop a contemporary social theory that is true to its classic themes and motifs but that addresses contemporary realities. These realities include not only the economic situation that Marxists would emphasize, but also the clash of civilizations, the revival of fundamentalist religions of all sorts, the vastly expanded cross-cultural communication enabled by fast travel and the internet, global migrations, and a host of other issues.

The deep themes that Confucianism needs to develop in a contemporary social theory are humaneness (*ren*) and ritual propriety (*li*). The importance of these themes makes it impossible for Confucianism to adopt the discourses of the two most important families of social theory. One of these Confucianly impossible families says that power is the key to social relations. Marxism and postmodern deconstructionism are examples of the approach to social understanding through power, although that has been characteristic of much European thinking since Thomas Hobbes. Power relations, of course, are real and need to be conceptualized accurately. But a Confucian social theory would want to understand power relations as judged by criteria of humaneness, and it would suggest that the strongest kind of power in the long run is that which is embodied in ritual structures. The other family of approaches to social theory that Confucianism should not befriend is the social contract theory that bases itself on conceptions of a state of nature prior to civil society. Confucians know that there is no state of pre-socialized nature for human beings and that ritual, and therefore civil society, permeate everything human. Social contract theories represent human nature, in a state of nature, as being essentially selfish, either aggressively so as in Hobbes's theory, or acquisitively so as in Locke's. As Xunzi pointed out, only infants and people who have learned no ritual are essentially selfish. The sad effect of social contract theory is to create rituals within which selfish behavior is tolerated and even made normative. But this is inhumane. In this point lies a profound Confucian critique of the interpretation of capitalism based on social contract theory.

What is the shape of a viable contemporary Confucian social theory? This extremely complicated question depends upon many forms of analysis of the social conditions of our time. For instance, family structure is very different now from what it was in the times when Confucians developed their classical notions of family. Perhaps other institutions such as places of employment and educational institutions perform some of the work that ancient agrarian families were supposed to perform. I believe that the key to understanding our current social conditions is to identify the ritual behaviors that are in them and ask critical Confucian moral questions about whether the rituals make humane life possible in those conditions. If they do not, what rituals would improve them? If no rituals would improve them, can the social conditions themselves be improved?

Stepping back from the analysis of particular social conditions in Confucian terms, I believe that the central theoretical principle of a contemporary Confucian social theory is a reversal of a certain point in social contract theory. In British social contract theory, of either Hobbes's or Locke's sort, people were construed to have no responsibilities at all in the state of nature. They have desires, instincts, passions, and fears, but no responsibilities. According to the social contract theory, people enter into civil society, surrendering some of their power to the government, in order to be able to get more of what they want and avoid more of what they fear. Once people are in civil society, they then have responsibilities for being citizens of that society, responsibilities such as obeying the law, respecting authority, honoring business contracts, and taking part in government so as to make the best possible civil society that would let everyone get more of what they want and avoid more of what they fear. Even in civil society, in which social contract theorists admit we always are, there is nothing normative, nothing good or bad, about our desires and fears except when they are prohibited or commanded by civil law. The bottom line in social contract theory is that people are free to do whatever they want so long as it does not interfere with others doing the same as this is defined by the laws of the civil society.

Now I suggest a Confucian reversal of this point. I hypothesize that everyone by nature (which of course includes our ritual constitution) is responsible for everything that ought to be done in a society except where the rituals of civil society assign the responsibility to some specific people. Where social contract theory says that no one is responsible for anything unless assigned the responsibility by civil society, I say everyone is responsible for everything unless civil society channels it elsewhere. If there were no civil society, no ritual structure, which says that you are responsible for feeding your family and I am responsible for feeding mine, then I have the responsibility to feed your family. This is because it is objectively better for your family to be fed than to starve and, if no one else will attend to it, the obligation becomes my responsibility. Of course, this is an impossible situation—I cannot feed everyone and neither can you. So human societies are all structured somewhat to assign general obligations such as getting people fed to the responsibilities of specific people or specific roles. We would not have evolved into human beings without our primitive ancestors developing some division of labor, that is, ritualized societies. Looked at this way, our societies are ritualized in a remarkably good way, and rituals are very basic adaptive necessities for the evolution of human life.

Nevertheless, in some social conditions people do starve. Perhaps it is because there is no one around whose role it is to feed them. Perhaps it is because the division of labor in agriculture cannot produce enough food. Whatever the reason for the failure, it becomes everyone's responsibility once again to do something about it. Of course, we say that we have governments to take on these responsibilities when the ritualized social system breaks down; but sometimes governments fail too. When the ritualized societies, including their governments, break down, then responsibility devolves again on everyone to do something about that. When someone starves to death, we are all a little guilty, even when it is not our assigned role in society to feed that person.

The reason Confucianism should invest in this reversed social contract discourse is because of its commitment to humaneness. Where people are hurt by a broken social system, it is inhumane not to help them. The Confucian heart "cannot bear the sufferings of others." All the social sciences should be brought to bear to understand why a social system is broken or inadequate for humane life. The Confucian use of those sciences, however, is governed by the search for the possibility of humaneness. Confucianism is famous, infamous in the eyes of Moists and some Enlightenment moralists, for its principle of "love with differences." This was taken to mean that one should love one's family more than the village and its laws, and one's village more than the empire, and one's empire more than people in other empires. Confucianism rejected universal love of Mozi's sort. I believe that what was presupposed, though not acknowledged, in the "love with differences" idea was a working ritualized social system that clearly defined responsibilities in family, village, empire, and for the barbarians. When that system breaks down, it is inhumane not to care for the barbarian. In Confucius's time the social system was very broken. His response was to teach rituals for reestablishing family responsibilities, productive friendship, local government, and a culture of proper ministerial responsibilities within the empire. He recognized that it was impossible to help all the villagers and barbarians even though it was inhumane not to do so. His remedy was the improvement of the ritual structures of society. So, a Confucian approach to social theory should focus on examining how the ritual structures that institutionalize society make humaneness possible, or fail to do so. All the sciences of society are at its disposal.[11]

I fear that I have both talked too long and said too little about any one topic to have been enlightening. My point, however, has been only to sketch some new directions for the development of Confucianism in the contemporary world. As a Confucian myself, I affirm the need to understand and honor the history of the tradition. Yet we also have the responsibility to extend the tradition to meet the needs of philosophy today. My own work for many years now has been in the development of the discourses in metaphysics, philosophical cosmology, human nature as interpretation, and social theory that I have discussed here, and footnoted so shamelessly. The chief strategic argument of this first chapter is to justify my hope that the body of my philosophic work, which looks so Western, is in fact a direct contribution to the development of Confucianism in the twenty-first century. I thank you for allowing me to invite you into this Boston Confucian family of discourses.

2
The Significance of Confucian Values

THE INTERACTIONS OF WORLD cultures have changed over the centuries.[1] In the nineteenth century European imperialism overran the globe, and it had a strong, though by no means universal, tendency to impose European values on the subjugated cultures. Historians say that the twentieth was the American Century. Americans had a far greater appreciation of cultural pluralism than the Europeans of the previous century, partly because so many cultures are represented in America. Korean culture is very powerful in the United States. But America also sponsored a global economic system that internally expressed many values of late-modern Western society. I am reasonably sure that the twenty-first will be the East Asian Century, dominated by China and Japan in addition to Korea. The economic systems of the East Asian Century are the clear outgrowth of Western capitalism, tailored to Asian cultures; nevertheless, native East Asian values will play increasingly powerful roles in guiding world societies and thus transforming their economic structures.

VALUES FOR THE GOOD LIFE: CONVENTIONAL, YET NORMATIVE

With this historical situation in mind I want to reflect on the significance of Confucian values for one particular question, the nature of the good life. Of course there are Confucian values for many other issues, and the nature of the good life is only a small part of the scope of personal and social ethics.

Nevertheless, certain important considerations about the good life can illustrate how Confucian values are now entering the larger philosophic discussion that moves beyond Confucian cultures to various global societies.

The question of the "good life" seems to be tied irrevocably to the particularity of cultures. Indeed, one of the defining marks of a culture seems to be what it defines as the good life. Yet our global situation is characterized by a plurality of cultures, each with its images of the good life, and these images often are in real or potential conflict with one another. Because our cultures interact so vigorously, the question of the possibility of a tolerant pluralism of images of the good life has become urgent. My thesis here is that an approach to the good life can be devised that, on the one hand, respects cultural differences and, on the other hand, builds ways of integrating them into a process that aims at a rich world civilization. The resources for advancing this thesis come from Confucianism and American pragmatism, often with parallel ideas.

First, however, I want to consider and reject three approaches to the good life that might seem good candidates to accomplish civilized integration while acknowledging cultural pluralism.

The most obvious is the economic approach to the good life that arises from capitalism, now practiced in one way or another in most of the world's societies. Advocates of global capitalism note that successful participation in capital markets and production raises everyone's standard of living and leaves them freer to pursue whatever cultural ideals for living they might choose. Every culture includes some ideal of comfortable living in its sense of the good life, however differently cultures draw the lines of poverty and wealth. Interpreting the capitalist economic approach to the good life is extremely complicated, including assessing whether the claim that everyone benefits is true, but I will not pursue these issues here. Suffice it to note that successful participation in a capitalistic economic market requires transforming cultures so that economic success is possible. The Qur'an, for instance, expressly forbids usury, lending money for gain, a policy that fosters societies based on the value of production and work, not investment. Yet it is virtually impossible for such a society to exist successfully in a capitalist market that so often defines itself as investing money for the sake of gain. Contemporary Muslim cultures do enter the capitalist market, but grudgingly, bitterly, muttering that "capitalism" is another word for avarice. Some Confucians feel the same way. The capitalistic economic approach to the good life does not tolerate the freedom to pursue all local cultural values, only those that make for successful economic competition. Moreover, because the international market forces of investment blindly and necessarily send money to where it is perceived to be likely to make the greatest gain, each society needs to work to its utmost to be competitive. Otherwise all the other things it prizes will be undercut when investments go elsewhere. So the capitalist economic approach to the good life in the end defines the good life as the competitive life. Few people would accept this because nothing is enjoyed in such a "good life" for its own sake, except more winning. Korea has successfully transformed its economy to be marvelously competitive. Perhaps its Confucian heritage can prevent this transformation from coming to believe that the only good life is the life of winning.

The second possible approach to the good life is the democratic ideal of freedom, so often associated with the capitalist economic approach. The ideal of freedom, however, includes the viability of dissent, particularly dissent from unsavory or obsessive economic practices. In the hands of theorists such as John Dewey, the ideal of freedom requires the building of a rich social fabric that supports freedom. An international society of different cultures, each free to pursue its own ideals of the good life, requires a very complicated infrastructure, and that is possible, according to Dewey, as people cultivate the institutions of democracy.[2] While institutions of democracy are all to the good and are required in any approach to cultural pluralism, the ideals of democratic freedom are not sufficient for the good life because they are always instrumental to something else. They suppose that something relatively more private than the institutions of democratic process is that for the sake of which democratic freedom is pursued. An approach to the good life needs to define itself publicly as well as privately, as Dewey himself knew very well; perhaps the distinction between the public and the private is itself inimical to approaching the good life.

The third possible approach to the good life is to define it religiously, with each religion contributing its ideals. Surely there is great truth in this approach, and religious ideals inevitably need to be taken up into approaches to the good life. Nevertheless, thinkers in every religion recognize now the disparity among religions with regard to what counts as the good life, and every religion thinks its candidates are the best. Any conception of the good life does have to represent itself as normative in some sense, and not merely conventional. Subsequent scholarship will determine whether the apparent disagreements among religions are matters of substance or only of differing conventional modes of expression, or perhaps only of different stresses for different contexts. At the moment, no scholarly consensus exists. Therefore the apparent pluralism of religious approaches to the good life makes the religious approaches poor candidates in the first instance for a viable conception of the good life in our situation.

Nevertheless, the case of religious approaches offers a clue to how to proceed. Religious thinkers of sophistication now recognize the paradox just mentioned. On the one hand, each religion believes its conception of the good life (and of much else besides) is normative; moreover, each religion knows the others believe that their conceptions are also normative. On the other hand, viewing other religions, each religion recognizes that the conceptions of all religious ideals of the good life are conventional. Each is expressed in the language and symbols of particular cultures with particular histories. Many religions admit the conventionality of their conceptions when they attribute them to revelations, as in the case of Daoism, Judaism, Christianity, and Islam, or to the genius of great teachers, as in Confucianism, most forms of Hinduism (where the teachers interpret the revealed Vedas), and Buddhism. Religions regard their commitments concerning the good life to be both normative and conventional. How can this be?

A CONFUCIAN SOLUTION: RITUAL

The Confucian theory of ritual, especially as expressed by Xunzi and his line of interpretation, offers a fine answer to this question.[3] To summarize his theory briefly and in contemporary terms, Xunzi observed, in his essay on Nature (*Tien*) and elsewhere, that nature endows human beings with biological, emotional, and personal governance systems that are seriously underdetermined.[4] Our bodies, for instance, have a very wide range of motion. This wide diversity is illustrated in the fact that different cultures teach children different postures, ways of moving, gesturing, and making eye contact. But a child cannot learn by using all ways at once: some specific ways need to be taught and learned, and these specific patterns of movement are conventional. Different cultures have different conventions. The most obvious illustration of this is with the wide range of possibilities for making verbal noise, and the need to learn some specific language in order to communicate by noise. Many different languages exist, all of which are possible for infants to learn, though with maturation the physical possibility to make sounds in unused languages diminishes, as those know who try to learn a foreign language in adulthood. Xunzi pointed out that all infants have a wide range of emotional expressions. But their capacity to make appropriate emotional responses is underdetermined, and they have to learn what is funny and what lamentable, what is dangerous and what is fruitful, what to love and what to fear. People also are born with a capacity for will and desire, but underdetermined with regard to what is appropriate to will and want.

Xunzi pointed out that if there were no conventions that gave specificity to these naturally underdetermined capacities, civilization would be impossible. People would never get beyond the spontaneous selfishness of infants.

Xunzi's understanding of convention was what he called ritual (*li*). The most obvious paradigm of ritual is court ritual, or religious liturgy. But Xunzi understood ritual to be so pervasive and basic as to determine styles of movement, gestures for communication, language, the habits forming social institutions, and the formal and informal dances of social intercourse. This conception of ritual finds almost exact parallel in Charles Peirce's conception of semiotics or sign-behavior.[5] A sign, like a ritual act, is general and is determined through a system of signs. To "signify" in a specific instance is to particularize the general sign, although the meaning of the signification comes from its generality. Moreover, to particularize the general sign is also to add something to the sign, some more meaning. Signs that are used tend to generalize further, Peirce said, with a growth of meaning. And signs within a semiotic system that are not used in particular significations tend to drop out, thereby altering the sign system itself. Although individuals make specific significations, the meaning and ramifications of the significations involve other people also participating in the semiotic system or ritual dance. The dance or system evolves as it is used in new situations and by new generations of dancers or participants in the cultural system defined by the shifting semiotic code. A contemporary Confucian theory of ritual has access to all the sophistication of pragmatic semiotics. By the same token, pragmatic semiotics has access to all the rich culture that lies within the Confucian approach to ritual. A central part of contemporary Confucian moral thinking is the analysis and criticism of the rituals that shape our societies.

A solution to how conceptions of the good life can be both normative and conventional is now in sight. All cultures are conventional in the sense that they are shaped by semiotically defined signs, that is, by rituals. Any behavior or thought wherein cultures might be different within the common underdetermined natural capacities of human beings is a matter of convention. But not all cultures have the conventions required for high civilization. They might have counterproductive conventions, or no relevant conventions at all. So, for instance, every culture needs conventions for how to make eye contact so as to convey an intended attitude; without ritual, eye contact is meaningless or confused. If an eye contact ritual conveys only belligerence or fear, for instance, then expressed attitudes are limited to belligerence or fear. Every culture needs rituals of greeting so that encounters are not always violent; a bow would do, or a handshake. But if there are no rituals of greeting, only fight/flight responses, then the culture is impoverished. Copulation can bring children into the world, but without family rituals, raising them is very difficult, and without good family rituals, the civilized values of family affection, care, support, and learning are impossible. Men can cooperate on the hunt, but without the rituals of public life, civilized government is impossible. Without rituals, friendship is impossible, the arts are impossible, and all the excellences involved in social cooperation are impossible. Confucius lamented that in his time, the rituals that obtained were simply incapable of sustaining high civilization. They were counterproductive and led to war, disorder, and famine.

New rituals were necessary, or as he tried to sell the point, the excellent rituals of the ancient sage-kings needed to be recovered.

Confucius recognized that rituals are conventions. Chinese is not the only language for speaking within high civilization. Sanskrit might do, or Greek or Hebrew, perhaps even English. But the languages of the nearby barbarians were too crude for high civilization. The barbarian languages simply could not express what civilization requires and would have to be expanded. The great Neo-Confucian Wang Yangming had direct experience civilizing the barbarians by teaching them an expanded ritual repertoire.[6]

HIGH CIVILIZATIONS: COMPETING VALUES AND GLOBAL RITUALS

Judging whether conventions are normative, of course, requires knowing something about what constitutes high civilization. The temptation is to think that we are in a vicious circle here: we judge the normativeness of rituals according to whether they make possible high civilization, and yet high civilization is defined differently by the different ritual systems of cultures. Nevertheless I think it is not the case that this is a vicious circle. The issue rather is that high civilization cannot be *appreciated* without the rituals that make it possible. The cultures that have appropriate rituals are able to articulate high civilization and set specific goals for civilizing specific contexts. Without the rituals, we would not recognize high civilization if we saw it.

Among the most important rituals for high civilization are those that constitute what we roughly think of as social institutions. Institutions are organized and clustered so as to make possible the achievement of excellence in important dimensions of civilized life, dimensions that themselves are defined ritually (or semiotically). An informal list of such dimensions includes education, economics, science, religion, the arts, morality, and government (including defense and judicial institutions as well as collective care for social problems). Each of these dimensions exists in a given culture because of a host of institutions that give it actuality. Education, for instance, in modern societies includes schools and universities, but also certain ritual habits of child-rearing and community organization, rituals of prestige, rituals of economic reward for education, and many more institutions. Cultures differ in the institutions they have at these levels, yet the institutions are normative in each culture if they enable the culture to achieve excellence in education.

Most of our societies are like Confucius's situation in an important respect. That is, the ritual institutions work well enough for us to feel that something is missing, that some excellence should be possible that is not. So we search for ways to improve our rituals, particularly our institutions of ritualized behavior. As I alluded to earlier, Confucius interpreted this as a memory of the good old days of the sage-kings. A better interpretation, I believe, comes from John Dewey who, in books such as *Human Nature and Conduct, Art as Experience, Experience and Nature*, and *The Quest for Certainty*, articulated the process of interacting with nature and social institutions with judgment and imagination. In particular, he stressed the importance of perceiving a situation as problematic and imagining various ways of resolving it. Imagined resolutions are subject to a kind of aesthetic judgment in which we can appreciate, through imagination, the plusses and minuses of value that the pursuit of them would entail.

The institutions of the various dimensions of civilized life closely interact with one another. So a lively social imagination needs to be able weave its way through the intricacies of the interactions of the relevant social institutions within all the valued "epitomes" of high civilizations, as Whitehead referred to art, science, religion, morality, education, and the rest.[7] Among the most important rituals of a culture are those that lead thinkers to dance through the connections among the institutions of high civilization.

Just as there are rituals for moving imaginatively among the institutions of a high civilization, we now are developing rituals for moving imaginatively among high civilizations themselves. These rituals are by no means highly developed. Leaders of government, commerce, education, religion, the arts, science, and morality recognize that the institutions of these dimensions of civilization reach across national boundaries. Global capitalism is a glaring example of this, although capitalism itself is but one rather abstract, albeit powerful, institution among the rich panoply of economic rituals. Samuel Huntington's warning about the clash of civilizations is only half the story.[8] The other half is the commingling of civilizations in so many areas of the world. To negotiate this world of commingled civilizations requires new inventions of ritual diplomacy in the various dimensions of high civilization.

Therefore we are at a moment of urgent need for Confucian ritual masters in all the dimensions of high civilization. Experiments in ritual-making are hypotheses about patterns of interaction in which people who disagree about fundamental things are still able to work together. The rituals proposed might fail, as any hypothesis is fallible, according to pragmatism. Nevertheless, the process of developing rituals itself transforms the situation. The rituals need to be sensitive to the differences among cultures regarding education, economics, the sciences, religion, the arts, morality, and government, as well as perhaps other important dimensions. To attain such sensitivity requires a steep learning curve in cross-cultural matters, which itself develops new ritual habits of thought and action. In religion, for instance, the current situation calls upon every religion to develop a detailed "theology of the other religions," for no religion now can think only about itself. A new kind of religious thinker, therefore, is being educated, one with rather deep sensitivity to other religions; scholarly work to establish comparative categories for relating religions is proceeding at a breathless pace. The power of fundamentalism in American Christianity, in Islam, in Sri Lankan Buddhism and Hinduism, and elsewhere might seem to be a countertrend, an insistence on one way of religion regardless of the others. But precisely because these fundamentalisms mirror one another, fundamentalism itself is a cross-religion or cross-tradition dimension of religious life more generally. Rituals for relating to fundamentalisms are an interreligious need, not something peculiar to any one religion. One of the most significant values Confucianism contributes to the contemporary world is the importance and use of ritual.

To return to the question of the good life, I suggest that a preliminary and necessary step toward it is participation in the rituals of high civilization that are relevant to one's situation. These include the nascent rituals that allow one to negotiate among the institutions of different cultures that express what each civilization regards as the epitomes of human excellence. To participate in these culturally integrative rituals does not mean that one has to agree with or approve the institutions of all the cultures, or of any culture beyond one's own, or even of one's own culture. Nevertheless, to engage all the relevant cultures in an appropriate ritual of negotiation does bring one to appreciate the values that the ritual institutions of each culture make possible. Just as it is impossible to appreciate the worth of a high civilization until one can play the rituals that make that civilization possible, to participate in those rituals reveals the worth of that high civilization. To the extent that we have the skills to appreciate what of value is at stake in each of the civilizations or cultures with which we ritually dance, we can employ Dewey's method of imagination to see how they compare, how they might be integrated, or disentangled, or rejected in favor of other values, and so on. At the very least, with the cross-cultural negotiating rituals we can arrange the dance so that every participant can understand and respect the others for what they are.

The Confucian moral to draw from all this is that living the good life means being first a ritual master. Not all of us have the vast responsibilities of the Secretary General of the United Nations, the global ritual master. But many of us work in educational institutions, for instance, and have the responsibilities of understanding the many cultures in which education is important, the cultures in which various people need to be educated, the styles of learning of our students who come from various cultures, and how the institutions in which we work relate to other institutions of education with which they interact.

Living the good life is always particular; we live as individuals in particular communities. So it is important to remember the distinction between a ritual itself and the individual and corporate playing of the ritual. The good life lies not in the ritual itself but in what is enabled by the playing of it. Our lives, in one sense, consist in the individuation of the ritual roles our situations call for.

Herbert Fingarette's brilliant interpretation of Confucianism famously pairs the emphasis on ritual with the emphasis on humanity (*ren*), or humanization, or humaneness, or human-heartedness, or love. I have stressed ritual, both because it is generally neglected by Confucians enamored too much of Mencius, and because it is the signal contribution Confucianism can make in our time to understanding how to approach the good life that is at once culturally particular and integral to the interactions of cultures. Nevertheless, before concluding I want to emphasize that the rituals themselves support content, and that the content of the good life is humaneness as that is made concrete in the actual living through the rituals of civilization, whatever one's culture.

A HOMILY ON HUMANENESS

Permit me to close with a brief Confucian homily on humaneness, which I gloss in terms of four characters, the first three of which come from *The Great Learning*.

The first character of humaneness is "manifesting the clear character." The discipline for achieving such public sincerity, or transparency of heart through actions, or authenticity, is very complex and involves eradicating both selfishness and incompetence from one's self. The point I wish to emphasize here is that manifesting the clear character requires developing a personal ritual that integrates all the orientations and rituals by which one relates to the myriad things. Manifesting the clear character itself requires a ritual that allows all the parts of one's life to dance together. Popularly this is called personal style, but the notion of ritual integration does the idea better justice.

The second character of humaneness is "loving the people," and I follow Wang Yangming in construing this as establishing such appreciative connections with things that one feels as if one were one body with the whole world. In particular I follow the general Confucian line that to treat everyone lovingly means addressing them singularly as who they are, not procedurally as if they were equal or the same. This means that, although ritual connections such as family kinship or explicit social roles might determine one's orientation to another, that person needs to be addressed as how he or she individuates those ritual connections. More than that, the person needs to be addressed in terms of how all his or her ritual connections are individuated and connected according to some personal ritual for manifesting the clear character. Rituals provide general forms for meaningful life; persons are how they individuate those ritual forms.

The third character of humaneness is "abiding in the highest good," by which is meant steadfastness in the pursuit of excellence in all one does. Following from the previous discussion, this means being able to make concrete the practices and institutions of one's life, family, and community that are sensitive to the highest values of one's culture. One's culture might be one among many cultures, and different from the others in significant ways. Yet in our time it is important to include within one's culture the special ritual connections that allow for appreciating how the other cultures themselves are high civilizations, along with the ritual ability to interact with those cultures.

The fourth character of humaneness is to "be creative." This is perhaps a more Western than Confucian notion, although it is the main theme of Zhu Xi's essay on humaneness or *ren*, which interprets humaneness as the root of the cycle of originating things, letting them flourish, and drawing determinate consequences from them.[9] Creativity is the influencing of the processes in the environment in such a way as to produce harmonies or values that were not present before, or that are threatened by changing circumstances. Creativity is obvious in art, but is also called for in all walks of life in which human effort can make a difference for better or worse. In light of the previous discussion, creativity is called for today especially in the development of new rituals that allow different and competing individuals and cultures to relate to one another with respect.

Of course most of us are good people with very murky characters, extremely imperfect love, little steady connection with excellence, and with lazy habits that turn rituals to stultifying repetition rather than creativity. We need to accept one another as such flawed creatures. Yet we should admit that insofar as we accept this status for ourselves, we have abandoned the approach to the good life. Instead of the good life, we settle for the goods of life that satisfy for a while but that depend for support on the rituals and humane strivings that constitute high civilization. The contemporary Confucian vocation is to become a sage with ritual mastery and humaneness, because this is what the good life is all about.

Perhaps my discussion of the contemporary significance of Confucian values is not what you expected. That is, I did not address traditional Confucian values until the very end in the little sermon on manifesting the clear character, loving the people, and abiding in the highest good. Confucianism has values even more basic than these, for instance those of filiality, friendship, and seriousness, which I did not discuss, although I prize them greatly. Rather I focused on the value of ritual, as that value has been elaborated with such subtlety in Confucianism, because I think that this is the uniquely Confucian value that our world society needs. The special contribution of Confucianism to world society is its conception of ritual that unites theory and practice, that provides a sharp tool for moral analysis, and that makes possible the pursuit of such questions as the nature of the good life.

Ritual carries with it the Confucian conception of high civilization, a conception that embraces all those other Confucian values I failed to discuss in detail. My concluding thesis is that Confucianism's greatest value, which gives the tradition such a rich conception of the good life, is ritual life that allows for the full expression of humaneness from the intimacy of home to the public responsibilities of government, from the simplicities of personal care to the achievements of the greatest art and high civilization.

3

Ritual in Xunzi

THAT XUNZI WAS MARGINALIZED in the tradition of Confucianism framed by Zhu Xi's edition of *The Four Books* had a worse result than relative neglect by East Asian and Western scholars.[1] The genius of his original philosophy has not yet had the impact it deserves on framing the contemporary philosophic discussion.[2] The scholarly neglect is being remedied with great efficiency at the present time, building on the modern edition and translation into English of Xunzi's works by John Knoblock and exemplified by a burgeoning commentarial literature.[3] The purpose of this chapter is not to contribute to the scholarly retrieval of Xunzi but rather to his philosophical retrieval.

After some initial remarks on themes in Xunzi, I shall develop three main points of contemporary interest to which Xunzi has much to contribute. The first is an intriguing connection between ritual theory (especially in Xunzi) and semiotics, mentioned in the previous chapter. The second relates ritual to the proper formation of desire. The third addresses the question of diversity and integration of desires and relates this question to a religious thesis about ritual connecting the "depths" with civilization and joy.

INITIAL CONSIDERATIONS OF RITUAL IN XUNZI

Ceremony is one of the meanings of ritual for Xunzi, as for the rest of the Confucian tradition. Ceremonies fall into five sorts in Xunzi's thought, as Knoblock has pointed out:

those dealing with such auspicious occasions as sacrifice and marriage; those dealing with inauspicious occasions such as mourning and the loss of the state; rites of hospitality involving tribute offerings and appearances at court; usages involving warfare, especially the display of weapons, types and decorations of chariots, and the use of banners; and festivities, notably serving elders, showing respect for the aged, making offerings, presenting gifts, and giving daughters in marriage.[4]

Late-modern societies have versions of all these ceremonies, if you count retirement parties as "respect for the aged" and remember "giving away" modern daughters in marriage (paying for the wedding is still a custom, if not a ceremony, even when daughters do not want their fathers to give them away). Modern democratic societies may have more ceremonies for political transitions than Xunzi's Chinese states had because of frequent formalized elections of officials. Late-modern societies observe a sharp distinction lacking in Xunzi's culture between political or court ceremonies (secular) and religious ceremonies, based on the modern Western division between public and private spheres of life.

Ritual (*li*) means far more than ceremony, however, for all of Confucian thought. Knoblock points out that in Xunzi's thought it includes "the highest sense of morality, duty, and social order as well as the most minor rules of good manners, the minutiae of polite forms, and insignificant, it seems to us, details of costume and dress."[5] I have developed a more elaborate spectrum of meanings of ritual as convention starting with penumbral conventions such as eye contact, posture and movement, semiotically coded signs such as language and gesture, sign-shaped behavior the very exercise of which constitutes social institutions, manners regarding the playing of socially defined roles, the cultivations of personal relationship, and the practices of etiquette, and then explicit ceremonies themselves.[6] This list obviously can be subdivided and extended, reaching to all thought and practice shaped by learned conventions.

The clue to the broad extension of ritual in Xunzi is his conception of human nature and what is added to its biological givens, as Edward Machle has pointed out and was mentioned in the previous chapter.[7] Heaven and Earth (jointly constituting nature) provide human beings with their bodies, their various senses, a range of emotions, and a mind capable of governing the natural elements and relating them to external things such as food.[8] Simply as given by Heaven and Earth, these elements are too underdetermined for human life. Given the range of possible postures, for instance, people can stand with their feet parallel (the ritual way in East Asia) or with the toes angled a bit to the side (the European way). Given the senses, everything is a cacophony, a "blooming, buzzing confusion," in William James's celebrated phrase, without learned discrimination and a sensibility as to what is important.⁹ Emotions as given have little or no measure and no intrinsic connection with proper objects. Conventionally learned signs and sign-shaped behaviors are required to determine the naturally underdetermined givens of nature in order for human life to be possible.

I take ritual (*li*) to encompass all conventions, all learned signs and sign-shaped behaviors. For Xunzi, these human-building conventions are what need to be added to Heaven and Earth in order for human life to be possible and, as constituting the human, they complete the potentials of Heaven and Earth. This is Xunzi's version of the Trinity of Heaven, Earth, and the Human.¹⁰

The importance of the ancient kings and sages of old is that they handed down the conventions that determine human nature so as to make civilized human life possible. Lacking a strong evolutionary view of nature and society, Xunzi and many of his sophisticated colleagues avoided supernaturalistic explanations. The popular culture perhaps within which Xunzi worked had a supernatural view of the culture-building imagination of the ancients: the rituals had to originate from somewhere. In any historical situation, the rituals need to be given and learned. Xunzi did not conceive a sharp boundary between the merely natural and the elementary human. He said, "The inborn nature of man is certainly that of the petty man."¹¹ Without tutoring, such a petty man will be selfish and contribute to chaos. Even selfishness requires a modicum of internal organization and regulation, and capacity to relate to things outside. So he would admit that a purely unritualized or untaught person would be impossible. But sageliness requires learning the sophisticated rituals and learning them well. "The sage purifies his natural lord, rectifies his natural faculties, completes his natural nourishment, is obedient to the natural rule of order, and nourishes his natural emotions and thereby completes nature's achievement."¹² Not just individual perfection but civilization itself depends on ritual mastery in the sense that humaneness cannot arise unless there are ritual social habits that allow of its expression. Without ritual there is no family life, only procreation, no division of family responsibilities, only the desire to get free as soon as possible, no political life, only strongman rule, no loyalties to a political entity larger than proximate community (e.g., the nation or empire/emperor), only clan-based self-serving. Civilization involves the move from face-to-face (usually clan) organization to more nearly universal role-based behavior, which means ritual. The great Confucian contribution to contemporary philosophy is calling attention to the moral weight of rituals that undergird every other sense of the social meaning of moral actions.

Our own late-modern science is very different from Xunzi's, emphasizing evolution and biological continuities up through sign-shaped behavior and language.¹³ Nevertheless, his point is well taken, namely, that the causal processes of interpreting signs are different from causal processes that are merely natural and do not have signs, to put the point a modern way. Many human processes are mixtures, with some elements best understood in terms of chemical reactions, say, and others in terms of signs. Human life is a kind of biopsychic dance. Chemical states cause the stomach to contract and growl, stimulating thoughts of food, purposeful eating, pleasurable digesting, and chemical metabolic nourishment; most meals also involve social interaction. Any explanation or understanding of this process that leaves out the chemical patterns of causation or the semiotic ones is stupidly reductive. Insofar as semiosis is involved, there is an element of Xunzian ritual.

RITUAL AND SEMIOTICS

Rituals across the spectrum are conventions. Conventions are not innate but are signs that need to be learned. The upshot of this is that semiotics, the study of signs, should be brought in to the *paideia* of religious studies in an important way. The semiotic theory most attuned to the ritual point is that of Charles S. Peirce for whom it is closely connected with his pragmatic theory of engaging the world and also with his metaphysics of nature.[14] Implicit in my argument here and drawn out elsewhere is that religious symbols serve to engage us with realities where otherwise we would have no handle. Other theories of signs take them to be distancing substitutes for addressing the realities. The chief distinction between Peirce's semiotics and that of the European tradition associated with Saussure is that, whereas the latter takes the interpretation of texts to be paradigmatic, Peirce takes the interpretation of nature to be paradigmatic. For Peirce, interpretation is the process of engagement with realities. The interesting question, then, is not so much the decoding of signs within semiotic systems, the European preoccupation, as the analysis of how signs arise within semiotic systems, how they take on definiteness, and sometimes lose definiteness. The reasons for this "genetic history" of signs have to do with pragmatic concerns for their roles in engaging realities, that is, whether they make proper discriminations for the contexts and purposes of interpretation.[15] That signs "grow" within semiotic systems illustrates Peirce's metaphysics according to which there is a cosmic propensity for growth of connection and relationship, which is what signs produce. All of this resonates with the contextualism of Xunzi's theory of ritual that marks its conventionality. For instance, ritual for him was seasonable; he adjusted periods of mourning to the station and importance of the deceased, as well as to the resources of the family.[16] He knew there were alternative calendars and different classifications of social merit, all conventional distinctions but articulating something real.

Peirce's semiotic theory introduces many distinctions that are obscure or wholly nonexistent in Xunzi's theory of ritual. Peirce said there are three main topics of semiotics. One is the analysis of signs themselves in their meanings relative to one another; Xunzi does some of this, as in 19.7a–b. A second topic is the context within which signs are used. The context determines the respects in which the signs stand for objects, thus what is taken to be important in the context. Context connects what is important in the object with what is important in the purposes and values of the interpreters. Xunzi is massively brilliant in analyzing the appropriateness of ritual behaviors for particular situations, dealing on the one hand with the objective occasion for ritual and on the other with the nature and contexts of the participants. The entire Confucian tradition has important contributions to make to this theme of contextual interpretation, so important to the pragmatic tradition. The theme was particularly important for John Dewey, and the fact that he failed to address the connection with Confucian culture was a significant missed opportunity.[17]

The third main topic of semiotics, according to Peirce, is reference, and he distinguished at least three kinds, conventional (which he called symbolic), iconic, and indexical. Conventional reference means that signs refer according to the ways their semiotic systems define, the way language does. Any kind of sign that can be talked about is at least conventional. Iconic reference takes reality to be like what the sign says. Simple iconic reference is like an isomorphism between the form of the thing and the form of the sign, as a cross is an icon of Jesus's crucifixion (to use Peirce's example). More complicated kinds of iconic reference go all the way to descriptions in which the words paint a picture, if you will, or present a theory, of the way the referent is supposed to be. Xunzi recognizes iconic reference in saying, for instance, that the cost and elaborateness of funerals should be in proportion to the importance of the deceased: "The funeral of the Son of Heaven affects all within the four seas and brings together the feudal lords. . . . The funeral of a castrated criminal does not involve uniting his family and neighbors, but brings together only his wife and children. . . . As soon as his body is interred in the earth, everything ends as though there had never been a funeral."[18] In his discussion of music, Xunzi relates instruments to great themes. The general idea of correlative thinking in ancient Chinese, especially Confucian, culture is a kind of iconic reference.[19]

Indexical reference, the third kind, is most important for Confucianism. Signs can refer by pointing, which is to say they can establish a causal relation between the object and the interpreter, like getting the person to turn and look. More significantly, many signs refer by requiring deep and important changes in the interpreter. This is especially significant for religious signs upon which people meditate or that guide religious practices: only long practice can transform the person enough properly to engage the object as the sign would require. The Confucian theme of the rectification of names should not be understood as an attempt to get the right icon or description, but as the attempt to get the right index.[20] The right index causes the interpreter to be properly comported toward to object, treating it according to its true nature and worth. A description might be involved in a rectified name, but then again the descriptive or iconic elements of the "right name" might be quite fanciful, plainly false if interpreted literally. Chad Hansen's "Daoist" interpretation of language can be seen as rightly emphasizing the indexical as opposed to iconic character of reference, according to Peirce's categories.[21] With this distinction in hand, a major new research project opens up for extending the Confucian analysis of the rectification of names.

Perhaps the most important connection of Xunzi's theory of ritual with semiotics has to do with ritual performance and semiotically shaped behavior. Speech act theory derived from Austin and Searle distinguishes the performative function of speech acts from cognitive statements, questions, and so forth.[22] Peirce's pragmatic semiotics treats all speech and sign-shaped acts as performatives, functioning to engage the interpreter or actor with the realities interpreted in one way or another. Distinctions between kinds of engagement, some quite physical and others purely contemplative with a vast array in between, are made on Peirce's theory in terms of considerations of meaning systems, interpretive contexts, and dimensions of reference. Sign-shaped behaviors are analyzed as habits whose guiding principles are interpretive signs that can be understood semiotically, and objectified in consciousness as a thought conceived as a thought. Xunzi's spectrum of rituals across all kinds of conventionally shaped actions and thought lend themselves to a Peircean analysis of performatives rather than a speech act analysis that distinguishes performatives from other locutions. Like Peirce's theory, Xunzi's supposes and manifests a unity of thought and action characteristic of Confucianism and pragmatism alike.[23]

One final point needs to be made about the semiotic character of ritual theory, which is that rituals as sign-shaped behaviors are vague and require individuation or specification in their performance. As Xunzi pointed out, there is a dance-like quality to rituals.[24] The dances have formal "steps" that integrate many people's movements and those steps can be learned. As vague, however, each performer has to make them specific to individuated actions. Underdetermined human nature can be determined greatly by the conventions of sign-shaped behavior; but that determination is still vague and needs individuation. Whereas individuation in Western philosophy has often been interpreted in terms of matter, or the haecceity of actualization, Xunzi's approach is through the analogies of music. Tones are entirely specific, and the major tone in a song sets all the other relations. Moreover, for Xunzi specific cooperation in integrating society does not come only from laws or precepts, though surely from them too, or even from just the modeling of a life, but from the ruler being like a singing master who provides the tune so that the others actualize an appropriate harmony.[25]

RITUAL AND DESIRE

Xunzi opened his essay on ritual principles with the question of the origin of ritual, by which he meant its founding utility as well as its historical origin: what is ritual basically good for? He answered by pointing out that people are born with desires, which prompt action to achieve their satisfaction. The action of seeking satisfaction has no measure, he said, leading people to fight over the means to satisfy their desires. That fighting leads to disorder, which in turn leads to the impoverishment of the society. The ancient kings abhorred disorder and wanted their people to have satisfaction in their desires. So they invented ritual regulations that appropriately related desires to the goods that might satisfy them. "In this way, the two of them, desires and goods, sustained each other over the course of time."[26] Note that desires are not bad. Nor is the fact that the pursuit of their satisfaction is unmeasured bad in itself. The drawback of unmeasured pursuit of desires is that it leads to conflict that diminishes wealth so that the desires cannot be satisfied—poverty is bad for the satisfaction of desires. The rebalancing of Xunzi's ill-founded reputation as a dour misanthrope who thought human nature is bad requires this point to be emphasized. Desires are often good and should be limited by ritual only so that their satisfaction might be maximized. Discussing music as ritual, Xunzi puts the point even more positively: music is joy and leads to joy.[27] Moreover, being full of joy, a person will start singing and dancing, exercising the ritual forms of music and dance.

The problem Xunzi recognized with desires is that they are inchoate, powerful, and underdetermined, to continue the point made previously. With our evolutionary biological understanding we can see this as the problem of stimulus-response organization. Animals have evolved so that complex defensive, aggressive, or appetitive responses are triggered by specific immediate stimuli like a flash of light or sudden sound that makes one jump. Reptilian brains are triggered to fight, flight, devour, or copulate by basic stimuli with relatively little mediating interpretation. Amphibians, for instance, lack the mental capacity to rotate a visual image in the mind's eye so as to imagine the backside of prey or a predator; a frog on a lily pad flicks its sticky tongue at tasty bugs in its field of vision, but cannot imagine creeping up behind one (and is not built to creep). Human beings have old "reptilian" brains, but these are overlaid by many other organs of the brain that mediate kinds of data that can suggest alternative modes of response to fighting or fleeing; we do not eat everything that looks good (after about the age of two) nor copulate on impulse. The frontal and temporal cortices, in fact, have evolved to readiness for semiotic interpretation with capacities for extraordinary mediation according to long-range personal and social values. Contemporary science is a long way from clearly demarcating the "merely biological" from the semiotic elements in the biopsychic dance, though we understand that there are a great many human functions in which basic biological or chemical interactions are ordered at a higher level by semiotic considerations. Stomach contractions register as hunger pangs that in turn motivate people to stop work and go to lunch, debating whether to have Chinese or Turkish food.

Wherever the semiotic organization of behavior reaches down into the biopsychic dance, Xunzi's point about ritual obtains. Without the culturally learned signs, the behavior cannot take on the kind of organization that signs allow. Hence desires can be only immediate responses to stimuli rather than interpreted responses that take the stimuli to stand for states of affairs beyond themselves. Xunzi commonly described human nature as that which people are born with, in contrast to what people subsequently learn.[28] Like babies they are selfish and irritable. "The inborn nature of man is certainly that of the petty man."[29] He described the natural human faults as adult vices such as aggressiveness, greediness, envy, and hatred; natural desires are crudely sensuous.[30] The characteristic of all these faults is lack of semiotic (*li*) ordering, like a baby. A person who grows up to exhibit the adult faults remains a baby in the failure to learn the rituals that allow proper mediating reference to others and to the real goods and evils of the social and natural world apart from immediate stimuli. Xunzi called this lack of deference, or inattention to the nature of other things.

Mencius's mistake, according to Xunzi, was to believe that desires could grow their needed semiotic focus from within. Because Xunzi believed that the semiotic or ritual elements derive from human contributions (e.g., the ancient kings) rather than the biological impulses given by Heaven and Earth, he rejected Mencius's theory of internal exfoliation of virtue as simply wrong. Moreover, by expecting people to become rightly related to others and nature simply by letting their natural impulses grow uncorrupted, Mencius's theory in practice would lead to adult babies, selfish and aggressive, envious and hateful. Or it would smuggle in ritual training disguised by romantic posturing. At any rate, to Xunzi, Mencius was literally irresponsible, failing to recognize the responsibility to acculturate desires ritually or semiotically so that they can attain their right objects and focus of activity. Only ritual can allow one to desire dancing with desirable others in a dance of civilized beauty.

Today we recognize that the biological is not prior to the semiotic in any simple sense. Only because primitive human ancestors had rudimentary signs could they evolve with Homo sapiens' brains, and thus develop even more complex signs so as to desire civilized ways of life and satisfaction. The ancient Chinese did not conceive of the interaction of semiotics and biology in evolution. Nevertheless, Xunzi is right over against Mencius about the movement from primitive desire as response to immediate stimuli on to authentically human and civilized desires, relating our capacities for sensation to their best proper objects. That movement requires human learning, especially ritualization into conventional organization that mediates immediate stimuli to larger human meanings. The moral, as obvious to us late moderns as to Xunzi himself, is that failure to pay attention to ritual and teach it intentionally results in merely "natural" behavior that falls short of the human.

RITUAL, INTEGRATION, AND RELIGION

The notorious problem with desires is that they conflict and lead to such disorganized behavior that even those whose fulfillment is possible and easy remain unfulfilled. This problem is as bad when the individual desires are clearly articulated with regard to sophisticated identification of their real fulfillment as when they are foolishly immediate. Xunzi, of course, was late in a long line of philosophers East and West who have recognized this point, for instance Plato in his discussions of eros. What parent of an adolescent can miss the difficulty?

The tempting response to the problem is to find a theory or overall pattern by which the many desires properly suitable to a person and community can be integrated. Patterns are usually conceived to be static, however, with the result that appetitive behavior is forced into fixed forms that are inattentive to the constant shifts in the natural and social environment, as well as to the psychological and physical development of the individuals. The better response is to conceive of the integration as a ritual dance, with the competing desires all having their roles to play according to appropriate timing and reactions with other desires, the desires of other people, and the shifting terrain for the human performance. A healthy and properly deferential individual has a rich internal ritual life that allows the measured satisfaction of all important desires required for personal fulfillment and social obligation.

From our evolutionary standpoint we can sort levels of ritual integration that Xunzi might recognize as ready to handle his examples. We have already noted the very primitive ritual level that integrates basic posture and movement with "styles" of determining the underdetermined biological potential. Closely related to this are the ritual dances imposed to clamp down on the immediate fight, flight, devour, embrace responses. Likely this is not a happy dance but, as Freud pointed out about learning physical and impulse control, closely akin to forcing oneself to withhold or expel feces contrary to impulse. As Plato said, elementary as well as sophisticated discipline is the application of one's aggression to oneself.[31] As Xunzi said, no one would undertake this naturally but needs to be taught with tough lessons.

Beyond impulse control the affective life of an individual needs to be organized so as to constitute an integrated personal style, a personality. This is done while yet a further level of integration is learned, namely, the roles the individual plays in the larger family. The Greeks, like the Confucians, stressed the back and forth movement between learning to play roles in the family and learning to integrate personal style. Just as immediate impulses need to be forced into a dance that allows for personal integration, one's personal interests need to be forced into a dance that allows for family functioning, which in turn defines personal interests. The Confucian ritual problematic of filiality, as important for Xunzi as for others, traces the development of personal and familial integrating rituals.[32]

The fortunes of families themselves are not naturally integrated in a larger community and need a further level of ritual integration. Left to themselves, competing for short resources, honor, and dominance, families feud, and a civil society with a king is needed. Civil ritual cannot be reduced to law imposed by the royal army alone. It is a function of a learned dance that acknowledges authority and subordinates the designs of families for their own blood to the needs of the trans-family whole. The ritual dances of public society are never without a supplementary police force, however much Confucius himself hoped they might be. Xunzi was never in doubt about the point. Public rituals need enforcement. No good king would tolerate the crude public policies of Mozi; the Way of the King is music![33]

Perhaps there is an even higher level of integration than that of public life, namely the exquisite beauty of the arts. As mentioned, Xunzi praises music for its sheer joy, punning on a homophone for music, joy, and delight. Music and the other arts call for the special organization of public life to support them, and they in turn shape public life. Our category of "art" is too narrow for the ancient Chinese conception, and for the reality too. Living, doing, making, and enjoying things that are intrinsically valuable and appreciable is a kind of perfection of civilized life, and this requires a further complex of rituals or socially shared and exercised conventions.

Although the image of levels of integration is artificial, belying many causal and ritual crossings from one level to the next, it does make a powerful point about human life that Xunzi would acknowledge quickly. Each level achieves a ritual integration and intensity by weaving a pattern on the lower level. But that is a kind of force, a constriction. The lower levels pay a price by being integrated into the dance of the higher levels. Brute impulses are constricted for the sake of personal integration; personal interests are subordinated to family integration; family interests are limited by public order; public order is given shape and justification by the goods and ways of life most nearly appreciable for their own sake. The ritual dances order their components by keeping them under pressure. When things work well, the pressure is released in the performance of the higher level. Or at least the pressure is managed. Confucians generally and Xunzi in particular have known that human life is organized with pressure and control. If Confucians have seemed a bit stiff and forced to Daoists, it is because they know and are willing to pay the price for impulse control, personal discipline, family flourishing, public order, and the high arts. Daoists generally count on Confucians paying the price for them, or pay themselves by shifting into a Confucian mode. The price is generally thought worthwhile because each level of integration brings a richer level of personal or civilizational satisfaction.[34]

But things rarely go perfectly well for long. The economy gets tight and the public schools cut out the arts budget. A crisis in public confidence causes representatives of families to vote for school vouchers rather than public schools. Then children rebel against the family's attempt to force its version of the social microcosm upon them. Untaught, they are defeated by their own impulses and wallow in selfish, aggressive, envious, hateful, and narcissistically immediate desires. Cut off on the freeway, even the patriarch burns white-knuckled with road rage, a velociraptor in a Volvo. The reptile erupts through all the levels of civilized ritual meaning and accomplishment. What most sets Xunzi apart from Mencius is that he knew this:

> Thus a warped piece of wood must first await application of the press-frame, steam to soften it, and force to bend its shape before it can be made straight. A dull piece of metal must first be whetted on the grindstone before it can be made sharp. Now, since human nature is evil, it must await the instructions of a teacher and the model before it can be put aright, and it must obtain ritual principles and a sense of moral right before it can become orderly. Nowadays, since men lack both teacher and model, they are prejudiced, wicked, and not upright. Since they lack ritual principles and precepts of moral duty, they are perverse, rebellious, and disorderly.
>
> In antiquity the sage-kings took man's nature to be evil, to be inclined to prejudice and prone to error, to be perverse and rebellious, and not to be upright or orderly. For this reason they invented ritual principles and precepts of moral duty. They instituted the regulations that are contained in laws and standards. Through these actions they intended to "straighten out" and develop man's essential nature and to set his inborn nature aright. They sought to tame and transform his essential nature and to guide his inborn nature with the Way. They caused both his essential and inborn natures to develop with good order and be consistent with the true Way.[35]

This sums up Xunzi's view that the normative Way of being human, that which the *Chongyong* says is Heaven sent, is not *given* in Heaven and Earth's biological or "natural" donation, but in what the sages have learned about the conventions or rituals that humanize. The Way for humans is conventional but not arbitrary in the sense of being the result of capricious will. For Xunzi the ancients figured out how rituals make the achievements of human life and civilization possible and developed rituals that do this; his moral crusade, like that of Confucius, was to recover those rituals so as to restore the possibility of high civilization. Whereas we take a more evolutionary view as to the development of those rituals or signs, we can accept the main point: without ritual semiotics, we are not human, we are more like reptiles.

Whereas Xunzi would resonate with the analysis of ritual as organizing desires to be attuned to proper objects, and also as organizing different levels of integration and achievement from the merely biological to high civilization, he seems not to have addressed the breakdown of the levels and the eruption of the pressures of the lower through the higher. He would not know what to do with the velociraptor in the Volvo, nor would his tradition generally. The traditions of West Asia, Judaism, Christianity, and Islam have been more sensitive than the Confucian to the situation of the pressures of life's hierarchical organization.

The situation, I have argued, is twofold. On the one hand, human life at each level feels the pressures of the lower levels. Cumulatively this is felt as guilt, the layers of prices paid to achieve higher organization. Rarely if ever is this guilt personally culpable, and hence it fails to register in the Western Enlightenment mentality. But one's impulses pay a price to be integrated into a personal style, which pays a price to live within a family, which pays a price to function in a public society, which pays a price to bear a high culture. To be a human being at all in a high society is to be a great expense for other things and the feeling of that price paid is guilt. Christianity carries this idea furthest in its idea of original sin. Xunzi himself held that a sage could harmonize all these elements, but I think that for him harmony includes holding things in tension, balance under pressure. Although I have developed his ideas in a contemporary language shaped by Freudian and Nietzschean sensibilities, obviously anachronistic in a sense, I suspect that part of the Neo-Confucian wariness of Xunzi came from an accurate apprehension of high pressure beneath his correct manner.

On the other hand the reaction to the pressure, doubled by the feelings of guilt, is destructive disruption of the levels of ritual organization in individuals and society, usually violent evil. Confucians generally have attempted to account for human evil by saying that it is the result of selfishness obstructing what otherwise would be naturally appropriate responses to things. Xunzi weighed these things differently from the Mencian tradition in Confucianism. He said first that selfishness is not a learned vice but the natural state of untutored desire that has only an immediate responsiveness. Failure to tutor the desire with ritual leads to infantile selfishness lasting into adulthood. But, second, Xunzi recognized that the ritual tutoring of desire itself puts infantile desire under pressure. Learning involves work, force, and control. When it fails, those infantile desires under pressure can explode. Xunzi does not go so far as to describe evil in this explosive way, although he does appreciate the pressure that ritual education applies to the merely natural and always remains suspicious of the natural alone and its threat to civilized life.

Ritual has a religious dimension that Xunzi and the ancient Confucians may not have fully recognized. If one imagines layers of ritual dance organizing horizontal levels of biopsychic human reality, one also can imagine vertical rituals that weave up and down through the horizontal levels. My hypothesis is that religious rituals connect otherwise incommensurate strategies of integration.[36] They release pressures. They reestablish broken dances. They acknowledge disruptions, tragedies, collapses of entire dimensions of human life. They rewind and set the clock so that things can go again. The paradigmatic religious ritual is the sacrifice in which something's or someone's lifeblood is drained and body parts rearranged as if rearranging some broken personal, social, or cosmic body. Emperors and parents function as priests to perform the humanly healing sacrifices and other religious rituals that realign the levels of semiotically meaningful human reality.

Of course Xunzi did not have this late twentieth-century, psychoanalytically and anthropologically oriented theory of ritual. But he did understand the role of the Son of Heaven, the chief sacrificer, to be to order the human world and fulfill Heaven and Earth, integrating both horizontally and vertically.[37] The emperor's diet, constituting his life and endurance, has abundant meat from the sacrificial animals.[38] Sacrifices were offered to the legendary sage emperors who invented the rituals that harmonized society (by creating hierarchical relations).[39] Few Chinese thinkers in the Confucian tradition had as much sensitivity as Xunzi to the ways by which the best laid rituals might slip. Whereas Mencius would say that people with uncorrupted human nature unfolding throughout life would employ ritual as the external expression of internal humaneness, Xunzi would warn that rituals need to be taught, imposed, and enforced for humaneness to develop at all out of the chaos of desires.[40] The perceived threat of a collapse back into personal and social chaos led some of Xunzi's followers to legalism, a move Xunzi steadily declined. But I would not be surprised if his insistence on returning to ritual in the threat of chaos did not have some hope in the purgative and restorative powers of sacrifice.

To distinguish a religious dimension from others within ritual is anachronistic in reference to Xunzi and his milieu. Nevertheless, to bring Xunzi into the contemporary discussion where that distinction is indeed very important is to play to his strength relative to other Confucians. For Xunzi in contrast to the Mencian line, the virtues of humaneness are achievements of harmonious determination of underdetermined human nature by ritual broadly conceived, and are as fragile as their ritual medium is fragile. Where Mencius would interpret the social collapses in Rwanda, Congo, Zimbabwe, Yugoslavia, India/Pakistan, Ireland, and Iraq as failures of ritual to allow the proper expression of humaneness that would otherwise naturally unfold, Xunzi would see those collapses as preventing the formation of humaneness out of inchoate immediate and aimless desires. Moreover, Xunzi would recognize, and approve as necessary, the pressures required to bring the desires to order and integration. But he would expect, and lament as tragic, occasional explosions of ritual organizations under those very pressures, thereby deconstructing the very essence of the human. In the face of this threat, Xunzi advocated ever more rule and control by the government.[41] But this should not be exercised by military strength, he said, only by strengthening the king's personal inner and outer power, accomplished through ritual.[42]

Ritual should not be overstressed in Xunzi so as to make it seem as if he lacked the Confucian commitment to humaneness or doubted that human nature derives from Heaven. But he did insist that the normative civilization made possible through ritual derives from Heaven only indirectly in ways requiring the creative discernment of the sages, not in what Heaven contributes to human biology, which includes "a bundle of 'unlovely' desires and impulses."[43] So for him, as for many contemporary thinkers, semiotics is required to understand how the human organism becomes a human being.

4
Daoist Relativism, Ethical Choice, and Normative Measure

FOR MANY OF OUR CONTEMPORARIES, Confucianism is not an attractive resource, precisely because of its emphasis on ritual. Rituals easily become merely formal and spiritually deadly. The social enforcement of rituals often is observed to be wickedly conservative and oppressive. Of course that sense and function of rituals is different from what I have mined from Xunzi and the other ancient Confucians. Nevertheless, at various times in Confucian cultures of East Asia, ritual life has indeed become a reinforcement of the status quo, a point made forcefully by Confucianism's critics in China in the early twentieth century.

Instead, many of our contemporaries look to Daoism as a far more attractive philosophic resource, precisely because it popularly is associated with spontaneity, rejection of the artificial (read *ritual*), and a humorous mockery of uptight Confucians. This popular contemporary vision of Daoism as the polar opposite of Confucianism is a great exaggeration, to be sure. They were not seen as radically opposing schools until the ninth century when Han Yu and Li Ao sharply attacked Daoism in the name of Confucianism, beginning a Confucian revival; even then, subsequent Neo-Confucianism adopted many Daoist themes. The earlier, third-century thinker, Wangbi, is usually accounted a Daoist because he wrote a commentary on the *Daodejing*; yet he developed the concept of substance-and-function, and that of Principle (*li*), basic Confucian themes. One of Xunzi's own students, Han Feizi, is usually associated with Daoism and Legalism, despite his teacher's place in the Confucian lineage; Han Feizi was one of the earliest thinkers to develop the Confucian notion of Principle (*li*). So it is only from our own vantage point that popular imagination can evoke the sharp contrast between ritualized Confucianism and spontaneous Daoism. Nevertheless, from our vantage point, Daoism is an important resource.

Daoism, like Confucianism, seeks to find a contemporary voice in a cultural world vastly different from that of the era of its founding vocabulary. By Daoism here I refer to the contemporary philosophic and spiritual movement that constructs its lineage from the classical texts of the *Daodejing* and *Zhuangzi*, especially as interpreted by Wangbi. This is different from, and sometimes hostile to, the institutionalized medieval Daoism that also developed from those texts but that eventuated in an elaborate supernatural cosmology and a highly ceremonial and medicalized practice, with monastic life and clerical officials. Even less than in the case of Confucianism can we recover the cultural context of the pre-classical founding of Daoism.[1] The contemporary Daoists whose development I wish to consider here are those who relate to the classical texts as representing a school that had more in common with the Confucian, Moist, and Legalist school than with the line of development of institutionalized religious Daoism, which also has contemporary development. I recognize that the image of the ancient school of philosophical Daoism might be as much the reconstruction of later philosophers who were competing with Confucians and others than a historical reality. A social scientific historical study of Daoism would have to give primacy to the line of development through institutionalized medieval Daoism, down to the present time. Nevertheless, the philosophical rendering of Daoism in competition with Confucianism and other philosophies has had a life of its own from Wangbi and Guo Xiang through Zhou Dunyi and Zhuxi down to Wu Kuangming and David L. Hall in our time.[2] Chang Chung-yuan represented this philosophic Daoism as both a translator and a philosopher of culture.[3] Regardless of founding contexts, both Daoism and Confucianism bring texts, trajectories of interpretation, and accumulated intellectual institutions to the contemporary global philosophic discussion. Moreover, they bring baggage.

The most prominent piece of philosophic Daoist baggage is the conviction that it is relativistic or amoral. Therefore it seems unhelpful, on second thought, for ecological ethics, for human relations to the natural and artificial, and for the conditions and obligations relative to the beauty and repose of life for which philosophic Daoism so forcefully recommends itself on first thought.[4] I've met no one who has read the *Daodejing*, for instance, without being moved in a threefold way: first, to sense an ideal of harmony and authentic relation to reality; second, to recoil from the suddenly illumined disharmony, clutter, and counterproductive inertias of the situation at hand; and third, to resolve some path of therapy aiming at natural wholesomeness. The resolve might not go far, but even undergraduates usually straighten their dorm room and rearrange the furniture, or else abandon the dorm and take some herbal tea to a secluded park. This threefold effect occurs even when people have been warned that the book is about politics, not about grooving on nature. The reason for the effect is that the *Daodejing*, like the *Zhuangzi*, displays an existentially sharp contrast between the ideal and real so perfectly general that every individual is named by it.[5] So we rightly expect help on the great issues of harmony and disharmony in contemporary life and are surprised to discover in Daoism, on deeper reflection, a denial of objectivism in morals and a rejection of moral earnestness (to be discussed more further on).

The alleged relativism of Daoism is not entirely unfriendly to some European movements of philosophy.[6] Since the early modern period many scientifically minded thinkers have distinguished sharply between "facts" and "values." The former are real, because modern science is the kind of knowledge that knows facts but not values; the latter are often thought to be subjective projections of the mind without justification in the objects on which they are projected.[7] Daoism can be taken to have an affinity with value-neutral naturalism and with parallel trains of humanistic thought that advise on how to keep perspective in a world with no objective human meaning.[8] In this essay I shall not analyze these claims for the virtues of relativism or the degree to which they can be found in Daoism. Instead I shall argue that philosophical Daoism has important contributions to make to moral and valuational issues in ecology, in the human relation to nature and the artificial, and in understanding the beauty and repose of human life.

A METAPHYSICAL DAOISM

The first step in my argument is to present a contemporary metaphysical interpretation of the Dao. Of course this is supposed to be impossible and intrinsically un-Daoistic, but everything depends on what you mean by *metaphysics*. The *Daodejing* opens with the famous lines "The Tao that can be told of is not the eternal Tao; The name that can be named is not the eternal name."[9] These and the immediately following lines would seem to say that you cannot do metaphysics about the real (eternal) Dao. But the line does indeed tell something of the unnameable Dao, namely that it is unnameable. The first stanza talks about the nameable and unnameable, and makes the point quite common in Western apophatic metaphysical theology that the ultimate can be discussed mainly by means of negations and indirections. Thomas Aquinas, more metaphysical than whom it is hard to be, made much the same point in claiming that the Act of Esse is not in a genus and is so simple as to have no nameable distinctions or definiteness except that it is the ground of everything else, all definiteness. The third and fourth lines of the *Daodejing* are "The

Nameless is the origin of Heaven and Earth; The Named is the mother of all things." Any metaphysical Neoplatonist could accept those lines, although the Chinese cosmology is quite different from the European theories associated with Neoplatonism. The apophatic character of heavy-duty Western metaphysics is as old as Parmenides and Plato and as recently chewed as Heidegger and Rahner. Only if metaphysics is restricted to the kind of scholasticism Kant attacked can the label be refused of the *Daodejing* and some of the writings of Zhuangzi.

The practice and form of metaphysics in the sense I mean here is the development of hypotheses about the broadest characteristics of reality and their conditions. This theory of hypotheses was developed by Charles S. Peirce, the American pragmatist, and used explicitly for metaphysics by Alfred North Whitehead, the great process philosopher.[10] The subject matter of metaphysics I take to be anything real, and reality is anything we can be wrong about. Positions, such as that metaphysics is impossible because reality flows too much (*pratitya samutpada*) to be described, are themselves metaphysical because they make claims about reality and refute alternatives by saying that reality does not sustain the alternative interpretations. Even the Madhyamaka claim that ontological reality cannot be referred to, or that reference cannot be made to anything ontologically real, is a metaphysical position on the nature of reality and reference that says alternative positions are wrong about reality and reference.

Plainly metaphysical interpretations of the *Daodejing* are ancient. Wangbi's (226–249 CE) is one of the oldest commentaries on the *Daodejing*, and it glosses the previous sentences:

> All being originated from nonbeing. The time before physical forms and names appeared was the beginning of the myriad things. After forms and names appeared, "Tao (the Way) develops them, nourishes them, provides their formal shape and completes their formal substance," that is, becomes (or is) their Mother. This means that Tao produces and completes things with the formless and nameless. Thus they are produced and completed but do not know why. Indeed it is the mystery of mysteries.[11]

A contemporary metaphysics, as argued in a previous chapter, needs to be attuned to contemporary knowledge in the sciences and practical arts and thus will be quite different in some respects from ancient metaphysics, Greek or Chinese. Moreover, it will have to reflect instruction from the intervening philosophic traditions from all cultures that have developed ancient motifs so as to enter the contemporary discussions. Nevertheless certain contemporary metaphysical points can be made that pick up on ancient Daoist themes so as to give currency to a philosophic Daoist approach to normative issues.[12]

First, a contemporary metaphysics needs to acknowledge that everything determinate is subject to explanation by science, not that current science has all the explanations, but that the what, why, and where of things, their determinate characters, are what need scientific explanation. "What, why, and where" are not to be given commonsense interpretations in dealing with astrophysics and particle physics, but those questions still are of the scientific sort calling for tests that decide among alternatives. "What" asks whether it's this or that; "why" asks for reasons that it's this rather than that; "where" asks about this rather than that existential location. These kinds of questions look for answers through the imaginative, often mathematical, construction of arrays of possibilities to be sorted through controlled experiments. Measure, especially mathematical measure, is the Western ideal for expressing determinateness. A contemporary metaphysics needs to be vague with respect to any plausible scientific findings or theories. That is, a contemporary metaphysics needs to be able to tolerate the truth of anything the sciences or other routes of knowing might find to be true of their determinate subject matters, even when those scientific theories are at odds with one another. In Daoist terms, everything determinate is the "nameable" and has "physical form."

Whereas scientific and related inquiries study the what, why, and where of determinate things, metaphysics also studies why there exists the array of determinate things in the first place, whatever they are and whatever their mathematically expressible principles of causal connection. Stephen Hawking, the famous mathematical physicist, wrote:

> What is it that breathes fire into the equations and makes a universe for them to describe? The usual approach of science of constructing a mathematical model cannot answer the questions of why there should be a universe for the model to describe. Why does the universe go to all the bother of existing?[13]

The Chinese and Western intellectual traditions have rather different basic metaphors and intellectual habits for addressing this ontological metaphysical question of the contingency of the nameable. The Western tradition generally has elaborated monotheistic metaphors into accounts of divine creation, with several typical models at hand, for instance the Neo-Platonic, the model of creation ex nihilo, and the participationist theory of Thomas Aquinas. The Chinese traditions, with no clear demarcation of Daoist from others in this respect, assiduously avoid agency language for ontological causation and insist instead that being and beings originate from nonbeing. The priority of nonbeing or the nameless is clear in the texts quoted previously from the *Daodejing* and from Wangbi's commentary.

The emphasis on nonbeing (*benwu*) or "not having properties" (*wuji*) is clear in its rejection of a prior agency in a Creator that (or who) is determinate in any sense. Nevertheless, the Chinese tradition affirms a strong ontological dependence of everything with characters on nonbeing. In fact, it uses the causal language of nonbeing as the origin of everything, of producing, as in the texts quoted.[14] The ancient *Great Learning*, subsequently affiliated with the Confucian tradition, employs the metaphor of "roots and branches" that is interpreted and expanded in many ways throughout the Chinese philosophic discussions.

I have argued extensively for a contemporary metaphysical hypothesis for ontological causation that develops the concepts of creation ex nihilo.[15] My hypothesis agrees with the Chinese tradition in denying any agency to an antecedent divine being, arguing instead that the creator takes on the characteristics of creator only in creating. Therefore, if ontological causation were to be expressed in temporal terms, first there is nothing and then the creative act brings determinate things into temporal existence. But ontological causation should not be expressed in temporal terms because time, temporal relations, and time's flow are all among the determinate things that must be created. Ontological causation is a wholly eternal act, on my hypothesis, giving rise to time and a temporal order that might well proceed from the Big Bang to some final entropic dissolution, whatever the best scientific hypothesis says. The eternal ontological act is not to be modeled on present time as a *totum simul* specious present (e.g., Augustine), or on past time as making a completely determined temporal history (e.g., Leibniz, Laplace), or on future time as achieving externally given form or value (Plato, Aristotle). The logic of eternity is simply different, and not difficult once one abandons the attempt to express it in temporal metaphors.

Nevertheless, because we do live within time that produces new occasions each moment, we need to ask how ontological causation manifests itself within time. The manifestation is precisely in the novelty.[16] At the very least, each moment is new relative to the past. To the extent determinism obtains, what happens in the moment and where is determined by antecedent conditions. Determinism seems not to be complete, at least in the sense sometimes sought in the nineteenth century. Determining conditions are often best expressed on the physical level in terms of statistical aggregates. Quantum mechanics in its several interpretations denies clocklike mechanical determinism. From the human perspective, many situation exist that could have been determined but are not and that depend on human intervention, choice, and action. When and wherever a situation is underdetermined by antecedent conditions, the decisive determining is spontaneous relative to the past, and is the locus of ontological causation. The spontaneity in a given present happening is part of the eternal ontologically creative act whose other parts are elsewhere and in other times. If every happening is partly determined by antecedent conditions and partly by spontaneous creativity, and antecedent conditions themselves are composed of past happenings similarly determined in two ways, then the sum of all determinate existence equals the sum of all spontaneity, namely, the ontological creative act. But within time, ontological creativity is manifest in the spontaneity that moves the moments forward. We can look to eternal ontological creativity and also to its temporal manifestation.

This distinction is neatly expressed in the Daoist distinction between the eternal, unnameable Dao that is the origin of all nameable things with form and the nameable Mother Dao that "completes" things in the flow of time. The temporal Dao embraces the exquisite continuity between the inertial determinations of processes at hand and the spontaneous accretions by which they are brought to novel developments, harmonies, and dissolutions. The ancient Daoists would have thought about this in the following ways. On the one hand are the patterns of change through which things are passing, as in the hexagrams of the *Yijing*. Modern science would interpret this as natural structures and laws. On the other hand is the spontaneity that fleshes out these patterns in particular ways and, in the realm of human affairs, offers the opportunities for human intervention and control within the patterned lines of force. The Dao is not only the patterns or laws, and hence science does not know all the Dao; the temporal Dao is the interplay between structured inertial forces and spontaneity, so mysterious and subtle as the *Daodejing* says.

The philosophic advice of the *Daodejing* is to locate the tiny and subtle places in the cosmic, social, and personal processes where there is an opening for spontaneity. These small openings are not only of utilitarian use but are where the eternal ontological power of creativity is to be found, that which in its vastness is responsible for everything. Livia Kohn and James Miller state the point in the following way:

> Dao is not really "infinite" or "transcendent" but rather infinitesimal, the faintest, most imperceptible of breaths, the darkest shade of light, the smallest possible contrast that, in its infinite fractal-like recursions, multiplies to constitute the shocking wealth of cosmic power. This is the ultimate mystery of Dao: that subtle void and intangible formlessness should be the root of all becoming . . . the insight of the *Daode jing* is that only by becoming small, low, weak, imperceptible, quiet, desireless, and empty we can ever get close to the heart of this truth of cosmic reality. The process of ultimate transformation, therefore, begins in attention—making ourselves so small that we are able once and for all to grasp the staggering spontaneity of all around us.[17]

NORMATIVE MEASURE

The Daoist adept, perhaps a spiritual master or a military general, can locate the existential nodes of spontaneous opportunity and tie in to the cosmic creativity whereby very small subtle moves can result in large differences, shining with the vitality of spontaneity.[18] The charge of Daoist relativism usually comes at this point. Here the amoral adept has extraordinary power to do whatever he or she wants in a heroism of spontaneity. Confucians fume at the lack of commitment to corrigible norms for the exercise of this ontologically based power.

The account I've given here of spontaneity and power in the moving Dao is incomplete, however. Throughout the texts of the *Daodejing* and the *Zhuangzi* are remarkable evocations of harmony, balance, and reciprocity. Things are attuned to one another, and when they are not, there's trouble. Chang Chung-yuan's little modern classic, *Creativity and Taoism: A Study of Chinese Philosophy, Art, and Poetry*, makes this case in beautiful and compelling ways.[19] The case is argued on more strictly philosophic grounds by David Hall in his *Eros and Irony* that contrasts encompassing logical order with aesthetic orders that are always perspectival and insistent on particulars. The aesthetic orientation is the ground of the normative, ultimately moral orientation, I suggest.[20]

Permit me to add more detail to a contemporary metaphysics of the temporal Dao, with references to classic Daoist motifs. Every nameable thing or situation is a harmonic achievement with four elements. The first element is form or pattern, either static or developmental (most likely a combination of both). The second is a congeries of components that are integrated within the form, components that have their own inertial trajectories and might come together only temporarily within the form, or on the other hand might depend organically for their very existence on the other things with which the form environs them. The third element is the existential location of the harmonized thing or situation within larger space-time relations. The fourth is the value achieved by having these components harmonized according to this form in this existential location; the value would be different with different integrating forms, different components, or different locations. Because harmonies have existential location, value is always perspectival, for instance from the standpoint of the harmonized thing itself, from that of the past to which it gives meaning and outcome, from that of future things it can impact, and such like. The summary value of a thing, its value from all perspectives combined, is not perspectival but eternal, combined not in a finite determined existential grid but in the nonfinite act of ontological creation and therefore not separable from the values of other things (more on this later).

One dimension of the temporal Dao is thus the achievement of value-laden, existentially located harmonies of swarms of component inertial processes with specific forms or patterns. Experiential contemplation of the flow of things around us can focus on the exquisite composition and siting of things that achieves the particular values that can be apprehended. As David Hall puts it, "The aesthetic perspective is one which concentrates, no matter how extensive the context, upon the harmony of insistently particular details."[21]

But another dimension of the temporal Dao is the existential *dis*location of those achieved harmonies in bursts of spontaneity large or small. The inertial trajectories of components don't stay tethered in harmonic forms, and the achieved harmonies are weakened, shaken, exploded. More energy is needed to put them back together, or to achieve a different harmony with perhaps somewhat different forms, components, location, and value. Whereas Confucian lovers of Heaven or Principle and Aristotelian teleologists celebrate the lure and obligation of achieving harmonic value, Daoists delight in the dislocating transgressions and playful tricks of spontaneity. The Great Robber Chi was a true criminal, destructive of achieved value, but also a licensed operative of the Dao's spontaneous destruction of such achievements as straw dogs. The Dao can be conceived as having a kind of pulse, achieving harmonies and then loosening them to form new harmonies. Modern physical cosmology registers this as the expenditure of energy to achieve some order and then entropic dissolution, calling for more energy to reorder things. One of the most ancient Chinese metaphors registers this with a reverse twist on the expenditure of energy: yin-movement is a kind of relaxing into harmony pulsed with yang-movement that extends energetically beyond the harmonic matrix.[22] The Daoist adept does not merely celebrate the Puckish destructiveness of the Dao's spontaneity, except to annoy Confucians. Rather the Daoist focuses on the nisus or interplay of achieving value and then adventuring beyond that.[23]

The importance of the Daoist focus on the interplay of achieving harmonic value and then releasing it in adventure lies in its treatment of perspective. I said earlier that value is always in some perspective, first the perspective of the harmony achieving the value, and then in the various perspectives of the components that go into the harmony relative to their own trajectories and careers, and also in the perspectives of the many things that might be impacted by the achieved harmonic value. Zhuangzi was particularly exercised to point out the divergences in appreciation of things from different perspectives, sometimes divergent to the point of incommensurability. The monstrous fish-bird that flies overhead does not notice the sparrow in the bush, nor does it register in the sparrow's perspective, as he said in the first chapter of his book. The stories of the dreaming butterfly, the happy fish, and three-in-the-morning monkeys work changes on the issue of diverse perspectives. The annoying problem of ordinary (Confucian) consciousness is that the perspective of some single elegant achieved harmony, such as one's combined elite education, scientific knowledge, aesthetic background, and social class, is taken to be the fixed point for evaluating the present, past, and future. Not only do the components within one's perspective have their own different perspectives, but one's own situation changes with the Dao's pulses of spontaneity and no longer has the same existential location, or even the same form and components, as the previous achieved perspective. So, even the subtlest of us easily gets out of date and existentially alienated. Whereas contemporary deconstructionists get excited about the plurality of perspectives and the tendency of some one perspective to dominate others with power, the Daoist sensibility has focused rather on the existential shifts that dislocate the commanding or conscious perspectives leading to confusion or self-deception about what is important. The ideal is to let perspectives go and achieve new ones as the situation does the same with achieved value, deferring also to others who should be doing the same thing. To say all this, of course, is but to have one more perspective, common to all who inhabit the contemporary cross-cultural philosophic situation, nuanced differently by the trajectories we each bring to that situation—not many from dialectical metaphysics I wager—and made quite specific by our individual locations within that situation. I am here urging, by means of a comparative philosophical construction, a new element in our cross-cultural philosophic situation that consists in an appreciation of Daoism ancient and contemporary for certain contributions to ethical issues. Our contemporary perspective is shifting but emerging with a kind of harmony.

What is the normative element in Daoism that contributes to ethics and does not reduce to relativism? Joseph Grange calls the concept "normative measure," a phrase from Plato's *Statesman*.[24] Plato contrasted normative measure with "standard measure" according to which one appeals to principles to mix elements as in a recipe. Normative measure means getting "just enough" of each ingredient to bring about optimal harmony in the existential situation. The Platonic case at hand is that of the statesman who needs to cultivate different proportions of gentility and bravery in the society, mixing them according to the needs of domestic flourishing and defense. Those needs are constantly shifting, and so the art of normative measure depends heavily on timing.

Similarly, the Daoist moral focus is not on the structure of harmony that would be ideal for the situation, but rather on catching the underlying beat of the shifting situations and intervening with the rightly timed subtle, infinitesimal dose. The Daoist point is not to step back to a perspective that catches a long-term developmental pattern, although discerning such patterns is helpful. The Daoist rather wants to discern the rhythm with which the Dao's pulses change perspectives, achieving and then loosening harmonies to press on toward different achievements. The danger in the high integrative perspective focused on a long-term developmental pattern is that it misses, or obscures, or deliberately misrepresents the subtle openings of spontaneity, the empty places of nonbeing where real intervention can be made. Long-term perspectives when planned out in patterns reduce to crude instrumentalisms that cover over real novelty and spontaneous possibility and often resort to forcing affairs in the direction of predetermined goals. As the *Daodejing* says, it's hard to beat the inertial forces of the Dao, so nonaction in the little openings of nonbeing's spontaneity is far more effective, moving with the cosmic forces of creation rather than against them. Daoism does not recommend a moral theory in the sense of goals, rules, or virtues, but rather a way of life attuned to the pulses of shifting perspectives and to the openings all around for ducking flying decayed matter and bringing things to a new achievement of value. The rhythm of shifts in perspectives of value is more important to moral life, in the Daoist account, than attainment of a unified vision of harmony. The art of normative measure is closer to catching the beat in a dance, combining set steps and improvisation, than to deliberating about means to achieve an end.

DAOIST ETHICS

Daoists are likely to be annoying participants in committees to legislate environmental policy, to balance nurture versus nature in federally fundable "family values," or to establish a sex education curriculum in a public school system. Legislative decisions usually require adopting a pattern that is taken to determine the whole and articulate the relation of means to ends relative to the goals chosen, even when the goals are compromises. Daoists are likely to insist on taking into account another point of view just when everyone else is ready to vote.

In contrast to legislative participation, Daoists make great administrators. Actually engaging in political realities, interacting with the environment, with cultural conflicts about nature and nurture, and with the conditions that make life rich and meaningful for different kinds of people, Daoist executives can pick up on the beat of the processes at hand. They can discern shifts in situations that realign perspectives from which the important things are assessed. They appreciate the difference between the perspectives of their own judgments and those of people whose trajectories of inertial force they need to accept and integrate for the optimal harmonic rhythm of the whole. They are sensitive to the sudden openings in the inertial flows of things so that they can act on new opportunities without being blinded by previously established policies or goals. They can shift course radically when such new opportunities arise. They are rightly accused of having no principles, of failing to stick to long-range policies, of being untrustworthy regarding legislative mandates, of being opportunistic, and of being deceitful when required to talk in terms of public patterns that everyone is supposed to sign on to. Insofar as a long-term situation has general overriding needs, a Daoist might well sustain a vague long-term policy. But the Daoist will duck battles that cannot be won, retreat under attack, turn in new directions that seem not to approach the long-term goal, and redefine the goal by those directions. A discerning and effective Daoist executive will optimize the opportunities for intervention to achieve harmonic values that would not be realized without intervention, will bend the forces at his or her disposal to avoid destructive detritus of decaying situations, and will find the best that can be brought out of the mixture of inertial and chaotic trajectories of things.

A Daoist adept attuned to the rhythm of achievement and adventure, ordering and disordering, is the very opposite of a relativist in one sense, and very much a relativist in another. Daoism is the opposite of relativism in its extreme realism. Perspective on what is important in the pulse of things, combining form and components place by place to achieve individuated value, is itself a function of existential location. Intelligent people enlarge their existential location as much as possible, including as many perspectives as possible within it. But each situation remains individuated, and its perspective on what is really valuable is equally individuated. By this means, it is possible to be extremely realistic about what is worth what from the perspective of one's genuine engagement. Moreover, the (non-Daoist) perspectives that inform long-term policies with fixed patterns, however attuned they might have been at one point, quickly become ideologies imposed on the new situations as factors slowly change what is important to register in discerning the opportunities of the Dao. Every perspective is partial, interpreting the situation in certain respects only; an engaged perspective picks up on the important elements to interpret. When the situation changes so that different things are important, the old perspective becomes unrealistic, an ideology. Daoism is extremely realistic in its shifting engagements with changing situations, alert to the rhythm of the dance and the sudden openings for nonbeing to make something new.

On the other hand, Daoism is relativistic in the obvious sense that appreciation of what is important is always relative to an evaluative perspective. No neutral, perspectiveless evaluative standpoint is possible short of eternity. Personally, we attempt to make our evaluative perspectives as inclusive as possible of the perspectives of the past and future possibilities, as well as of present modes of enjoying and suffering. Public life is even more rigorous in defining the terms of conception and discussion so that as many different people's perspectives can be registered as possible. But inclusiveness of perspective is always a gain at the price of individuation by advancing toward vague tolerance. The vague perspectives can be filled in and individuated by included perspectives, but at the price of their vague flexibility. Even the most inclusive public perspective for reflecting on moral affairs needs to be viewed as just a hypothesis, hopefully the best, for grasping what is at stake from many perspectives at each nisus of the Dao. Daoists insist on riding such hypotheses through the pulses of their transformations. No absolutes exist because there are no absolute perspectives from which the achievements of the Dao can be appreciated and assessed.

The *Daodejing*'s distinction between the eternal unnameable and the temporal, mothering, completing, nameable Dao needs to be recalled. The latter combines inertial trajectories with spontaneity to complete things, but there is no fully complete thing within time that does not loosen and venture to something new. The loosening of achieved value surely need not be replaced by a *better* value. Nothing in Daoist metaphysics suggests a hint at inevitable historical progress. The scary part of the loosening of achieved harmonic value is that the resulting chaos might not come to a new order half so good. On the other hand, it might get better. A clever Daoist minimizes loss and optimizes opportunities but always rides the dragon. The dragon is the cosmic power of ontologically creative nonbeing that emerges spontaneously in the infinitesimal fissures of entwined and colliding inertial forces.

If ontologically creative nonbeing were an agent, we might hope that it constitutes a perspective in which the values of all things might be measured together, reconciled in cosmic determinate harmony. Many forms of monotheism attempt to articulate such a hypothesis in their theories of the infinite mind of God. Whitehead's great idea of God's infinite conceptual capacity to reconcile any achieved value with any other whatsoever, indeed reconciling all actual achieved values in a wholly determinate form that constitutes the divine actuality, is the latest grand monotheistic hypothesis of this sort.[25] But ontologically creative nonbeing is not an agent and does not achieve the determinateness required for a perspective except in the determinate nameable things within the temporal Dao that it originates. The eternal Dao that cannot be named is unnameable precisely because its only name comes from what it does, namely, originate the nameable. Using Wangbi's *ti-yung* construction, the substance of reality is nonbeing and its function is the unfolding of the ten thousand things. The diverse achieved values of the ten thousand things, flowing through their completions in the Dao, are largely incommensurate from their own determinate perspectives. Ontologically prior to their distinction within the produced temporal order, they cannot be registered as anything except infinite possibilities. Wangbi dutifully noted, in the text quoted before, that even undifferentiated being, containing only incipient possibilities, is dependent on nonbeing which is nothing, nothing, nothing, totally unnameable, apart from being named by its origination of everything else.

For the Daoist normative adept, to become so subtle and fine as to grasp and manipulate the openings in the great trajectories of forces is an ontological dragon ride. On the one hand it is the most realistically possible grasp on what is important and how to deal with that. On the other it is in touch with the infinite ground in which nothing important is differentiated, the abyss of nonbeing and vacuity. The connection between the undifferentiated ground and the differentiated array of normatively relevant forces is spontaneous creativity itself, wild, undetermined, unnameable but naming. Daoist mysticism is not nature romanticism about achieved harmonies, nor Buddhist or Neoplatonic flight to nothingness itself, but scorching identification with the asymmetrical origination of the Dao that can be named from the Dao that cannot, manifested in spontaneity (*tsu-jan*).

DAOISM AND CONFUCIANISM COMPARED

Confucianism and Daoism share a fundamental respect for the Dao, the Way the world goes. Philosophers of both traditions have given differing specific accounts of the Dao, but I suggest that solid, if vague, agreement exists on the following, which generalizes the previous discussion. The Dao is to be understood as the intertwining of two dimensions, a temporal horizontal dimension and a somewhat nontemporal vertical dimension.

The horizontal dimension is the inertial power of the unfolding of natural forces through time. To be in conformity with the Dao is to ride that inertial power, and to be in competition with it is to try to fight against it. A tree that bends to the wind is in harmony with the Dao, whereas one that stands without bending will be broken by the wind's inertial force. Modern science understands inertia to be uniform—a body in motion tends to remain in motion and move in straight lines unless deflected. Of course the modern Chinese have adopted that science. Yet the more ancient view of inertia was that changes have diverse patterns of unfolding, like the hexagrams discussed in the *Yijing*. The inertial power lies in the pattern of unfolding, not straight-line motion. So finding harmony with the Dao requires grasping its patterns at the macroscopic and microscopic levels.

The vertical dimension is the sense that the temporal flow of patterned processes arises from a deeper source, not some other process or even a determinate thing. Rather, it arises from a mysterious and subtle fecund nothingness. The opening lines of the *Daodejing* make the point. The Dao that can be named is the swarm of patterned processes that give shape and existence to all things. The Dao that cannot be named, the eternal Dao, has no nature (name), and yet gives rise to Heaven and Earth, that is, to the patterned processes. Wangbi, in his commentary on the *Daodejing* quoted previously, put the point plainly: "All being originated from nonbeing." Although Wangbi is famous for his commentary on the classic Daoist text, he could well have been classified as a Confucian for his original formulation of the substance/function (*ti-yung*) construction. Surely on the Confucian side was Zhou Dunyi, who began his *Explanation of the Diagram of the Great Ultimate* with the striking passage quoted in the first section of chapter 1. I take the sequence he spelled out there to mean a complicated origination of the horizontal Dao of patterned inertial processes through a series of steps that begin with nonbeing and are not fully temporal until the seasons move.

The intertwining of the two dimensions of the Dao, the horizontal and vertical, produces the following situation. Although the unfolding of patterned processes proceeds with a kind of inexorable inertia, the patterns are underdetermined. Gaps in the patterns abound, there are openings for human intervention, and precisely at those openings human beings have access to the vertical spontaneity to fill in or redirect the inertial forces. The wind will break down an unyielding tree: but make the tree into a mast on a boat and its very unyieldingness will propel the boat in many directions. The directions taken cannot go contrary to the force and direction of the wind; but by means of adapting the force of water on rudders and keels, and shifting the angles of sails on the mast, the boat can be made to tack into the wind, almost contrary to it. To be in harmony with the Dao means more than going along with the dominating patterned processes. It means being subtle enough to spot the openings for spontaneous intervention, for changing directions by bringing the Dao of straight wood sliding through water to bear upon the Dao of wind on the sails. The patterns of process give the Dao a kind of rhythm, a beat. If one knows the beat of the Dao, its repetitions of yin-yang harmony, one knows where the openings are to intervene. An adept of the Dao knows the subtle ways to adapt the Dao to his or her purposes.

With this common understanding, Daoists and Confucians nevertheless differ somewhat regarding the nature of the human response, or responsibility, to the Dao. Briefly put, the Daoists look to the patterns and beat of nature, and the Confucians to the patterns and beat of institution and character building.

Consider the Confucian case first. I and most of the likely readers of this book participate in academic life. The rhythm of my school is set by the yearly calendar, two semesters, summer school, and summer vacation. Once a semester starts, the courses are set: innovation in courses usually requires prior planning for a future semester. The rhythm of the semester is set by weekly classes, about fifteen weeks a semester. Faculty have to abide by courses that can be taught in fifteen weeks; but within that limit they can exercise much creativity. Academic administrators' responsibilities run to the beat of accreditation reviews that come every ten years; early in the ten-year period they can experiment wildly with curriculum and policies for admitting students, but toward the end of that period they need to bring everything into harmony for the review. A chief administrator's greatest responsibility is the hiring of the faculty, and the timing for that is set by the faculty retirement schedule. New administrators step into a process that had been set in many ways years before, but which has openings for improvements, some weekly, some semester by semester, some in decades, and some over the career life of individual faculty members. Confucian concern for building an institution looks at long, slow pulses of institutional change.

When it comes to the building of personal character, a preoccupation of Confucians, you have to wait through infancy to teach the motor skills of children; you have to wait through adolescence to teach the virtues of young adulthood; you have to wait through the years of middle age when a person is overwhelmed with family responsibility to learn the powers of meditation and repose. Character growth takes place in its seasons, and the seasons are long. For a Confucian to become adept at living responsibly with the Dao requires taking the long view of things.

This is precisely what annoys philosophical Daoists. Daoists enjoy nature in its tiny moments. The forces with which they would conform and use to their purposes are the subtle shifts in nature like changing breezes, rocks crumbling with water's flowing and freezing. Daoists look to few processes for manipulation larger than the rotation of seasons. Perhaps the paradigmatic social activity for Daoists is making war, watching for opportunity on the battlefield, having the patience to let the enemy run afoul of nature's forces. Daoists see the Confucian emphasis on institution and character building to be a kind of deliberate inattention to the subtleties of process now. By staring into the future, Confucians overlook the openings at hand and thus seem to be pompous and clumsy. The weakness of Confucians is that by thinking on the large and long scale of the Dao's rhythms, they become blunted to the opportunities for spontaneous life now. The weakness of the Daoists, of course, is that they are not much good at institution building or character development, at least insofar as that would derive from their Daoist philosophy.

A metaphysical point underlies this distinction between Confucians and Daoists. For the Confucian tradition, the Human forms a trinity with Heaven and Earth. For the Daoist tradition, the Human is to be merged with the forces of Heaven and Earth. The Confucian argument, for instance as expressed by Xunzi in his chapter on *Tian*, is that the products of Heaven and Earth in human nature are underdetermined. What makes the human an independent though related cosmic principle is the elaboration of conventions or rituals. Human civilization depends on ritualized behavior or conventions, which supplement the biological givens of Heaven and Earth to make them humanly determinate.

Therefore, for the Confucians the long natural pulses of institution and character building are deeply involved with ritual making, ritual modification, and ritual exercise. No less than the Daoists, the Confucians look for the openings in the Dao, but they are openings for the criticism and practice of ritual behavior on which high civilization lies. The Daoists, of course, fear the easy degeneration of ritual behavior into meaningless form and, worse, control. Whereas ritual in its ideal form makes possible a high kind of civilized life that can be sensitive to nature in all its nuances, and gives rise to freedom, in actual practice, ritual can be deadening.

I believe that our own world desperately needs philosophers and statesmen who are sensitive to the Confucian concern to build rituals of peace, free exchange of ideas, and the flourishing of many cultures defined by different conventions. This point is important to emphasize in societies that have come to see virtue only in modernistic rationalism and functionalism. Yet we also need the Daoist critique of ritual pretensions.

As to the metaphysical issue, I think the Confucians are right about civilization depending on well-functioning rituals and conventions. Because Daoists such as the authors of the *Daodejing* and *Zhuangzi* are sophisticated people, masters of the rituals of writing, thinking, and statecraft, I suspect they too recognize the positive Confucian point. The Daoist glorification of nature as that into which human life should be absorbed is a bit playful and insincere. At least that is a good way to read the texts from the standpoint of philosophies that accept evolutionary theories of nature and society. The contemporary reappropriation of ideas from classical Confucianism and philosophical Daoism can understand them in light of many other things we also know.

Confucians have long known the seductive power of the Daoist enthrallment with the junction of the forces of inertia and the creative spontaneity of what appears within time merely as opportunity. The corrective Confucian project is to settle in for the long haul of building the human sphere through the establishment of rituals and conventions that give substance to civilization and humane living. However genuinely engaged and realistic Daoists might be about the beat of the dance and the shifting importances of the Dao that complete things, they are flighty when it comes to sustained effort. The very reality of the human sphere, constituted as it is by a dance of conventions played ritualistically, requires long-term projects and constant effort to build a human semiotic culture and reinforce it by nature's wild beat. For the Confucians, the Daoists are not realistic at all about what is important in the human cultural sphere because they do not easily recognize or register a cultural reality whose rhythms require long beats of intentionally driven effort that are blind to many of mere nature's transformative openings. Being serious about the human requires a slow rhythm whose beat cannot easily be discerned if distracted by the fast-shifting perspectives of nature's pulses.

Are we not fortunate to have two and a half millennia of East Asian effort to get the Daoists and Confucians to dance together with the incommensurate rhythms of their different perspectives? This is the way to build a civilization attuned to discordant realities and best possibilities alike.[26]

5
Chinese Influences in English-Speaking Philosophy

ALTHOUGH MOST ACADEMIC philosophy departments in Great Britain and the United States at the present time do not consider Chinese philosophy to be part of the mainstream curriculum, a recognition is growing among the broader community of philosophers that the traditions of China (and also India, Islam, and Orthodox Christian civilization) are necessary components of the contemporary public discussion of philosophy.[1] Chinese philosophy is indeed part of the mainstream curriculum in English-speaking philosophical studies in Hong Kong and Singapore, and also at the University of Hawaii; many American philosophy departments have at least token representation of Chinese philosophy. And although academic philosophy in the United States and Great Britain has become narrow in its self-definition of method and topic, the broader philosophical issues such as have been important in Chinese philosophy are frequently and rather thoroughly addressed in American departments of religious studies.

The influence of Chinese philosophy on the West is not recent. It began in modern times with the reports of Marco Polo and Christian missionaries to China that were read by European philosophers such as Leibniz. Leibniz was fascinated with China from his youth, corresponded and visited with missionaries, and edited a book of missionary reports; he also wrote essays or long letters on Chinese theology, Neo-Confucian metaphysics, Chinese morality, and on the Chinese approach to mathematics in the *Yijing* and the writings of Shao Yung.[2] Joseph Needham cites the influence of Leibniz's interpretation of Chinese (especially Zhu Xi's) theories of natural law and organicism on Whitehead's organic process philosophy, although his interpretation is not universally accepted.³

SCHOLARLY INFLUENCES

The widespread knowledge and use of Chinese philosophy in the English speaking philosophical world has been made possible by the achievement of a critical mass of translations and scholarship in intellectual history. Perhaps the single most important event for Chinese philosophy in the West was the publication in 1963 of Wing-tsit Chan's *A Source Book in Chinese Philosophy*.⁴ That volume, over 850 pages long, contains sober scholarly translations, with straightforward explanatory notes, of the whole or large selections of the *Analects*, Mencius, the *Great Learning*, the *Doctrine of the Mean*, Hsun-tzu, Lao-tzu, Chuang-tzu, Mo-tzu, the School of Names, the School of Yin-Yang, Legalism, Tung Chung-shu, Yang Hsiung, Wang Ch'ung, Huai-nan Tzu, Lieh Tzu, Wang Pi, Ho Yen, Kuo Hsiang, early Buddhism, Seng-chao, Chi-tsang, Hsuan-tsang, Hui-ssu, Fa-tsang, the *Platform Scripture of the Sixth Patriarch*, Shen-hui, I-Hsuan, Han Yu, Li Ao, Chou Tun-i, Shao Yung, Chang Tsai, Ch'eng Hao, Ch'eng I, Lu Hsiang-shan, Chu Hsi, Wang Yang-ming, Wang Fu-chih, Yen Yuan, Tai Chen, K'ang Yu-wei, T'an Ssu-t'ung, Chang Tung-sun, Fung Yu-lan, and Hsiung Shih-li. In hindsight some scholars have criticized both Chan's selection and his interpretive notes for expressing his own Neo-Confucian reading of the tradition. But whatever the validity of that criticism, the volume put before the English-reading public a serious representation of the vast array of philosophic thinking in China's history. With that volume alone, British and American trained philosophers could come to engage major ideas of the Chinese philosophic tradition in critical fashion. Meanwhile, for decades departments of history or East Asian languages and cultures in universities such as Cambridge and Oxford in Britain and Columbia, Yale, Harvard, Princeton, Wisconsin, Berkeley, and Stanford in the United States, and Toronto in Canada, have been producing graduates whose typical dissertation is the translation of some important Chinese text in a critical edition with a historical commentary. In the last decade or so these graduates have replicated the translation-historical-philosophic studies programs at many universities and colleges of hitherto lesser reputation for Chinese studies. The result is an ever-increasing flood of good translations and increasingly sophisticated historical studies of Chinese philosophy in English so that non-Chinese reading philosophers can engage Chinese philosophical ideas and movements just the way they can European ones. Of course, philosophers in Britain and America who cannot read Chinese cannot be *scholars* of Chinese philosophy, just as they cannot be scholars of Plato, Aristotle, Epictetus, or Augustine without reading them in the Greek or Latin originals. But just as most English-speaking philosophers engage the ancient Western philosophers in translation, so can they now engage the Chinese. The question is how they engage it.

How the English-speaking world engages the Chinese tradition depends on how it is presented. I suggest that there are three imperfectly distinct ways: through the work of interpretive philosophers (often translators), through bridging philosophers, and through philosophers who inhabit the Chinese tradition as contemporary philosophers. Regarding the last group, I shall discuss the work of Roger Ames and David Hall, Tu Weiming and Cheng Chungying, and Wu Kuangming.

Interpretive Philosophers

The work of Wing-tsit Chan has already been mentioned, and it includes far more than the *Source Book in Chinese Philosophy*. Under his inspiration and editorship a number of major scholars published *Chu Hsi and Neo-Confucianism*, and his own *Chu Hsi: New Studies* has helped supplant the earlier commentary by J. Percy Bruce.[5] Chan has a translation of Zhu Xi's *Reflections on Things at Hand* and also a full translation of Wang Yangming's *Instructions for Practical Living*.[6] In all these translations Chan has copious historical and philosophical commentary. A new generation of historians writing in English, such as Hoyt Cleveland Tillman, suggests that Chan and his followers overemphasize philosophy in the Neo-Confucian project to the detriment of their social involvement.[7] But that does not detract from Chan's contribution to the philosophers' understanding of the Neo-Confucian tradition.

Just as important as Chan has been William Theodore de Bary who for many years was professor of East Asian thought at Columbia University and trained a great many of the scholars of Chinese philosophy now working in the United States and Canada who have made and are making the translations of the important works; he was for much of the same time the provost of the university, living the life of the Confucian scholar-official. For many years he has run the Columbia University Seminar on Neo-Confucianism, which has been the intellectual meeting ground to discuss Chinese philosophy of many persons of a scholarly and or philosophical bent. He edited the *Sources of Chinese Tradition* and then edited and contributed significantly to a number of conferences volumes, among which the most important are *Self and Society in Ming Thought* and *The Unfolding of Neo-Confucianism*.[8] His recent work, for instance *The Liberal Tradition in China*, has focused on historical backgrounds in philosophy for contemporary philosophic debates in China, such as over human rights.[9]

Although Confucians by temperament, like Aristotelians, might be more prone to translation, scholarly editions, and interpretive commentary, the Daoist traditions have had their representatives in interpretive work. The *Daodejing* has been translated into English more times than any other Chinese classic, and there are many beautiful editions of translations of the *Zhuangzu*. Herrlee G. Creel's *What Is Taoism* is a classic study, and the early works of Wu Kuangming, *Chuang Tzu: World Philosopher at Play* and *The Butterfly as Companion: Meditations on the First Three Chapters of the* Chuang Tzu, are deep interpretations oriented to the Western problematics of philosophy.[10] Daoism, of course, is not only a philosophy in the Western sense, although Laozi and Zhuangzi are usually interpreted that way, as the previous chapter noted. The religious dimensions of Daoism have received brilliant interpretive attention from Norman Girardot in *Myth and Meaning in Early Taoism*, from Isabelle Robinet's *Taoist Meditation*, from John Lagerwey in *Taoist Ritual in Chinese Society and History*, and from the extraordinary translations and interpretations of Livia Kohn, *Early Chinese Mysticism*, *Taoist Mystical Philosophy*, *Taoist Meditation and Longevity Techniques* and *The Taoist Experience*.[11]

Bridging Scholars

Far and away the most important recent book on Chinese philosophy for Western philosophers is Herbert Fingarette's little gem of 1972, *Confucius: The Secular as Sacred*. Fingarette is a distinguished philosopher in the analytic tradition who has written on many topics within the Western problematic.[12] His book on Confucius was significant because it contrasted and paralleled the Confucian notions of *ren* (humanity, love) with those of *li* (ritual propriety, decorum). Whereas Western philosophy since the European Enlightenment has taken quite a dim view of ritual as associated with religious superstition, authoritarian court etiquette, and an evasion of plain speaking, Fingarette drew upon notions usually associated with John Searle to show how ritual is a performative act. Suddenly, Confucianism, and also institutional Daoism for that matter with its emphasis on ritual, became intelligible to Western philosophers as philosophically significant. He showed how the function of ritual is to make social relations possible and how, in the structures of ritual, lies the medium of ethics. Suddenly it made sense to Western philosophers for Confucius to have responded to the lawless anarchy of his time with a call to retrieve civilizing rituals.

David S. Nivison is another analytic philosopher who has entered into detailed Sinological studies of the history of Chinese philosophy, but who has also made explicit expositions of thinkers in that tradition as contributing to the solution of contemporary Western philosophical problems. His principal interest has been in ethical questions, and he mines the Chinese tradition from the most ancient times to the Ming, as in his book, *The Ways of Confucianism: Investigations in Chinese Philosophy*.[13] Another analytical philosopher who has dealt extensively with Chinese philosophy as a source for contemporary thinking is Antonio Cua. His *Dimensions of Moral Creativity* involves an extensive treatment of Confucius.[14] *The Unity of Knowledge and Action* is a brilliant interpretation of Wang Yangming as a moral psychologist and ethical thinker with contributions for the contemporary debate.[15] *Ethical Argumentation* is a study of Xunzi as a moral thinker, equally apt for the contemporary discussion.[16]

Philip J. Ivanhoe is a scholar who also relates Confucian thought to contemporary philosophical problems, again mainly ethics but not entirely so. His view of Western philosophy is somewhat broader than the analytic tradition, but he writes with the clarity about particular arguments often association with analytic thought. His *Confucian Moral Self Cultivation* studies six thinkers, Confucius, Mencius, Xunzi, Zhu Xi, Wang Yangming, and Dai Zhen, showing the contemporary relevance of their thought; this volume is not technical Sinology, which might be daunting to Western philosophers, yet it rests upon very exact Sinological research.[17] His *Ethics in the Confucian Tradition* is a careful study of Mencius and Wang Yangming; after this book there is no reason for Western philosophers not to respect those thinkers as they do Plato and Descartes.[18]

Perhaps the most explicit bridging interpreter is Lee H. Yearley, whose *Mencius and Aquinas* sets the standard for careful comparison.[19] His topics are theories of virtue and courage in those two thinkers and he handles masterfully the issues of bringing together thinkers from separate traditions and vastly different epochs of time. It is interesting that, because neither Ivanhoe nor Yearley limits Western philosophy to the analytic tradition in the twentieth century, both were for a time in a department of religious studies (at Stanford University). Religious studies departments are often the locus of nonanalytical philosophy in America.

Most of the bridging interpreters of Chinese philosophy pick up on the Confucian side. One of the earliest and most inventive, however, relates primarily to Daoism, Chang Chung-yuan, long a professor of philosophy at the University of Hawaii. His *Tao: A New Way of Thinking* is a translation of the *Daodejing* with extensive commentaries on each chapter.[20] He explicates the meaning of that book in connection with Western philosophy though he hardly mentions analytic philosophy and his major dialogue partners are Heidegger and Whitehead. His *Creativity and Taoism: A Study of Chinese Philosophy, Art, and Poetry*, is a genuinely creative philosophical essay in which he retrieves major Daoist themes for what is essentially a study of the Western problematic of imagination.[21] Although Chang's work is fundamentally a kind of bridging interpretation of China to the West and vice versa, its originality as a philosophical synthesis anticipates the later work of Wu Kuang-ming.

Any number of contemporary philosophers could be cited for their engagement of current philosophical issues with the resources of Chinese philosophy. As I have argued before, for most practical purposes the Chinese tradition of philosophy is as available to Western thinkers as the Greek and European, even if the cultural context is understood less well. And in matters of understanding cultural contexts, recent critics such as Michel Foucault have made even the Western tradition unfamiliar to Westerners. I might discuss the important work done by the late Charles Wei-shun Fu, or the interpretive system of Liu Shu-hsien, or the creative new approach to field theory of Lik Kuen Tong. Many of the thinkers discussed earlier for their interpretive and bridging work could be reconsidered for their own philosophical thought, especially Chang Chung-yuan. But in recognition of influence and of the distinct type of their contributions I shall discuss three projects: Roger Ames and David Hall as a collaborative team, Tu Weiming and Cheng Chungying as parallel approaches to making Chinese philosophy relevant, and Wu Kuangming. All are North Americans of European or Chinese ancestry and have had the major part of their teaching careers at American universities.

ROGER T. AMES AND DAVID L. HALL

Roger T. Ames and the late David L. Hall have collaborated on three extremely influential volumes, *Thinking Through Confucius*, *Anticipating China*, and *Thinking from the Han: Self, Truth, and Transcendence in Chinese and Western Culture*.[22] Ames is professor of philosophy at the University of Hawaii and edits the major comparative journal *Philosophy East and West*. The Sinologist of the pair, Ames is expert in ancient Chinese political philosophy and is the author of *The Art of Rulership* and *Sun-tzu: The Art of Warfare*.[23] The late David Hall was professor of philosophy at the University of Texas at El Paso, a classically trained (Yale) Western philosopher whose topic was philosophy of culture and whose bent was to lift up the aesthetic dimension over Western preoccupations with ethics and classificatory metaphysics and epistemology. This was the burden of his first book, *The Civilization of Experience: A Whiteheadian Theory of Culture*, and he deeply mined the resources of Chinese philosophical Daoism in the aesthetic philosophy of culture in *The Uncertain Phoenix* and *Eros and Irony: A Prelude to Philosophical Anarchism*.[24] *Eros and Irony* contains an extraordinary critique of conceptions of regular order, which he attributed to European thought, from the perspective of aesthetic order that he found in Daoism. His preference for the aesthetic stance over the assertive or foundationalist prompted an appreciation of Richard Rorty's conversational neo-pragmatism, expressed in Hall's *Richard Rorty: Prophet and Poet of the New Pragmatism*.[25]

The collaborative work of Ames and Hall in *Thinking Through Confucius, Anticipating China*, and *Thinking from the Han*, is the first full-blown philosophy of culture in the West to be undertaken primarily from a Chinese perspective. To be sure, Western thinkers such as Ralph Waldo Emerson, Max Weber, Friedrich Nietzsche, and Ernst Cassirer had some knowledge of Chinese culture, and often brilliant insights. Chang Chung-yuan began a Chinese-based philosophy of culture, as mentioned earlier. But Hall and Ames bring that project to brilliant, if controversial, fruition.

Their central idea is to contrast Western and Chinese cultures more or less as wholes, generalizing each to certain essential characteristics. No summary can do justice to their detailed and learned argument, but roughly stated, the contrast is this: Western culture, in its Greek and Semitic roots and European flowering, is based fundamentally on ordering principles that transcend what is ordered. The West finds meaning in the asymmetrical relations between God and the world, for instance, or between metaphysical or scientific explanatory principles and what is explained. In ethics, the West searches for transcending grounding principles, and in science it explains things by antecedent causes and universal laws. Western culture thinks in terms of linear ordering going from ground to consequent, from earlier to later in narrative. This leads to the cultural instincts that take the abstract to be more real and perhaps better than the concrete, and valorizes orders of dominance and submission.

The Chinese cultural assumptions, by contrast, are based on what Ames and Hall call, following A. C. Graham, "correlative thinking." They point to reciprocal notions such as yin and yang, to the explanatory habits of identifying the classifications in which things fall, and to the classifications themselves arranged in correlative orders such as the eight directions plus center, the cyclic interactions of the five elements—fire, earth, metal, water, wood—their directional orientations—water/north, wood/east, fire/south, metal/west, and earth/center. Chinese science, medicine, cuisine, politics, and philosophy all exhibit correlative thinking. Moreover, they do not exhibit transcendent or asymmetrically linear thinking of the sort characterizing Western culture. As a consequence, the Chinese sensibility is primarily aesthetic, concerned with wholeness and patterns and interpreting difficulties as matters of attaining or restoring harmony. This contrasts with the primary Western sensibility, which is to see what follows from what and to set things straight according to transcendent norms.

In my rough sketch of Hall and Ames's philosophy I have neglected their subtle qualifications. Of course there are many nontranscendent and aesthetically oriented elements in the West, and many unidirectional, transcendent, and morally authoritarian elements in China. They are particularly careful in *Thinking Through Confucius* to limit their claims to Confucius himself, admitting that later developments introduced more transcendent and less correlative matters. In *Anticipating China*, they provide narratives of how Western and Chinese cultures developed the ways they did to their general characteristics. But in the end, their project is to cause philosophers to become aware of the general traits of the two cultures, overriding special exceptions and providing differing contexts of cultural assumptions. Awareness of the difference reduces false familiarity, both about the other and about one's sense of one's own tradition. Above all, Ames and Hall argue subtly for the superiority of the Chinese cultural tradition for doing philosophy of culture.

I cannot resist pointing out a certain irony in their procedure. One of their most telling points is that the aesthetic order in Chinese culture emerges from within concrete experience and is not imposed from the outside, as they accuse Western culture of doing. Wu Kuangming, in *On Chinese Body Thinking*, makes a similar point about concrete interior order.[26] Yet their method of contrasting cultures by generalizing to basic principles and trivializing exceptions follows the Western Aristotelian strategy of developing a grid of categories, for instance the Four Causes in Aristotle's case, and locating thinkers and cultures within them. The recent exemplars of this method are Richard McKeon, F. S. C. Northrop, Walter Watson, and David Dilworth. The aspects of a thinker's thought or of cultures' traits that do not register in the categories of the scheme are ignored, and what is most important is not the concrete but the abstract ways in which the cultures are transcendence-oriented on the one hand or correlative-oriented on the other. This is surely an imposition of categories from without to the neglect of the concrete, a matter they would consign to the West. Even in the West, however, that strategy is typical only of the Aristotelian strain: the Platonic tradition has been far subtler in its dialectical relations of the concrete with abstractions that allow for discriminations within the concrete.

The chief contribution of Hall and Ames's collaboration is not to do interpretive or bridging work, although of course their work does that too. Rather it is to move all philosophy into a sensibility of culturally constructed assumptions in which there are real and pervasive differences between traditions that can be known and adjudicated. Moreover, even if their method and intent are classificatory in an Aristotelian sense, their cultural resources and sensibilities are most favorably Chinese. Or to put the matter more plainly, after their work no philosopher in China or the West can innocently assume his or her own cultural assumptions. Rather those assumptions relative to the others constitute a philosophic problem.

TU WEIMING AND CHENG CHUNGYING

Tu Weiming and Cheng Chungying are contemporary philosophers who are unabashedly Confucians. Although both interpret Chinese culture, neither does so as a philosopher of culture like Hall and Ames. Both have as their intent to develop Confucianism and Chinese philosophy as a viable tradition for addressing contemporary problems, and both are "scholar-officials" who work to institutionalize Confucianism's place in the contemporary scene.

Tu Weiming is a contemporary American philosopher whose principle intellectual roots are both Chinese and Western. Trained at Harvard University where he now teaches in philosophy and intellectual history, Tu's intellectual project is to develop the role of the Confucian intellectual in the contemporary world. His early work in many respects is an updated version of the Confucian commentarial tradition. *Neo-Confucian Thought in Action: Wang Yang-ming's Youth (1472–1509)* is an intellectual biography of that great thinker in which Tu lays the groundwork for the claim associated with his teacher, Mou Zhongsan, that the Mencian line of Confucianism comes down through Wang rather than Zhu Xi.[27] *Centrality and Commonality: An Essay on Confucian Religiousness* is a commentary on the *Chung-Yung* (the *Doctrine of the Mean*) advocating it as of contemporary truth and interpreting it according to the Mencian emphasis on *ren*.[28] *Humanity and Self-Cultivation: Essays in Confucian Thought*, *Confucian Thought: Selfhood as Creative Transformation*, and *Way, Learning, and Politics: Essays on the Confucian Intellectual* all contain essays that are interpretive in genre but programmatic in intent: the program is to lay out the task for a contemporary Confucian intellectual.[29]

That task is unusual in several ways, perhaps the most outstanding of which is that the contemporary Confucian need not be in East Asia nor even East Asian. Indeed, the Confucians or Neo-Confucians of the generation of Tu's teachers were mainly Chinese expatriates in Taiwan, Hong Kong, or America who fled the Communists in China. Tu's own generation is mainly Western educated, even where the content of their education was the Chinese, especially Confucian, tradition. Tu, like many others of his generation, has had a dual education, Western and Chinese at once, and he is as at home in Western intellectual history and philosophy as in the East Asian traditions.

Another way in which the task of the contemporary Confucian is unusual in the West is that it does not conform to the Western academic distinctions between philosophy, religion, history, social analysis, and practice. I have called Tu a philosopher, and that he is; but he is also a historian, an expert in social scientific analyses of the current situation, and quite deliberately an active player in the formation of a political and intellectual conversation about contemporary global society. He is famous for contending that Confucianism is a religion. Whereas most contemporary Confucian (and Daoist) philosophers are content to live the academic life, Tu, along with William Theodore de Bary, devotes much energy, shaping his career, to the creation of a public community and discourse. He is in this respect a scholar-official. The writings most illustrative of this aspect of his career, perhaps, are his editing of two volumes of

Daedalus, "The Living Tree: The Changing Meaning of Being Chinese Today" and "China in Transformation," volumes that bring together China experts from many fields.[30] For many years, Tu has been the director of the Harvard Yenching Library.

The trajectory of Tu's thought has moved from interpreting the Chinese classics, especially in respect to *ren*, to manifesting the contributions of the Confucian intellectual in the present world conversation. Along the way he has focused on the nature of the self and its existential process of taking on the way of the sage. From the beginning this existentialist orientation has always been with regard to the way of the sage in the modern world, not the world of Confucius, Zhou Dunyi, or Wang Yangming. Sensing the anomaly to Western thinking of the Confucian (and Daoist) emphasis on ritual, Tu has argued that ritual propriety is the set of external forms required for *ren* to be expressed in human relations. Without ritual propriety or decorum, human relationships could not be established that might be quickened by *ren*. Tu has always been clear that the way of the sage is not merely a matter of personal self-cultivation but also of the cultivation of one's relationships.

In his later thought he has turned more to the issues of cultivating a community within which life can flourish under the conditions of modernity within a global society, defined by economic and other interactions, but with a conflict of competing and fractured cultures. Specifically, he has examined the European Enlightenment project and its challenges to Confucianism. Part of this concern is expressed with respect to the modernization of China, with Marxism, liberal democracy, and modern science seen as expressions of Enlightenment. Another part of the concern has to do with the effects of Enlightenment thinking on family structures and personal relationships so crucial to the Confucian conceptions of self and society. Yet another part has to do with the critiques of the Enlightenment project itself. Some of those critiques are external, as from postmodernists on the one hand and nativist reactionaries on the other. Others are internal critiques such as the self-destruction of communist governments, the apparent difficulty of liberal democracies to sustain the tolerance and pluralism they require for mutual cooperation, and the self-betrayal of scientific technologies by ecological crises of their own making. In all of this Tu argues for the relevance and importance of Confucian values, appropriately adapted to the conditions of our time.

Tu is not a philosopher of culture with an aesthetic bent, like Ames and Hall. Nor is he a political philosopher with a particular program, like a liberal democrat or a Marxist. He is not a metaphysical or ethical theorist aiming to provide a speculative perspective on things. He honors all these things and engages in them from time to time, but they are not the focus of his project. His focus rather is on the creation of a global intellectual conversation that registers and reflects Confucian values. That one would want to do this is itself a Confucian project: not by the arts or by laws or by abstract speculation should we try to govern ourselves but by the creation of a community of discourse in which all are respected, all cultures and perspectives, and the Confucian virtues of what Tu calls the fiduciary community can be practiced. Tu is the Confucian ritual master of important public conversation.

Cheng Chungying, by contrast, risks the limiting privacy of creative genius in his project of developing a contemporary speculative metaphysics and ethics funded primarily from the Chinese tradition. He too is a good Confucian, of Tu's generation and with many of the same teachers and influences, including a Harvard PhD. But whereas Tu's doctoral work was on Wang Yangming, Cheng's was on Charles S. Peirce, the founder of American pragmatism, as well as on Dai Zhen, the great thinker of China in the modern Ching dynasty and the contemporary of David Hume; see his *Tai Chen's Inquiry into Goodness*.[31] Rather than attempting to create a public global conversation in which Chinese philosophy plays a large part, Cheng's project from very early days has been to reconstruct Chinese philosophy so as to make it part of the world philosophical conversation in league with Western philosophy. His topics thus have been easily recognizable by Western philosophers, for instance, conceptions of being, causation, explanation, mind, morality, knowledge, art, and the like.

Cheng has been tireless in his work to bring together the institutions of Chinese and Western philosophy. He was the founding editor of the *Journal of Chinese Philosophy* and the founding president of the International Society for Chinese Philosophy. Although there are many venues in which Chinese and Western philosophers now interact, including conferences of many sorts and a variety of philosophical journals including *Philosophy East and West*, his journal and society are the most focused. He too is a Confucian scholar-official who has founded and cared for institutions.

Cheng's primary philosophical work, however, has been the construction of a philosophical system using key elements of Chinese philosophy. The major locus for this is his *New Dimensions of Confucian and Neo-Confucian Philosophy*, as well as many articles in books and journals.[32] Like most of us, the emphasis in his early essays was on interpretation, and in the later essays on speculative reconstruction and what he calls the hermeneutics of the present situation. The resources to which he appeals begin with the *Yijing*, which has been a continuing fascination for him; that very ancient book provides the themes in which Cheng sees China's distinctive philosophical identity and with which he engages the Western tradition of philosophy. He also takes seriously, both with hermeneutic intent and as resources for contemporary philosophy, the great writings of Daoists and Buddhists in China's history. In this regard he identifies clearly with the Song Neo-Confucians in their attempts to synthesize and criticize the vast range of texts of their past, not merely those identified as Confucian. But whereas the Song Neo-Confucians dealt with the Chinese cultural arena, Cheng incorporates into the synthesis and criticism the great texts of the Western tradition from Plato and Aristotle down to Whitehead and Heidegger.

Cheng provides an interesting contrast with the previous generation of Confucian scholars, such as Mou Zhongsan, who are sometimes called "New Confucians" because of the attention they paid to Western philosophers. That earlier generation pioneered in the interpretation of Western philosophy for the Chinese mind, but generally with the overall intentionality of showing how the West could bolster threatened ideas within Confucianism and Daoism. Mou's "moral metaphysics," for instance, made good use of moral and epistemological idealism to defend the Mencian project. Cheng, by contrast, is far less concerned to bolster any Chinese project than to employ Chinese resources to address issues that Western philosophers also address and that define the contemporary situation.

For instance, after two hundred years in which most Western philosophers have abandoned philosophy of nature, leaving nature to the natural scientists and restricting philosophy to philosophy of science, it has become clear that we need a philosophy of nature that puts scientific technology in perspective and defines an ethical attitude toward the environment. Whitehead and Heidegger addressed this in their very different ways, offering conceptions of nature, creativity, relation, time, space, value, and human existence. Cheng picks up these very themes and argues that Chinese philosophy has resources for even subtler theories regarding these topics. His fascination with the *Yijing* comes in part from his concern to develop a contemporary philosophy of nature.

Ethics in recent Western philosophy, especially its analytic branches, has suffered from being abstractly removed from first-order problems except when it deals nominalistically with case studies, and from depending on a consensus arising from antecedently formed common sense. The modern use of traditional Confucian ethics is surprisingly similar, being formulaic and therefore abstract, and resting on received wisdom. Our situation has so much changed, however, with global economies and ecologically insensitive technologies, not to speak of new social relations, that received wisdom needs to be rethought; the meta-theories that justified and embodied it need reconstruction also. Cheng's genius has been to see that a rethinking of ethics from a Western or Confucian standpoint requires a speculative rethinking of the conception of the world itself. This speculative metaphysics cannot be a repetition of old positions Chinese or Western, nor a mirroring of science, but a critical reconstruction of all these into a new vision. In contrast to Mou's moral metaphysics, it is helpful to think of Cheng's work as metaphysical morals: his intent, true to the Confucian (and Platonic) tradition, is essentially practical, but the practice needs to be informed by a new speculative worldview. Because of Cheng's efforts, whatever worldviews emerge to compete for our loyalties, they will include the themes of Chinese philosophy.

Tu Weiming and Cheng Chungying offer parallel and complementary ways of pursuing Confucianism today.

WU KUANGMING

Wu Kuangming differs from the aforementioned positions in many important respects. Taiwanese born, Yale educated with specialties in Kant and Kierkegaard, Wu has spent most of his career in the philosophy department at the University of Wisconsin at Oshkosh and recently has been at the University of Missouri. Deeply versed in Chinese culture, its art as well as philosophy, and the Confucian texts as well as Buddhist and Daoist, Wu considers himself primarily to represent the Daoist vision. He also takes that to be the essential Chinese vision, in contrast to those who identify Chinese philosophy and culture primarily with Confucianism; in this respect he is a fellow spirit with Chang Chung-yuan. Wu has slight patience with metaphysical speculation of Cheng's sort, and even less patience with Tu's kind of Confucian scholar-official concern for public discourse (since I myself am both a speculative metaphysician and a scholar-official, Wu finds me useless twice-over). He has in principle an affinity with Hall and Ames' philosophy of culture but does not see much in its generalizations and external application of classificatory categories.

Rather, Wu does what Ames and Hall say Chinese philosophy does generally, namely, work from the concrete to develop distinctions that can be expressed only in concrete terms such as stories, analogies, and telling metaphors. Because to assert something directly, Wu believes, is to distance yourself from it and thereby distort it, all serious expression is indirect and self-critically ironic. This is the position Wu developed as arising from Chuang Tzu in his *Chuang Tzu: World Philosopher at Play*.[33] It was the position he illustrated copiously with line-by-line essays on Chuang Tzu's text in *The Butterfly as Companion*.[34] And it is the position he explains by contrast and indirection in *On Chinese Body Thinking: A Cultural Hermeneutic* and *On the "Logic" of Togetherness: A Cultural Hermeneutic*.[35]

In both of the last volumes Wu unfolds the cultural hermeneutics that follows from something like this world-picture. Life contains only concrete processes, among which are we ourselves, and in these processes there is structure and grain, as in wood, but no abstract patterns replicable from one place to another. Unexpectedly, we can know other things, discriminate their structures, and comport ourselves so as to take these into account and behave appropriately. That is, there is a representative function in human life. How is this possible, given the concreteness?

Western culture has developed strategies of representation that involve asserting that reality is like the abstract structures of a proposition. To be sure, being *like* is not the same as being *the same as*, and many Western philosophies assert concreteness in the objects while marking that the representations are only abstract. Nevertheless, the typical Western representative strategies first assert an abstract character to reality and then might take it back. Some Western strategies do not take it back, for instance most of those of scientific knowing.

Chinese representative strategies, Wu maintains, generally avoid the abstraction-negation dialectic by subordinating representation to comportment toward things, guided or oriented by representation. We come through knowledge to move in concert with things, thereby establishing concrete inter-movements and wholes. In this Wu reinforces the linguistic argument of Chad Hansen that Chinese language primarily discriminates and orients rather than represents propositionally.[36] In this concrete dance, representation is not self-reflective as such. But of course the Chinese are as self-reflective as anyone else. So their reflection takes ironic forms of playing with the perspectives of the many things involved in the dance, allowing none the priority of being subject over the others as objects in representation. Hence butterflies cannot be engaged concretely except by keeping open the question of who dreams whom. More prosaically, Chinese culture and philosophy communicate more by telling stories that one understands to apply analogically to one's situation than by offering abstract descriptions. This is not to say that the Chinese cannot say how many people came to lunch, or that Western philosophers cannot use telling metaphors and analogies for which there is no better direct speech. But it is to give priority in the Chinese case to representing the grain of things so that people concretely can dispose themselves appreciatively and deferentially toward them, and in the Western case to getting the form of the thing in the mind, the form being at best still abstract. Body thinking is discriminating orientation and comportment, not getting the other thing in mind.

As Wu's philosophical project is coming to light in greater publications, it appears as a concrete working out of the Hegelian "labor of the notion" in respect to claims many have made about the immanence and concreteness of Chinese thought. Wu's argument, as often as not, is through analysis of Western philosophical positions. His very argument form is the abstract representation and criticism of philosophical positions. But unlike Ames and Hall who seek to impose abstraction in order to distinguish and classify, or Cheng who seeks to cultivate and express abstractions faithful to the Chinese as well as Western vision, Wu seeks to create a concrete apprehension of different grains in Chinese and Western thinking by a series of critical vignettes. In this he is like Tu who seeks to create a concrete conversation within which the Chinese vision can find expression and relevance beyond its world of origin. But whereas Tu strategizes the conversation, and awaits the concrete deliberation, Wu's philosophy attempts to *be* the conversation. Wu's philosophy is not a little like Hegel's total system, a logic, though in a different sense of logic from Hegel's, rather the way Kierkegaard is Hegel inverted. The potential limitation of Tu's strategy is that little might be said in the long run besides the representation of the sides. The potential limitation of Wu's is that it is a conversation complete in itself into which it might be the case that no one else will join, a *Chuang Tzu* tale tour de force that one can admire and affirm but not enter. My own critique of Wu is that concreteness itself is an abstraction except sub specie aeternitatis: we only engage things partially, in those selective respects in which our representations can interpret them. Things are always more than we ever engage even at our most real, and hence our existential relations are always abstract in various senses. Life's philosophic questions, I believe, are those of whether our partial engagements of things are in the most important respects rather than in trivial or irrelevant respects. I take the best Chinese philosophy as well as the best Western philosophy to be about that question rather than about concreteness.

6

Methodology, Practices, and Disciplines in Chinese and Western Philosophy

THE PROBLEM

THE THEME OF THIS CHAPTER, Chinese philosophy and analytic methodology, is as creatively ambiguous as it is important. Its importance lies in promoting scholarly comparisons of Chinese and Western philosophies as background for integrating both into a larger world conversation of philosophy. The ambiguities have to do with what counts as Chinese philosophy and what counts as analytic methodology.

The problem from the Western side for what counts as Chinese philosophy is that philosophy might be defined so narrowly as to exclude all genres of Chinese thinking. Lawrence E. Cahoone, for instance, has written the subtlest book to date on the internal struggle of Western philosophy to fulfill its essential aim, which according to him is to know everything, at least abstractly, and to know that we know and why we know.[1] His point is not to laud the Western philosophic tradition. On the contrary, he shows that and how it fails in the work of its great late-modern defenders: Peirce, Nietzsche, Wittgenstein, Buchler, Derrida, and Rorty, and he makes no comments whatsoever on Chinese philosophy. If Chinese philosophies were to be registered on the grids of his rather analytic classifications of philosophical "isms" and "ologies," most would fall within the position he calls "nonfoundational realism." Nonfoundational realism, as he defines it, claims philosophical knowledge about the world but does not claim absolute self-reflexive certainty or comprehensiveness.[2] He argues that nonfoundational realism is untenable and hence he would not have a high regard for nonfoundational realist Chinese philosophies were he to regard them as philosophies at all. He might admit them as inquiries into "practice" or "aesthetics," but that is not philosophy for him. If "analytic argument" is construed according to something like Cahoone's reading of the history and nature of Western philosophy, then there is no problem comparing it to Chinese philosophy because none of the latter exists to be compared, at least not in the dominant, enduring, and still-evolving reflective traditions such as Daoism and Confucianism. Most Western philosophers who think the Chinese tradition has no philosophy are crude in comparison with Cahoone, defining philosophy as Socratic skeptical epistemology and having little tolerance for other modes of philosophic reflection.

Over against this narrow and exclusivistic reading of the nature of philosophy, it is well to recall that in their own Hellenistic time the Platonic and Aristotelian schools, and their competitors the Pythagoreans, Epicureans, Stoics, Cynics, and, a little later, the Neo-Platonists, functioned as what we today would call religions, or religious communities. Similarly, early Christianity was called a philosophy.[3] They were ways of life, sometimes gathered into organized communities, based on conceptions of the universe, nature, society, and human life that were articulated in powerful ways and defended over time against one another. Only some were Socratic in their form of philosophical inquiry (and only some were theistic, which means "religion" has a broader scope than theism). But they all involved reasoned conceptions of the important things in life, with both theoretical and practical implications, and they had ways of defending those conceptions and developing them over time. Great thinkers amended the schools, reconstructed their histories, and often successfully borrowed back and forth among the schools. If we keep in mind the social context of philosophy, what it means to have a living tradition of influences and correction, devoted to asking big questions in theory and practice, then clearly all the thinkers in Wing-tsit Chan's *Sourcebook in Chinese Philosophy*, as well as those in Radhakrishnan and Moore's *Source Book in Indian Philosophy*, are philosophers.[4] For purposes of this discussion, the Confucian tradition arising in China and moving to Korea, Japan, Southeast Asia, California, and Boston will be the main example of Chinese philosophy discussed.[5] The entire question of what counts as philosophy, and how the philosophies of "different traditions" are connected, has been decisively transformed by Randall Collins, who demonstrates its social bases and structures and lays out many of the causal lineaments of its global character.[6]

The other side of the ambiguity is what counts as "analytic methodology." If that phrase is interpreted in a strict and narrow sense to mean Anglo-American analytic philosophy, in *contrast* to Continental, pragmatic, Marxist, and process philosophy, then there are not many interesting comparisons between Chinese philosophy and analytic methodology.[7] Formal and informal logic, conceptual mapworking a la Strawson,[8] positivistic debunkery a la Ayer,[9] and ordinary language analysis a la the late Wittgenstein,[10] Austin,[11] and Searle,[12] can all be construed as methodologies, and as such there is little to commend them for interesting comparisons with Chinese philosophy. Nor, I think, is there much enduring virtue in them as methodologies.

Those are all better construed, not as methodologies, but as philosophical positions generally sharing nominalism and an insistence on first-person empirical verification in ordinary untutored present consciousness.[13] As such, they can be grouped as various late outcomes of British empiricism in opposition to the various rejections of nominalism and the rejections of ordinary untutored present consciousness among their contemporaries, Peirce, Heidegger, Dewey, and Whitehead (not that those in the latter group agree with one another on many other matters).[14]

Perhaps *analytic methodology* is best construed, not as referring to so-called Anglo-American analytic philosophy, but as meaning only the general character of arguing positions closely from a variety of angles, being aware of dialectical differences, and prizing the precision that comes from making distinctions. In this sense Plato, Aristotle, and the other ancient philosophic schools are analytical, though with quite different styles of analysis. So are the Muslim philosophers influenced by Plato, Aristotle, and Plotinus.[15] So are the Christian and Jewish philosophers of the European medieval period. And so are the famous philosophers of European modernity; Pascal, Hegel, and Kierkegaard are as analytical in their own unique ways as Descartes, Spinoza, Leibniz, Hume, and Kant. In this generalized sense of arguing analytically, recognizing different genres of argument, there are many parallels with Chinese philosophy, for what they are worth. Zhuangzi has dialogues like Plato, and they can be understood only through dramatic intent. The Moists invented dull philosophic prose in China before Aristotle did in Greece. The Neo-Confucians were particularly fond of commentarial argument of the sort that would be recognized in medieval Europe and in discussions of the history of philosophy in the nineteenth and twentieth centuries. But these are the kinds of loose parallels we could hardly doubt would obtain between two great, imaginative, long, and interactive cultures such as the Chinese and European. How could it be otherwise?

METHODOLOGY AS A CONCERN

This generalized construal of *analytic methodology* seems to lose an interesting concern, however. For, *methodology* in a far more specific sense has been a prominent theme in modern European philosophy. Indeed, the concern for methodology has been a foundational philosophical doctrine for that strain of modernity that led from Descartes through Kant to modernism/postmodernism.[16] The vague statement of the doctrine is that valid inquiry should be like a syllogism, starting from premises known to be true, proceeding by argument-forms known to be valid, to conclude with results that are thereby guaranteed by the path through which they were reached.

Descartes was, if not the inventor of the doctrine of method, at least the emblem of its originating importance for European Enlightenment thought in his *Discourse on Method*. His *Meditations, Rules for the Direction of the Mind*, and even the *Optics* develop and defend that doctrine. The doctrine of method is complex but has the rough form of saying that, if a philosopher can work down to indubitable starting points, and move without introducing any connective tissue that is not thoroughly understood, it is possible to escape error entirely.[17]

In Descartes' case, there are two parts to the method. The first is working down to indubitable starting points, which means analyzing the topic down into simples. A simple is anything that can be understood all the way through, with no backside, as it were. The best examples are mathematical and logical principles.

Two metaphysical doctrines accompany this conception of attaining simples. One is that all reality is wholly positive and can be penetrated thoroughly in its positive character by what Descartes called the "light of reason" or the "light of nature": no backside or perspectivalism here, no darkside or internal nothingness, no dialectical negation—just positive things that are real in and as God makes them. The other doctrine is that such positive things can be taken apart from one another, separated in analysis, without changing their nature; nothing is internally defined by context or relations with other things such that changing contextual relations changes them. The modern notion of the *controlled experiment* depends on these two doctrines, and philosophers such as Hegel and Heidegger who strongly deny the doctrines are recognized as being hostile to science in the positivistic sense.

The other part of Descartes' method is to put the simples back together into the complex phenomena with which the method starts. Because it is the investigator that puts the simple parts back together, the only thing added to the simples, now themselves completely understood, derives from the will of the investigator. The investigator knows what is added because it all comes from the rational soul, not from any mystery in nature. Good investigation makes sure that every composition of simples by the will ought to be approved by the intuitive understanding first, so that the composition itself is made by simple steps. Error, for Descartes, consists in the will making judgments that the light of reason, knowing simple connections, does not inspect and improve. If the composition part of method is followed, with "constant summaries and reviews" to keep the whole argument in mind, then there is no chance for error to creep in, and science is built upon an indubitable foundation.

Descartes' was not the only version of the doctrine of method. Hobbes (*The Leviathan*), Locke (*An Essay Concerning Human Understanding*), and Hume (*A Treatise on Human Nature*) favored sense data over intuitions as the indubitable simple starting points. Spinoza (*Ethics*) pushed intuitive geometrical reasoning farther than Descartes dreamed. Leibniz (*Discourse on Metaphysics*) disagreed with Descartes about God. Descartes thought God creates possibilities and hence could make any possible world; therefore we need experimental science to determine which actual world God has made. Leibniz believed that God is constrained by both possibilities and goodness to create the best of all possible worlds; hence for Leibniz the appeal to the aesthetics of argument was far more important than would have seemed reasonable to Descartes. Having adopted the sense data theory of simples, Hume crippled the second, compositional, part of Descartes' method by arguing that the will (or imagination) could composite anything it pleases out of the data, and hence nothing in mind gives a clue to what is real outside the mind save for the data. Even more drastic, Kant (*Critique of Pure Reason*) completely refigured Descartes' particular method so that science is guaranteed to give certain knowledge of the world if it follows the way of controlled experiments: Kant redefined the world as what science knows when it conducts controlled experiments. Rationalist intuitions and empirical sense data were rejected as adequate simples, in Kant's scheme. What takes their place are categories of intellectual sensibility to which both objects and good thinking must be conformed; those categories define the form of the world and science fills in the content. However different from Descartes' particular method, Kant's is yet another example of the doctrine of method, namely, that if you can get to a certain starting point, and proceed without introducing mistakes, you can have certain knowledge at the end, a certainty guaranteed by the method.

The doctrine of method has had a predominant role in the history of modern European philosophy. Modernism, with its infamous foundationalism, dominated not only philosophy but the arts as well during the late nineteenth and most of the twentieth centuries. The logical positivists, with their concern not to be fooled by any nonsense, were modernists. So were the early and late Wittgenstein, the former in his assertion that where we cannot speak with "sense" (defined rather positivistically) we should be silent[18] and the latter with his view that language games themselves are something like privileged simples. So was the phenomenologist Edmund Husserl, whose *Crisis of the European Sciences* is a dirge for the failure of the modernist philosophic and scientific program.[19]

Yet the doctrine of method had its opponents. Hegel, in his criticism of Kant, said in effect that the doctrine of method knows too much. The kind of thinking that Descartes, and even more Kant, engaged in while defending their theories of method is something that does not fall within the method they allow. To know a boundary, Hegel said, means that you are already on the other side of it.[20] Hume's contemporaries and successor colleagues, the Scottish common sense philosophers, also rejected the doctrine of method.[21] In essence their view was that knowing is not building upon a certain foundation but rather learning to correct your errors, with common sense providing what Dewey called the "funded wisdom of the race" that gives you adequate truth by and large. Peirce and Dewey picked up on this alternative to the doctrine of method, and hence to modernism and its denial postmodernism, although of course they knew nothing of those terms. Their philosophies, though often preoccupied with method, took method to be the process of correcting ongoing views, not a method for building a certain scientific edifice.[22] To put the point more strongly, if vaguely, for the Romantic, pragmatic, and process philosophies, the "results" of inquiry are to be judged by the cases that can be made for them as they are made vulnerable to testing, not by the argumentative process of inquiry that gives rise to them. On the contrary, the processes of inquiry are to be judged by their results. Therefore, if the "methods" of Anglo-American analytic philosophy are applicable only to small technical problems and fail to provide much wisdom about the great issues of life or to engage the philosophic tradition, then those methods are wanting.[23]

If the comparative concern with Chinese philosophy is about the doctrine of method, that is a narrow concern. It would be like comparing Chinese philosophy with Western nominalism, with which the doctrine of method is closely allied. But suppose we contrast methodology in the sense of the doctrine of method with two related notions, philosophical practices and philosophical discipline.

PHILOSOPHICAL PRACTICES

Philosophical practices are typical or habitual modes of presentation, argument, and life, of the sort listed earlier. Written dialogues displaying debate with theses and objections are a common practice in Plato, Berkeley, Hume, and in modified ways in Kierkegaard. They are very common in Buddhist writing, both Chinese and Indo-Tibetan, and in writers such Mencius and Zhuangzi. Zhuangzi rivals Plato in the artfulness of the dialogue, using the full power of the dramatic context as well as the verbal content of the argument. Prose essays in which positive theories are put forward with internal defense and criticism of alternative views are the primary philosophic practices of Aristotle, the Mohist writers, and Xunzi, as well as later writers such as Wangbi. Wangbi's work can also be considered a commentary, as can many of the writings of the Neo-Confucians on the Classics, and the later Neo-Confucians on the earlier Neo-Confucians. Ching dynasty Confucianism was characterized by elaborate philological attention to the history of philosophic texts and the interpretation of philosophy as having a history. This anticipated a similar concern in European philosophy arising out of Hegel's approach to the philosophy of history and history of philosophy, and out of Jewish and Christian theologians' analysis of biblical texts.

Of course these and many other philosophical practices have analogies in both China and the West. With every analogy, of course, there are many dis-analogies that should be pointed out. David L. Hall and Roger T. Ames have made very strong cases for the dis-analogies in both philosophical practices and fundamental root metaphors between Chinese and Western thinking.[24] My concern here is not to trace out the analogies and dis-analogies but to indicate the recurrence of a wide variety of philosophical practices in both China and the West, often with interesting parallels. The difference in philosophic practice between Spinoza and his near contemporary Wang Fu-chi is not greater than that between Spinoza and Montaigne, another near contemporary, save in the fact that the Europeans had the same reference set of antecedent texts.

The practices discussed so far mainly have been genres of philosophical writing. Philosophies need also to be understood more concretely as practices within social settings. Mention was made earlier of the fact that the ancient classical and Hellenistic philosophical schools were organized as religious communities replete with rituals and initiations. Even earlier, Confucianism was organized as a religious community mainly for learning and practicing ritual.[25] In addition to the organization of schools with a religious cast, philosophers in the ancient world gathered into what we would call proto-universities where different schools would be represented and different disciplines would be gathered along with philosophy. Plato's Academy and Aristotle's Lyceum are famous Greek examples, and the Chi-hsia and Lanling academies of the same time are similar centers of learning.[26] Plato had once hoped that philosophy would be influential in the courts of political power, and established the Academy only after extreme disappointment in politics (he was sold into slavery!). Stoic philosophy was important for the Roman government for a brief period. If we count the philosophical aspects of Christianity and Islam, we can note the influence of Christian and Islamic philosophy during the medieval period in the courts of Europe and the Muslim world. Chinese philosophy has been much more deeply invested in determining political culture than Western philosophy, however. Confucius and Mencius wrote about advising rulers, and the *Daodejing* is a manual for government. Confucians, Daoists, and Buddhists, as well as despised Legalists, have vied for favor at the Chinese court, and in some periods, especially the Han Dynasty, have been actually instrumental in functioning as institutional philosophers. More often than not, however, the social context for Confucian thinkers especially has been that of being out of office, being exiled, being in official public retirement. The great Neo-Confucians Zhu Xi and Wang Yangming founded their teaching academies when they were pushed out of public life.[27] An ideal for Confucians, ever since Confucius himself, has been to be a scholar-official, an ideal no less powerful for the fact that circumstances often prevented its fulfillment. Nevertheless, from the twelfth century to the beginning of the nineteenth, the civil service examination in China was a *philosophy* test.

In contemporary Western society, philosophers have sometimes played the role of what we now call "public intellectuals." One thinks of John Dewey, Bertrand Russell, Martin Heidegger, Ralf Dahrendorf, and Richard Rorty. But often these thinkers are rejected as philosophers by fellow philosophers precisely to the extent that they take part in public life. This is likely because, just to that extent, they move beyond the boundaries of philosophy as a discipline. Public intellectuals are those who define the contours of their thinking by the needs of the problems they address, not by the disciplines they bring to their inquiry. So, public intellectuals are rarely pure enough for philosophers, or for social scientists or humanists for that matter. This guild disapproval does not necessarily diminish their worth to the public conversation, however, although few people nowadays, philosophic or otherwise, would approve of the public stance of philosophers like Heidegger (a Nazi mythmaker).

The discussion of philosophical practices serves to show both the diversity of practices and the fact that they are not distinguished particularly by separation into those of the West and those of China. The critical problem that arises in our own time is which forms of philosophical practice are appropriate. The nature of that problem can be sensed from a list of some of the issues to which philosophy needs to address itself in our world. Consider the following, arbitrary in a way, but also obvious.

The entanglement of world cultures. Although Samuel Huntington is extreme and oversimple in describing our situation as a "clash of civilizations,"[28] the realities of economics, global politics, and especially electronic communications require people to understand one another in terms of their background cultures, including their philosophic cultures. Therefore one great philosophic challenge for each of the world's philosophic cultures is to enrich its *paideia* so as to include understanding and interpretation of the others, eventually to enter into a global philosophic conversation inclusive of all cultural resources in philosophy.

Political thought for a global multicultural society. The world's philosophic cultures, in conversation, need to address questions of political authority and tolerance, including the distribution of power to manage economic and military affairs, in a world with many cultures. Western liberalism has a well-developed theory in several regards, but it itself is under attack from Western philosophy as well as from other philosophic cultures. A specific example is the debate over the differences between Chinese and Western liberal interpretations of human rights.[29]

Conceptions of the meaning and value of human life in a world understood according to the scale of modern science. A vast array of issues falls under this rubric, all arising from the destruction of "traditional" images of human meaning by the findings of modern science.

Development of conceptions of distributive justice for a global economy. Although most philosophic traditions have theories of distributive justice, nearly all assume distribution over an area to be ruled by a single government, not a world of global governments. Moreover, until the last century or two, too little was known about real economic causation for distributive justice to be a practical conception. Now we know something, because of advances in the social sciences, about how markets in one country affect life in another, and about what can be done to control these effects. The philosophic conversation needs to provide a normative account of this.

Ecological issues. Modern technologies have provided instruments for altering the human environment fast enough for it to be noticed, and science allows us to measure effects of technology that are far beyond the obvious, for instance, destruction of the ozone layer. Most philosophic cultures suppose that the problems of human life are to be worked out within the structures of a given environment. Recognition of the fact that human practices affect the environment means that new conceptions are required to understand how we are and ought to be "at home" in the environment.[30]

These are but a few of the issues to which philosophical understanding is relevant, and about which the world's philosophic (and religious) traditions so far have little to say. Each has analogies from which to work, of course, but the question is just how far the analogies extend and where are they inappropriate. Moreover, the public for philosophic discourse is making a case to anyone who has a philosophic interest, no matter what the philosophical culture of the thinker's background.

So what are the social practices appropriate for our global situation? I have three observations.

First, a principal, if not the principal, motivation for contemporary global philosophy engaged with the issues defining our world comes from religion, from the world's religions, from interreligious dialogue, and from religious activism. Contemporary religions have been at the forefront of coping with the entanglement of world cultures, urging political solutions to war and peace, imagining the place of the human in a world of vast scientific scale, coping with transnational injustice and oppression, and rethinking what it means to be at home on earth. In all the world's cultures except the European, philosophy is just the intellectual side of religious cultural life, and the practice of philosophy in religious communities is a natural and expected Way. In European philosophy, there has been a skeptical alienation of some forms of philosophy from religious life, and philosophy has been defined very much in epistemological terms that are not friendly to religious commitment; the discussion of Cahoone at the beginning traced one form of this. In Europe and North America, philosophy has come to think of itself as a separate discipline from religious thinking, and often in somewhat hostile relations with religion. Accordingly, Western academic philosophy has been the most tardy of the world's philosophic traditions to define its roles in terms of problems of the sort listed earlier, save in the case of questioning human life relative to modern science, and thinking about global justice. But Western academic philosophy will just have to come along and learn to think about the big important issues, or it will die out within its academic base as trivial. At any rate, philosophical practices will and should be affected by religious practices.

Second, the locus if not always the motivation for the contemporary practice of engaged global philosophy will include the academy—universities and colleges. This will likely be its most important locus. The reason is that the academy, at least in the instance of philosophy in most places, is a neat balance of research and teaching where leisure is preserved for getting it right. Criticisms from peers and demands from students press philosophy departments to be honest, thorough, historically grounded, and relevant. Other fields within the academy have not been so lucky. Most of the sciences are pressured by government and business to give them what they want. The very irrelevance of philosophy and some of the other humanistic disciplines gives them the leisure to pay attention to getting it right. So far, philosophy is able to respond to the demands for relevance to the issues rather than relevance to some social group's special interests, although any discussion reflects the social biases of its participants.

The third observation is that philosophy needs to be in close interaction with other disciplines in order to address issues of the sort mentioned previously. Obviously those include the natural and social sciences, and also the hermeneutical disciplines of history and criticism. All of these are to be found within the academy, and this is another reason why universities are likely to be the prime locus of philosophical conversations. Beyond "disciplines" in the academic sense, however, philosophy needs to be engaged with, learning from, and helping shape the various spheres of public life, including government and law; economics and production; cultural formation of communities, families, and persons; and religious practices. This is because, in the end, philosophy should not be defined as a guild with a special methodology but rather as the work of public intellect on the large issues of meaning and existence.

The vast extent of contemporary knowledge, however, makes impossible the ancient model of the philosopher as knowing everything important. Plato, Aristotle, Augustine, Confucius, Mencius, and Xunzi might well have known just about all kinds of elite knowledge for their day. Contemporary philosophers cannot know enough and therefore must think cooperatively with other "professionals." Philosophers are not alone in needing an interdisciplinary context: politicians too need economists, theologians, theater critics, and psychologists. Alfred North Whitehead pointed out the inevitability of philosophy operating in a field where the mastery of knowledge requires a plurality of professionals.[31] William Sullivan has analyzed the conflict internal to professionalism in thinking, namely, adherence to methodologies defining a guild and the engagement of issues that require more than that method, engagement often with a moral impulse.[32] So the practice of philosophy in the contemporary situation has to be situated in a multidisciplinary as well as multicultural context.

PHILOSOPHICAL DISCIPLINE

Surely the reader will have noticed the surreptitious introduction earlier of the notion that philosophy is a discipline, a profession. This needs analysis, for it surely is the real issue behind the problematic of "Chinese philosophy and analytic methodology." Can Chinese philosophers make cases for their basic claims being true, as Western philosophers have argued for their claims?

What is philosophic discipline? I suggest it is inquiry into philosophic issues involving three things. First, it is the study and appropriation of philosophic resources. These include previous philosophy and the other kinds of knowledge relevant for philosophic thinking. Second is the engagement of real issues. These can have a moral cast, as in the aforementioned examples. But the real issues are matters of wonder, a matter of curiosity because something should be understood that is not. Moral issues are a subcase of these. Philosophy can engage the meaning of existence, or being, or why there is anything at all, with the same urgency as it engages the problem of conceiving of distributive justice in the days of the United Nations. Wonder and curiosity are among the defining characteristics of human concern. Third, philosophic discipline needs to propose hypotheses about how to understand the issues engaged, and then to make a case for those hypotheses. Usually making a case means showing that they are internally consistent and coherent and then making them vulnerable to correction regarding their adequacy and applicability.

All three parts of philosophic discipline are necessary, I believe. Without mastery and appropriation of the resources for philosophic thought, philosophy does not take advantage of the best that it can be, and remains amateurish. Therefore much of philosophical education is devoted to getting oneself prepared through the appropriation of cognitive and perhaps spiritual resources. Philosophy does require a kind of guildmastery.

Without engagement of the real issues, philosophy becomes intellectual history or a play of technical methods. Anglo-American academic philosophers are often accused of being only guild masters, not real philosophers engaged with the issues that justify philosophic effort in the first place. This criticism is often overdrawn: great metaphysicians such as Paul Weiss and great political philosophers such as John Rawls have been academic philosophers.

Without formulating hypotheses and making cases for them, philosophy does not make claims as to the truth and defend those claims. Philosophy in China as well as the West goes beyond history writing and aesthetic criticism by virtue of making good on claims to get the truth about its issues.

To call philosophic claims "hypotheses," of course, is to reflect the rhetoric of the pragmatic tradition. Most philosophers never conceived of claims as hypotheses until that was spelled out in nineteenth- and twentieth-century pragmatism and process philosophy;[33] if they had known about those ideas, they probably would not have thought of their own views that way. But in retrospect, we can treat philosophic claims as hypotheses. So, for instance, the doctrine of method discussed previously can be construed as a hypothesis for arriving at true conclusions, and the case for it assessed. Plato was rather explicit about considering his dialectic as a ladder of hypotheses. Aristotle dismissed dialectic as bad logic, a point that itself can be treated as an hypothesis about logic, and assessed. Similarly, Confucius's views about humanity and ritual can be viewed as hypotheses about what ideals and courses of action to urge for the improvement of human life. Xunzi's views of nature or heaven can be treated as hypotheses about the natural context within which human direction and effort are to be understood, and so forth.

The chief significance of calling all philosophical views "hypotheses" is to point out that they are vulnerable to correction. Whether or not they would have thought of themselves as presenting hypotheses, every important philosopher's views have been vulnerable to correction. Sometimes that means merely the contradiction of them because they are not persuasive. But more usually it means the amendment and modification of them to be more nuanced, subtle, and articulate at getting around objections. In the long run, making a case for a philosophical hypothesis means making it so vulnerable to correction that it is responsive to every objection and has been modified so that nothing more can be said against it. To be vulnerable is to be correctable, and a hypothesis that has been thoroughly corrected has a good case. Only when something new comes up against it would its vulnerability again be tested and its fallibility displayed.

Now it is apparent that a philosophy has good discipline when it can make a case for itself in the relevant public. What is a philosophy's public? It can only be those perspectives and other positions that can interact with it and have an interest in the outcome of the discussion to which it needs to make its case. Its public therefore is historically contingent.

Ancient Confucians had to make their cases in a public that included one another—for instance the followers of Mencius relating to those of Xunzi—and also the Moists, Legalists, Daoists, and others. They did not have to make a case to the Platonists, Buddhists, Neo-Confucians, Cartesians, or Marxists. Contemporary Confucians do have a public that includes the whole of Chinese and Western philosophy, as well as that of India to which they have already responded somewhat through Buddhism. Similarly, Thomas Aquinas had a public including the Christian Platonists and Aristotelians as well as some of the great Muslim and Jewish philosophers, but not Zhu Xi or Kant; most twentieth-century Thomists, however, have been Kantians, and certain seventeenth century Thomists such as Matteo Ricci would have liked to have included Zhu Xi in their philosophic public.

If judged by the standard of making a case for their philosophy as being true, in the context of their actual philosophical public, Chinese philosophers throughout history have been as disciplined or "analytical in methodology" as any Western philosopher. The title of Angus Graham's introduction to ancient Chinese philosophy, *Disputers of the Tao: Philosophical Argument in Ancient China*, accurately indicates that the philosophers argued their cases within a vigorously disputatious public.[34] The subsequent history of Chinese philosophy expanded its public to include Buddhists and others, down to the last two centuries in which it has engaged Western thought. The modes of argument have always been historically relative to the perspectives involved in the public at hand. As argued previously, the genres of arguments have not been all that different from those used by Western philosophers in their own historical contexts. The content of the arguments has been quite different, especially in slant if not in topic.

In contemporary terms, the issue of Chinese philosophy and "analytic methodology," meaning good philosophic discipline, can be phrased in the terms laid out in the aforementioned discussion of practice. Do Chinese philosophies have something to contribute to the contemporary discussion of engaged issues, and can those philosophies be reconstructed so as to address the contemporary philosophic public? It seems obvious to me that the answer to this double question is vaguely yes, and that the case needs to be made for or against specific philosophic ideas in detail; other chapters in this book expand the point.

7
Metaphysics for Contemporary Chinese Philosophy

METAPHYSICS FOR CHINESE PHILOSOPHY is a topic at the edge of foolhardiness. Most prominent forms of philosophy today, both Chinese and Western, take metaphysics to be an unnecessary, outmoded, and distracting (if not perverse) enterprise. In the West this depreciation of metaphysics is a Kantian legacy maintained by both Continental and analytical philosophers, with a few notable exceptions. In East Asia it results from construing the Chinese philosophical tradition as primarily ethical and practical, not theoretical. Given this common depreciation of metaphysics, there would be little point in discussing various Chinese heritages in these matters, for that could be dismissed as showing that East Asia has the same dead ends as the West. What would be the point of inventing troubles for Chinese philosophy?

My argument, therefore, shall *not* be that Chinese philosophy has some interesting metaphysical ideas to offer the contemporary situation (although it does, and many are listed in previous chapters). My argument rather shall be that the common depreciation of metaphysics is misguided, as mentioned in chapter 1. Just as the West needs to develop better metaphysics, not to abandon that enterprise, so does Chinese philosophy, and for the same reasons. Moreover, I shall argue that the great themes of Chinese philosophy from the ancient to the modern periods require a contemporary metaphysics that needs to meet today's conditions of plausibility and truth. That these themes have been given traditional expressions that look, to Westerners, more like ethics than metaphysics does not gainsay the fact that, without a viable metaphysics, even their ethical expressions are impotent today.

THE NEED FOR METAPHYSICS

The world needs good philosophy about fundamental problems.[1] "Fundamental problems" need to be addressed at least two ways. The profound, slow, ruminative address to the problems is through reflection on and development of the historically deep ideas and metaphors of the great civilized traditions. This way reveals basic constitutive dimensions of reality and human life, however variant in cultural forms they might be. The other address is through appreciation of the urgencies of the crises of life and civilization, usually expressed in panicked ethical terms such as the "ecological crisis" or "the clash of civilizations."[2] Because the deep dimensions of reality are nearly always problematic for human life, they are nearly always expressed in crises of one sort or another. Crises appeal to journalists. The profundities appeal to scholars who take nothing seriously that does not have a core text and a scholarly tradition. Philosophy embraces and bridges both. Or at least it should.

Ours is a time filled with philosophical crises that themselves rest on a failure of classic sources (in the West Asian, East Asian, South Asian, and Islamic traditions) to address current problems. In this chapter I shall mention only the following contemporary crises for philosophy: Given the traditional cosmologies of the great traditions formed two to three thousand years ago, how shall we understand any lessons from those traditions in light of modern science and the imagination it forms? Given that we now understand something of the global causation involved in economics and politics, how can we understand distributive justice on a global scale and devise the political means to achieve it? Given our recently acquired ecological knowledge of the serious systematic effects of human life patterns on the environment, both local and global (and perhaps galactic if we start shooting nuclear waste into outer space), how should we conduct ourselves, legally and politically, with regard to ecological concerns? Given all of the aforementioned, plus the competitive and now sometimes abrasive encounter of world civilizations, how should we conceive of personal identity and fulfillment? Given all of this, and recognizing the plurality of human situations and cultural conditions, how can a global society of peace and fulfillment be devised, and with what kinds of governments?

Behind these crises are the following profound and enduring issues: What is reality and how can we conceive and imagine it in order properly to be oriented in truthful ways? What is justice in human causal interactions? What does it mean to be at home in the universe? What are the meanings, values, and goals of human life? Can human beings govern themselves responsibly, and how?

The contemporary world situation calls for philosophic answers to these questions on both the crisis and profundity levels. The crises descried in the media have the form of practical urgency. The underlying deep problems have the form of requiring deep reflection that calls upon the resources of the great traditions of thought. Neither the demand for timely solutions nor the mining of the traditions is enough for contemporary philosophy, however. Creative imagination and originality are required. Now is a time (like every other historical time) when thinkers are called to frame new directions out of old inertial vectors of force. Metaphysics is necessary to do this.

The Chinese philosophical traditions have major themes that can give life to important aspects of the contemporary discussion. Yet these themes are framed in ways that do not easily accord with modern science, that do not envision global economic and social causation, that have little global ecological sense, that do not address selfhood in a radically pluralistic situation, and that do not imagine global government in a democratic, multicentered sense, but only in the totalitarian sense of empire. If these Chinese themes can be brought to the current discussion, it will be in part by a metaphysics that directly engages the contemporary issues. The Chinese themes include a sense of the cosmos consisting of diverse processes plus normative order or pattern, an apprehension of each thing having a value that is accessible to human recognition and deference, a conviction of unity and continuity expressed in the phrase "being one body with the world," a habit of self-identity that consists partly in uniquely singular concrete developments of institutionalized social roles, and an understanding of responsible and just social interaction as made possible by ritual play.

Anti-metaphysical thinkers have several arguments that would short circuit a program of contemporary metaphysics that draws upon Chinese (or any other kind of) philosophy. The first, the Kantian argument, is that metaphysics is not knowledge. At most it can be only projection of some tradition's ideas and interests. The answer to this argument is the one devised by Charles Peirce, namely, that metaphysics has the form of a hypothesis, not an intuition from looking at reality or an a priori deductive argument from first principles (the two sources of knowledge Kant criticized). A metaphysical theory is a vastly complicated hypothesis, to be sure. It arises from the imagination of deep traditions of thought, and also from the spontaneity of intellectual creativity. It has canons of internal coherence and consistency, and it needs to be tested for applicability to reality and adequacy of explanation. I doubt any metaphysical theory can be complete, only better than its alternatives. The testing of such a hypothesis requires engaging reality in ways that are differentially shaped by the hypothesis. A person can do this over a lifetime, and a community of scholars can test hypotheses in cumulative ways. Living with a metaphysical hypothesis involves altering the hypothesis as new evidence comes in or new elements of reality show up that need interpretation. Although Kant read the history of Western metaphysics as a failed enterprise, it can better be read as the evolution of greater subtlety, more intense aesthetic vision, and grander scope. The other great metaphysical traditions can be read in a similar way, and part of the excitement of metaphysics today is that these traditions are being read together as reinforcing and criticizing one another.

The second common argument against metaphysics is the ethical one that metaphysics is impractical. Real human personal and social crises will be decided by practical exigencies, often by force and nearly always by at least partly arbitrary acts of will. Furthermore, the "philosophy" behind practical life is the ethos or culture of a society. Mining and adapting deep cultural values is the way to give what wisdom is available to social structuring; metaphysics just gets in the way. Charles Peirce, in a quasi-ironic mode, argued that with regard to "vitally important topics" we should keep philosophy out of the way and trust instinct that has developed over eons.[3] Many people take the Confucian tradition to be ethical and anti-metaphysical in this way. The counter-argument, however, is that unnoticed connections and unconscious presuppositions can be disastrous in ethically problematic situations. Modern science, communications, and technologies have led to causal connections that were not noticed in ancient philosophies: metaphysics involves the deliberate attempt to think things together by inventing abstract bridging notions. The assumptions that might have evolved or come to characterize the genius of a culture might be wholly inappropriate when applied to new situations, and can be recognized as such only when articulated in metaphysical form. Without saying that metaphysics alone will solve fundamental practical problems, we should say that the problems will be more obscure, possibly with great bias, without appropriate metaphysics.[4]

THEMES OF CHINESE PHILOSOPHY

The Chinese philosophical traditions share and differently punctuate ancient themes in cosmology. These include a deep sense of events or changes as the units of reality that can be known, an appreciation of process described in alternations of yang and yin, a binary sense of intelligibility consisting in interactions of malleable processes with patterns or some source of harmony, variously described as Earth and Heaven, or *qi* and *li*, material force and Heavenly Principle. Although this is not too distant from Plato's conception of processes of becoming made intelligible by forms of being, it is quite distinct from Aristotle's fundamental sense that reality consists of substances. Aristotle's theory entered modern science in the assumption that explanation means articulating the nature of atoms and showing how their behavior follows from their nature. Part of Whitehead's extraordinary philosophical contribution was to show that the Aristotelian metaphysical imagination could not account for the processes mathematical physics was articulating; it could not make sense of how mathematics applies to physical reality.[5] Whitehead's "Platonic" system was an attempt to remedy this by showing how properly abstract notions can be constructed that properly articulate form in process.

How can the themes of ancient Chinese cosmology be brought to the modern discussion? Some years ago certain scientists remarked about the similarity of ancient East Asian patterns of thought to the findings of atomic physics. Fritjof Capra's *The Tao of Physics* was the most popular writing of this sort.[6] These rough parallels are not enough, however. Daoist and Confucian philosophers need to articulate metaphysical systems as detailed and abstract as Whitehead's in order to show that the crude materialism of early modern science cannot dismiss the ancient Chinese cosmological themes as mere swarmy romanticism. Without a detailed and systematic contemporary metaphysical expression, the ancient themes must be dismissed as primitive protoscience. They are not proto-scientific in their philosophic range, however. They are abstractions with metaphysical range, and therefore must be given viable metaphysical expression so that contemporary science (and cultural encounters, the arts, etc.) can be given contextual orientation by them.

Nowhere is this more important than with regard to value. The early success of modern science was based in part on a sharp distinction between facts and values. Facts are knowable, and values are human inventions and projections. This is obviously false, because experience is filled with things that are worthwhile or dangerous, fulfilling or destructive, intrinsically valuable or positively wicked. We can be mistaken about what we say is valuable, from truth values to personal fulfillments to civilizational values. Anything we can be mistaken about is real. So values are real. The modern Western philosophic tradition struggled to hold to real values without saying that they could be known the way scientific facts are known.[7] But the upshot is that values were construed to be subjective, binding perhaps on a noumenal will that is not socially interactive, as in Kant's theory, and often merely the result of arbitrary will. The postmodern critique of all theory as mere power plays is one consequence of the assumption that nature is only factual.

The Chinese tradition is a powerful antidote to the fact/value distinction. Tu Weiming has pointed out that the Western project of liberal humanism is extraordinarily anthropocentric, and that the Chinese Confucian tradition (it works for Daoism too) has a cosmocentric locus for value.[8] This is true despite the common view that Confucianism in particular deals merely with the human sphere. It deals with the human sphere by orienting that sphere within the larger realm of nature and nature's values. "To be one body with the world" is not merely to assert a universal causal connection. It asserts a valuationally appreciative connection. When Wang Yangming elaborated that phrase, he said we feel pain when tiles and stones are broken.[9] Indeed, the universe contains nothing that in micro-and-macro-cosmic ways fails to orient the valuations of human beings who are sufficiently learned and sensitive.

Chinese philosophy thus demands a contemporary metaphysics that shows how things have value, and how their relations constitute obligations on human beings irrespective sometimes of whether human beings recognize those values. The ancient and modern ideals of sagehood or human worthiness involve the obligation to be so cultivated as to recognize one's obligations. Daoists and Confucians do this in different ways. None of this makes sense unless a contemporary viable metaphysics can be developed that articulates the ancient themes of pervasive and differential value that determines that to which human beings should defer.

Distributive justice and ecological concerns mark off two fields within which we should learn to defer. Distributive justice in Western thinking has usually been hung up on two conflicting principles, equality and historical right of ownership. The principles of equality suggest that everyone should start off with equal resources and opportunities, and this has guided many policy arguments. The principles of the historical right of ownership say that people have a right to their labor and its fruits, and to the possessions given to them by family and sometimes by cultural or social standing.[10] Most conceptions of property ownership pay tribute to rights of parents to give gifts to their children, to control what they make or inherit, and so forth. The supposition in this conflict over distributive justice is that people are either all the same or that they are unique in their claims.

The Chinese contribution, I wager, lies in its notion of deference combined with ritual. People are not equal, but they are bound together in social rituals that give them identity. Moreover they are subjects of humaneness or *ren* and therefore should be deferred to as human being each with their situation of being humane, with just their family and friends, and just their social projects and obligations, playing just their ritual roles. Whereas the West has seen the demands that individuals can make on distributive justice, China has seen the obligations of deference individuals have toward others related to them ritually. Deference in distributive justice finesses the conflict between equal rights of possession and historically defined ownership. Chinese metaphysics of value needs to be supplemented by a contemporary theory of deference and ritual interaction.[11]

Ecological concerns are obvious topics for a Chinese theory of deference. Without treating environmental elements as human beings, with something like "animal rights" or "ecosystem rights," we can learn the worth of things in ecosystemic interactions and defer accordingly. To defer is to acknowledge the value in something, its specific character, and to respond appropriately. Without a metaphysics that shows how things have value, such deference is impossible. Of course, metaphysics alone will not show how to defer in ecological matters. A far more elaborate theory of criteria of worth will be required, and also of markers of proper deference (with fines and other sanctions for failures of deference).

Another metaphysically important theme in Chinese philosophy is its general approach to the self. In contrast to Western approaches to the self as a substance or a subject in polar opposition to an objective world, the Chinese metaphysical imagination conceives the self to be a set of physical, psychological, and social structures through which a person perceives (or misperceives) the worthy things in the environment and with intuitive or innate appreciation responds to them appropriately (or inappropriately). Classic texts for this conception are the *Zhongyong* and Mencius's discussion of the "four beginnings." The pure center of the self is a readiness to respond aesthetically and harmoniously to the world, with appropriate purposes; Chinese schools have differed over whether this center is ever isolable, or is always perceiving and responding. An added dimension to the Chinese approach is that the self is or should be in process of transformation to perfect its response-ability to the world. This involves perfecting the physical, psychological, and social structures of one's state. Marks of perfection include naturalness and spontaneity, improving those affected by actions, being at home in a world with vastly diverse things in it, and being able to identify with the whole of things "as one's body."

If this complex theme of Chinese metaphysics of the self is to enter into contemporary discussions of justice and agency, it needs a metaphysical expression that can relate it to psychology, neurophysiology, and all the social sciences. Metaphors of "center" and the "ten thousand things" to which the center relates are simply not adequate to enter the conversation.

Yet another theme, already mentioned in the discussion of the self, is the Chinese, especially Confucian, conception of ritual. From a Western standpoint, ritual is part of ethics or religion, or maybe anthropology. From the Chinese standpoint, however, ritual has a fundamental metaphysical or ontological status, for, as we have seen in previous chapters, it is the principal element by which human beings "complete Heaven and Earth." The conception of ritual is extraordinarily important for bringing civilization to the chaotic world of clashing cultures, competing economic entities, national and ethnic rivalries, and so forth. Confucius was surely right that harmony cannot be brought to a conflictual pluralistic situation by force of arms that imposes a single order, but rather by the invention of rituals that allow people who hate one another and whose real interests are in conflict to dance together. The Chinese conception of ritual needs a contemporary metaphysical expression if its importance is to be seen.

METAPHYSICAL DIRECTIONS

Might we speculate about the directions to a contemporary metaphysics that can give a new rendering of the metaphysical imagination of the ancient tradition of Chinese philosophy in its various histories?

As Whitehead argued, metaphysics needs to work at the level of the greatest possible abstraction because it represents and integrates all the other abstractions that epitomize human reflections on science, the arts, ethics, politics, and religion. I suggest then that a key concept is that reality consists of processive events of harmonization. To stipulate a definition of harmony, it is the togetherness of components of at least two sorts, conditional and essential. Conditional components are all the features of a harmony that come from or are determined by other harmonies. The conditional components of a harmony are those traits by virtue of which it is itself and not those other things, or is a unique reordering and relocating of those other things. Essential components are the features that determine the unique own-being of a harmony by virtue of which it integrates the conditional components. At least three sorts of conditional components can be mentioned. One is the spontaneous creative features that give present existence in a specific place and time; Whitehead's theory focuses on creativity in this sense. A second are the features inherited from the past that give normative weight to the present; in human beings these are past actions and commitments that determine what is right or wrong in the present. A third sort of essential component is the structure of future possibility; present decisive creativity is bound by the structure of possibility as that is affected by other harmonies. By virtue of conditional components, harmonies exist only in relation to other things with respect to which they are determinate. Harmonies are not atoms. By virtue of essential components, harmonies have their own being and can have unique singular identity and existential location. Harmonies are irreducibly plural and not resolvable into relations alone. All the components of harmonies are themselves harmonies.

The real things of the world are not harmonies as if they were static but rather are processes of harmonizing and dissolving of harmonies. According to Whitehead, the actual occasions of the world are very small finite comings-to-be. I think rather that harmonizing events overlap in countless ways, to be plumbed by sciences and arts. The components of a harmony themselves have a trajectory of coming to be that depends on the trajectories of coming to be of their own components, and so on down. The harmony of a person's life requires harmonizing physical body with life circumstances; the physical body is a harmony of many organic processes, which themselves are harmonies of chemical interactions with constant nutrient inputs and waste products. Personal lives are components of social structures that are components of civilizations. Harmonies dissolve in time as their components go ways that are no longer compatible. Whereas some harmonies are brief and adventitious, others are reinforced by surrounding systems of harmonies. But all decay as their irreducibly plural components go their own ways, or themselves decay. The relative stability of our world comes from a rough rhythm of harmonization and decay, with the decomposing components going on to be components in new harmonies. Many patterns of harmonization and decay exist, nested inside one another, overlapping, perhaps resonating from one sphere to another. When harmonizing events occur, sometimes it is simply the result of the inertial forces of the components; but often energies from outside the harmonic process itself contribute to the process so as to sustain the harmony's role in some larger harmony. As a harmony begins to decay, more and more external energy is needed to hold it together.

The process of harmonization can represent the ancient notion of yang, which extends itself until its resources are used up. Yin is represented by the phase of deconstruction or decay of the harmonic event so that the components become resources for new harmonies. We articulate the processes of nature by understanding the various phases of harmonization and decay. Because the components of harmonic events are themselves harmonic events, rising and falling, reality is a vastly complicated, partly rhythmic, structure of yang and yin interactions, as the ancient Chinese said. The recurring patterns of harmonic interactions might be more complicated than the sixty-four hexagrams of the *Yijing*: nevertheless, that basic idea of patterns of change from ancient China is thoroughly compatible with late-modern science and might be a more fruitful way of articulating the processes of reality than the Western idea of classifying sorts of substances or particles.

Harmony is intrinsically a value notion. A harmony has the value of putting its components together. Sometimes that value is far greater than the sum of the values of the components if they were not together. I believe that the most plausible metaphysical way of understanding value is through the aesthetic properties of harmony. There seem to be two scales of harmonization, complexity and simplicity. Complexity is the diversity of things brought together in a harmony; simplicity is the ways those diverse ways reinforce one another. The togetherness of a purely complex harmony would be mere conjunction. The togetherness of a purely simple harmony would be pure homogeneity. Value is added to the mere sum of the components' values by simplicity added onto complexity so that new elements of value emerge.

The Chinese notions of Earth or material force can be represented by the maelstrom of processes that need harmonization. The notions of Heaven or Principle (in Neo-Confucian philosophy) can be represented by that which makes harmonies harmonious, whatever those aesthetic elements are. Without Principle, the plurality of processes would not gain harmony, and their subprocesses would not gain harmony either. There never is material force without the operation of Principle or that which makes things hang together with value. Principle cannot be conceived by itself because it has no determinate character without something to harmonize, some specific plurality. Some philosophers have made the mistake of thinking that Principle is just pattern, perhaps a Platonic grab bag of patterns. But that is to mistake the pattern that would make a given plurality harmonious for that which makes any harmony harmonious, such as the aforementioned aesthetic properties.

Because everything in reality is involved in processes of becoming harmonious or decaying from harmony, and related to everything else in similar process, everything has value. Insofar as people can relate to these processes in cognitive ways, they can recognize and defer to those values. Our new scientific understandings of ecological systems in nature point out new (for us) processes of harmonization and decay. Our new social scientific understanding of economic and other kinds of global social interactions, point out new (for us) processes of harmonization and decay. Both allow for the discernment of values missed before, and the development of modes of response that respect these values. Of course, this metaphysics alone does not answer the ecological and global distributive justice problems. But it does allow the classical Chinese ideas to be brought to bear in ways they could not if a fact/value metaphysics reigned.

A contemporary metaphysics of the self, if that is not too specific for metaphysics, needs three elements if it is to pick up on Chinese themes. First, it needs to show how human beings can grasp the values of things and respond appropriately. For this, an axiological epistemology is called for that exhibits how valuation is involved in sheer imagination, in interpretive judgment, in theorizing, and in practical reason. Dualistic philosophies of consciousness are not apt for this task. The naturalistic philosophies of Peirce and Dewey are far more promising. Warren Frisina has shown how pragmatic (and Whiteheadian) naturalistic nonrepresentational philosophies very nicely articulate the major themes of Wang Yangming, for instance.[12]

Second, a contemporary metaphysics of the self needs to show how the unity of a self consists not in an unyielding character but in a kind of poise for balancing out the many, often conflicting, orientations that a self requires to relate to its world. A person is oriented to family, friends, community, work, religion, day-to-day events, larger historical events, ongoing civilization, and even to the Heavens, to use Xunzi's point. Each of these and many others has its own scale and shape of response, and it is a mistake to treat one as if it were adequately oriented by another. Poise is the ability to keep all the orientations going in their proper places, and the maturation of a self involves attaining that poise.

Third, a metaphysics of the self, true to Chinese metaphysical themes on the topic, would have to show how the body, psyche, and social behavior of individuals are formed according to semiotic structures. That is, human beings learn a meaningful way of moving, of composing their emotional life, and knowing how to interact cognitively and socially with other people. Confucians emphasize the roles that people individuate as they mature. All of this falls under the rubric of ritual, which needs a metaphysical interpretation.

The mention of ritual brings us once again to the metaphysics of social interaction. I believe that an understanding of ritual is crucial for supplementing discussions of human agency, freedom, and social participation. The current conflicts and competitions in our world would be greatly enhanced by a greater appreciation of ritual, especially as it is seen to have metaphysical generality.

8
The Conscious and Unconscious Placing of Ritual and Humanity

THE UNCONSCIOUS AS A
PROBLEM FOR CONFUCIAN VIRTUE

THIS ESSAY IN CONTEMPORARY cross-cultural Confucian philosophy raises a question unlikely to arise from either Chinese Confucianism or Western philosophy alone. The Confucian tradition from ancient times has said that both ritual (*li*) and humanity (*ren*) need to be learned and practiced so much that they become spontaneous responses. Western philosophers would rightly understand this as a kind of learning that requires conscious attention at first but that becomes habituated with practice, like learning to ride a bicycle or being kind to elderly strangers. In addition, however, Western culture understands unconscious behavior to have a structure of its own that sometimes is at odds with the structure of conscious life. Two principal lineages of the Western notion of the unconscious have currency now. One is the Freudian, emphasizing unconscious psychological structures that cause us to do things other than what we consciously intend or think we are doing. The other is the Marxist, emphasizing real economic motivations based on social location and class structure that are often different from our conscious motivations structured by a self-serving ideology.

Both Western senses of the unconscious call for a Confucian rectification of names. With regard to the psychological sense of the unconscious, the Confucian project of embedding ritual and humanity in the deepest center of the person requires a transformation of unconscious structures. The techniques of ritual learning and becoming humane are Confucian contributions to psychodynamic procedures for transforming the unconscious, especially transforming it so that it does not mislead or betray important conscious intentions. With regard to the Marxist sociological sense of the unconscious, the Confucian project of education in ritual and humanity requires a transformation of our conscious structures and categories so that we admit honestly our true motivations stemming from social location and come to terms with them. The Confucian tradition also, of course, emphasizes the transformation of social structures and personal social location, although that is a different point from the one I am making here. The sagely project of becoming sincere (*cheng*) requires a contemporary Confucian to think through the tasks of transforming the psychological unconscious so as to be reconciled with conscious intentions, and transforming conscious beliefs about motives that are ideological in disguising real socially structured motivations. This continues the theme developed in chapter 3.

A final preliminary word should be said about why the Confucian virtues of ritual propriety and humaneness are so important in the contemporary world. As in Confucius's time, our world is sorely lacking in rituals needed for diplomacy, for common courtesy among persons and nations of different religions, and for harmonizing societies whose citizens have genuinely different interests and social locations. Part of the contemporary Confucian agenda is the identification and criticism of the dysfunctional rituals that are in place and the areas where rituals are simply lacking. A related part of the agenda is to devise, institutionalize, and teach improved rituals that address the situation. The contemporary promotion of the Confucian virtue of humaneness is especially important now because Confucianism is one of the two influential traditions to emphasize human responsibility for social structures as well as personal action. The other tradition is the Western Enlightenment thought that has become attached to the rationalism of the capitalist market economy, which is inhumane. Should capitalists seek to limit their rational profit-making in order to promote justice and humanity in some circumstance, they are ideologically self-deceived because the market is against them. The real market decisions are made by the millions of investors around the world, large and small, who move financial investments by way of the Internet to the places that maximize profit. Should a company choose to lower its profit in order to be humane, anonymous investments will be moved away from its production to some other company. Capitalism is not about to be dislodged soon as the world's economic system, and the alternative systems seem so much worse. Perhaps a Confucian promotion of humaneness can be integrated with the practice of market capitalism.

RITUAL AND HUMANENESS

Ritual and humanity are extremely complicated practices within the Confucian tradition, or better, the Confucian traditions. Diverse as Confucianism has become over the centuries, every branch of it needs to give an interpretation of ritual and humanity as cardinal virtues. With the different contributions of such a diverse heritage, the conceptions of ritual and humanity are impossible to describe accurately in a brief compass. As we apply them to new circumstances in global societies, outside the East Asian social and familial context in which they originated, those virtues are made even richer. A brief word, however abstract, can indicate their importance.

If we ask what Confucius actually did, the most straightforward answer was that he ran a traveling school for teaching young men rituals for all phases of life, quite a different model from Plato and Aristotle's seminar system.[1] What was the point of centering a school around the teaching of ritual? Confucius thought the calamitous times in which he lived suffered from such a decay of the ritual structure of life that harmonious and prosperous living was simply impossible. Because the rituals of government and public life had declined, only warlords could keep a peace that was dubious at best. Because the rituals of economic exchange within a deeply divided class society had broken down, the economy was unproductive and distribution was unjust. Because the rituals of family life had been neglected, people failed to learn how to be humane. Good rituals make civilized life possible. Without good rituals, no matter what the intent or how good the will of people with different interests, civilized life is impossible, according to Confucius. His points about the degeneracy of ritual in government, community, and family life have close analogues today.

The theoretical underpinnings of the ancient Confucian approach to ritual were expressed by Xunzi, as we have seen earlier. Xunzi pointed out that two kinds of ritual learning for the most part take care of themselves. The starry heavens move slowly around us and we cannot do anything about that except to respond with rituals of admiring deference; many religious rituals today have to do with simple awe and gratitude for the fundamental constitution of the universe. At the other extreme, the peasant society of Xunzi's time had rituals for coping with seasonal life that were learned with the mother's milk, as it were, from direct encounter, like learning a language; just about everybody today learns some language, though not all learn the subtleties so as to express themselves well. In between these extremes are the large problems of social life, such as droughts, floods, and sudden attacks from marauding barbarians: for these, the individuals, communities, and especially governments have to develop ritual institutions of coping. Clearly today we need to think about rituals for such problems as ecological management, international diplomacy, and global economic interactions, for we do not have successful ones. Politics sometimes is about particular actions, but more often it is about policies and laws that institutionalize rituals, say, for the care of the newborn or elderly, for dealing with breaches of contract, for public care of transportation, safety, the economy, and the like.

Western culture since the Enlightenment has had a love affair with grounding human values in nature, so that it has often viewed convention or ritual as merely artificial. The Confucians have the better understanding in their claim that the human completes Heaven and Earth, or to put it in Western terms, that nature needs to be supplemented by human convention or ritual in order to attain to the values of deep civilization. In fact, ritual behavior, especially in family life, was essential to the development of the current human biology that requires a long dependent nurturing period.

Humaneness (*ren*), the other Confucian virtue under scrutiny here, seems initially to be more familiar to Western notions. *Ren* has often been translated as "love," with associations with the Christian virtue. The Christian virtue of love is extraordinarily complicated, and good parallels exist at many points. Zhu Xi's "Treatise on *Ren*" gives it an ontological function similar to the Christian sense that God's creating and loving are the same.[2] *Ren* has also been translated as "human heartedness," a kind of feeling for others and the whole cosmos that best manifests human greatness and sensitivity. Roger Ames and David Hall translate it as "authoritative conduct or person."[3] *Ren* also has similarities to the Buddhist notion of compassion, particularly when the Confucian project of "becoming one body with the universe" is in mind.

What is distinctive about the Confucian virtue of humaneness comes from the institution where it primarily is learned, the family. In one sense a person learns to love by coming to understand how his or her parents love him or her. But in another sense, closer to the Confucian family practice, you begin to love mainly as a parent. Everyone automatically, almost biologically, loves a baby. As the baby becomes a child, you learn more complicated modes of loving through teaching discipline and coping with that fast-moving and fast-talking bundle of *qi*. Learning to love your adolescent child requires enormous patience and far greater subtlety. You love your grown children through educating them and setting them up in life, and then they leave you. You have to love them when they do that too. Your love is full only when you bring up your children so that they are free and virtuous. From their standpoint, the obligation of filial piety is not only to take care of you when you get old but to become so virtuous themselves that you are released from your obligation to bring them up well: a virtuous grown child sets his or her parents free. But of course a child cannot be fully virtuous, fully humane (*ren*) without raising children of his or her own. And so the parents' learning to be humane requires at least two more generations. To be sure, not everyone has an extended family or children, or even living parents, and the Confucian glorification of the family is overly romantic on one hand and bordering on totalitarian on the other. Many analogies for families exist in the social order, however.

The upshot of taking the family as the prime analogate for learning humaneness is that the Confucian virtue requires regarding other people as embedded in a multigenerational stream and individuated through a host of social relations that change with different stages of life. Confucian humaneness does not regard people only according to the situation, but construes that situation to be a focus within a field of a much more complex interactive life for those people, and indeed to be an incident in the life of those people that has a past and, hopefully a future. To put the point more strongly, Confucian humaneness treats as merely abstract the here-and-now situation of others and rejects the vision of others as merely in the situation. It insists that the other persons in the situation be addressed in terms of their larger life history and social network. To be humane to another person is to watch for the clues to that person's whole identity, past and future, filled with these relations and those. To be humane is to defer to that person's larger identity than appears in the situation, and to respond appreciatively to the whole.

Capitalism, according to Adam Smith's "invisible hand" theory, makes everyone better off than they were otherwise: the poor get wages they otherwise would not have, the rich get richer, and no one is forced to choose anything among real options that would not be to his or her advantage as best perceived in the economic situation. Confucian humaneness rejects this philosophy of the "optimizing choice points." It says that the real values in the choice points cannot be discerned without taking into account the network of social and cultural relations, the place in the lifespan of people, and the personal and communal participation in a multigenerational group. Very often, what is best for the individual in terms of contributions to the lives of others affected by his or her actions, and for growth in stages of life, might not be the choice that optimizes profit. Capitalism brutalizes the sensitivity to life's choices that a Confucian with humane virtue would make. Confucian humaneness can civilize capitalist definitions of optimizing profit.

Both ritual and humaneness can be described externally as behaviors. They also need to be acknowledged as matters of the heart. Mature ritual mastery and humaneness are spontaneous and fresh. Therefore we must look to their subjective embeddedness.

DECEPTIONS OF THE HEART: FREUD

Confucian ritual mastery and mature humaneness need to spring from the heart. In the case of ritual mastery this involves first learning the ritual and then practicing it so much it becomes a matter of unconscious and automatic habit. Rituals are learned in complex ways. Sometimes they are learned unconsciously by imitation, as children learn to walk and speak without realizing that they are doing so. Often we learn relatively isolated bits of ritual behavior, without realizing until later (if ever) that those bits fit into a larger ritual dance. The Marxist point about ideological self-deception puts a special twist on this common failure to appreciate the extent of the ritual in which we are involved. Sometimes we learn a ritual through a self-conscious search for a pattern of behavior that lets us interact with others, as when we first visit a foreign culture and look for ways to greet people, find lodging and food, buy and sell, without offending them: actions such as eye contact, body posture, volume of voice, and proximity of approach to people that mean one thing in our own ritual patterns might mean very different things in theirs. When whole cultures interact, as the Muslim and Western cultures are doing with such danger in our day, new integrative rituals need to be devised that respect the differences but enable both sides to dance together. Sometimes rituals are learned in the very invention of them.

A ritual mastered to the point of habit fits in with the other habits of a person's life, or of a group's life for that matter. It needs to be compatible with the other habits already engrained, or to alter those habits so as to make a place for itself. A person's life is articulated by a very great many habits, interpreting aspects of reality and responding in habituated ways. Some of these are tightly connected, and others less so. Because habits do engage reality and receive feedback, they are often changing and reshaping themselves. So for a new habit to fit in with the old ones is not just to find a place, but to find a balancing point so as to keep abreast the changes in all the other habits. Often habits are contradictory to one another and yet buffered by other habits. For instance, a person can have the habit of being deferential and kind to elderly people, and also have the habit of being demeaning to people of another race, with a contradiction in the treatment of elderly people of the other race. Avoiding elderly people of the other race buffers the contradiction. Where confrontation occurs, one habit must give way to the other. Many situations in life are so filled with ambiguities that the inconsistencies among our habitual responses are bearable. Our social rituals are often inconsistent, speaking respectfully, for instance, while standing in a disrespectful posture. Part of maturity of ritual mastery is making the ritual behaviors consistent. The higher forms of ritual provide behavioral patterns for being able to sustain many kinds of inconsistency, for instance those rituals that allow us to interact productively with people we hate, whose culture and social location are different from ours, whose objective interests compete with ours, and whom we misunderstand. Many of the paradigms of rituals come from court rituals that allow social intercourse to proceed productively despite various forms of deception, disagreement, hate, and intrigue: "courtesy" (from "court" rituals) does not require that you love your partners as your family.

The Freudian point about the unconscious, however, is that whereas you consciously believe that you love your family, your unconscious feelings about them are filled with infantile aggressions, jealousies, resentments, slights, desires to dominate or submit, murder or copulate. The unconscious has a structure of its own, a primary or infantile process that reflects your drive to life reacting to the persons, events, and situations that comprise your context. For most people, the unconscious has an extremely selfish infantile orientation to motives with regard to people, events, and situations. Its habits are not acceptable at the conscious level, and are expressed in overt action and speech only "by mistake," in what we, half humorously, call "Freudian slips." Freud's model was that the conscious ego is captivated by an acceptable story it tells itself about proper feelings and motivations, with proper images of other significant people, events, and situations. The alternative, unacceptable, unconscious structure of feelings and motivations keeps up a relentless pressure for expression, however, and sometimes breaks through.

A contemporary Confucian contribution is to see ritual as integrating the conscious and unconscious, motivationally different, sets of habits. At a superficial level we have many rituals that allow the underside its day in the light, a time of carnival, a ritualized drinking party, vicarious aggression toward those we unconsciously resent and hate through war or sports, even more through sports fanaticism. By jokes about "Freudian slips" we even ritually make acceptable in polite social intercourse the unacceptable feelings of the unconscious.

The Confucian point, however, is to modify the unacceptable unconscious feelings themselves by having those feelings participate in rituals of harmonization. The psychodynamic Freudian mechanism for modifying the unacceptable unconscious feelings has been to get them expressed and understood in a controlled environment, such as psychotherapeutic treatment. This mechanism has not always been very successful, and often the goal of treatment is just to learn to live with the unacceptable feelings. The Confucian tradition too has emphasized self-analysis and discernment. Nevertheless it has also emphasized practices of harmonious meditation, movement, and the development of skills such as calligraphy for the purpose of tranquilizing the violent contradictions of the unconscious heart. The ritualized practice of harmonious feeling and movement can bring infantile rage into peaceful repose. Of course, all this must be embedded in larger patterns of harmonious social and personal life, but that too is part of the Confucian project.

The next turn in this Confucian argument is to note that the harmonization of the unconscious is itself a condition for making ritual mastery spontaneous. To the degree that the unconscious forces in a person run counter to the social rituals that engage others harmoniously, the person cannot play those social rituals from the heart. Of course, the social rituals can be played, but with a kind of hollowness or false consciousness. This is not necessarily a bad thing. It is far better to play productive social rituals hypocritically than not to play them at all. Most of the time we do not realize that we are playing the rituals with a false consciousness. But even when we are thrown into a kind of self-loathing by the recognition that we are pretending to respect those we despise, it is a good thing to bear the self-loathing if the situation is made better by the playing of the ritual.

Nevertheless, the cost of self-integration and personal harmony is very high if we cannot participate in important social rituals without self-loathing or a feeling of inner contradiction. For that reason it is important to engage in the rituals that modify the infantile aggressive unconscious so that it harmonizes with the playing of the larger rituals in social life to which we are called. Although a person who has not brought unconscious feelings to harmony with the whole of life can play social rituals successfully, that play cannot be spontaneous as coming from the heart. Often other people will detect this and distrust the maturity of the person's ritual mastery. The Confucian project for this situation is to bring the unconscious into harmony with the whole.

At this point a comment is appropriate about the Confucianism of this argument. Since the Song and Ming Neo-Confucians, it has been common to place Mencius above Xunzi, which means, among other things, placing humaneness above ritual propriety. Tu Weiming, a contemporary Confucian in Boston, represents the Mencian line when he argues that humaneness is innate and that ritual is its externalized expression.[4] The argument in this chapter, by contrast, comes to humaneness through ritual. Like Xunzi, the Freudian perspective sees the infantile stage of human life and the unconscious infantile part of mature personality to be selfish and in great need of harmonization. Mencius was right that the heart can respond to things in their aesthetic and moral worth when it sees them with clear discernment. He was right that its responses in turn are harmonious and appropriate under the conditions of action that is direct and at ease with itself and the world. But those conditions, clear discernment and direct action, constitute sincerity (*cheng*) and are not natively given. They are the great accomplishments of the sage. Xunzi was right that the developing mastery of rituals is part of the means by which sincerity is accomplished.

As to humaneness in the unconscious, the unconscious needs to be brought into harmony if the heart is to be humane and express itself in humane attitudes and behavior. The West has had two principal models of love, which is part of Confucian humaneness. The Platonic model is that the loveliness in the object arouses eros in the lover. The Freudian model is that love, or sexual energy, is a force within the individual looking for an object on which to cathect. The Confucian model of the self combines both points in a broader picture. The heart innately is the special, Heavenly endowed human nature that is capable of grasping the worth of things and responding appropriately. On the one hand are the ten thousand things with values to be understood and respected. On the other hand is the heart that can appreciate those values and respond so as to create value and respect the values of the things affected. The grave human difficulty is clearing the path between the heart and the ten thousand things so that they can be seen for what they are worth and so that the heart's responsive actions can be carried out without deflection. Many obstacles of personality, emotions, cognition, and even physical development, usually summarized as "selfishness" by Confucians, lie in that path. Mencians emphasize the fact that the heart would automatically perceive and respond well if society had not taught selfishness. Xunzians counter that the connection between the ten thousand things and the heart itself needs to be created by appropriate rituals, or habitual meaning structures. If the learned rituals are bad, selfishness is reinforced. But if the person is relatively unritualized, the heart will be like the baby's infantile selfishness. The way to create a path between the world and the heart necessarily includes teaching civilizing rituals. Learning to be humane through the raising of children, and analogues to this, as mentioned earlier, needs to be supplemented by learning the rituals that allow the learner to relate with sincerity to those to be loved. Ritual, of course, is not the whole of learning, but it is a significant part.

DECEPTIONS OF THE HEART: MARX

The Marxist point about the unconscious does not focus on the infantile feelings of primary process but rather on the real but unacknowledged motivations for behavior that result from social location. Social location is a function of social class, Marx said, and social class is a function of economic structure. In Marx's view the main classes were the owners of the means of production and those who owned nothing but their work and hence subsisted on wages. Marxists and other thinkers have made this view of social class far more complex than Marx's original version, but the general point still stands: much of our behavior is motivated unconsciously by the interests of our social location, which includes not only economic class differences but cultural and age differences. Because the crude selfishness of social-location interest is unacceptable, and because we have to get along with others in competing social locations, our conscious thoughts about social relations are captivated by fictions that disguise the real motivations.

The result is that many of us live within a story of morality, social justice, and often religion that seems to give us moral projects and a righteous direction but that in fact justifies or leaves untouched real evils of social injustice. Marx was concerned that the poor would be misled by religion to accept their economic condition, and that the rich would think they were being moral by doling out charities to people whose poverty in fact was caused by the system that provided most advantages to the rich. The point can be generalized. Some American Christians use the religious ideology of righteousness to justify attacking so-called evil Muslim nations with assertive governments when the real motivation is Western dominance for the sake of oil. Some Muslim fundamentalists use the religious ideology of righteousness and divine will for Muslim law to justify attacking the Great Satans of the West when the real motivation is control of the oil, their economy, and a longing for lost empire. Most of us live lives motivated in significant ways by unconscious desires for advancement and dominance that are covered over by visions of the roles we play in moral society. In countless ways, the usually unconscious interests determined by our social location give us a false consciousness.

Marx was right that religion often is the teacher and reinforcer of the false consciousness of social location. He put too much emphasis on the theological or ideological parts of religion, however: the effective power of religion to produce false consciousness of social location lies in ritual. Religious rituals usually rehearse a certain approved stereotype of what social relations are, and people come to see those approved relations instead of the actual relations of competition and conflict among social locations. Moreover, many other areas of life involve rituals expressive of ideal social relations. The economic, artistic, entertainment, political, and neighborhood spheres of life are just as ritualized as the religious, and many rehearse the idealized relations of false consciousness as effectively as the religious sphere. In secular societies, those other spheres are far more important ritualizers than religion.

The first Confucian contribution to the problem of ritualized reinforcement of false consciousness of social location is through the analysis of the rituals actually being played. Because of their millennia-long emphasis on rituals and their meaning, Confucians should be adept at discerning just what the rituals do. In line with the Confucian theme of the "rectification of names," rituals need to acknowledge not only differences in social location but the injustices embodied in systems that cause certain social locations to oppress or exploit others. Marx's analysis, brilliant for its time, is far too unsubtle to grasp the intricacies of exploitation and oppression. Confucians in our time should bring their tradition to bear upon improving his analysis.

Perhaps the most obvious "ritual" act in recent history that exposes, expresses, and reharmonizes injustice between social locations are the Truth and Reconciliation trials in South Africa. In these encounters, staged in public before judges, members of the white South African apparatus for enforcing apartheid were forced to listen to their black victims describe their torture and oppression. The oppressors had to see what they had done from the standpoint of the oppressed. The oppressed, who had been silenced and marginalized so as to become almost non-people, were able to make their stories heard. The ritualized character of the proceedings allowed the deep emotions to be expressed in purging but peaceful ways. In societies as filled with confusions and injustices as ours, so riddled with secret corruptions and lies, many rituals are needed to bring to light those evils of bad relations among social locations. Not only should they be brought to light, they should be ritually examined, confessed, and amended. We need Confucian rituals of reconciliation, and those rituals need to be woven through the other rituals of religious, economic, political, artistic, entertainment, and neighborhood spheres of life. This is the second Confucian contribution regarding rituals of overcoming false consciousness.

Confucian humaneness demands that honesty about conflicts among social locations be achieved. False consciousness is a great evil because, among other things, it prevents people from seeing the humanity in persons who occupy competing social locations. Or rather, it presents a false picture of their humanity, one that does not express the aspects of oppressing and being oppressed that their social location bears. There is a huge and wicked false consciousness in "loving everyone" but not being able to see the details of the consequences of social location in the particular people around you. As previously argued, humaneness requires knowing people not only in the roles they play in specific situations but in their life histories and networks. Social location is part of life history and social networking.

In the contemporary world, in any place on the globe, to be humane is, among other things, to be able to relate to people in terms of the truth of their social location, especially as it is defined by one's own location. On the surface, this means being able to stand in the other person's perspective, to see how one looks from someone else's vantage point. More deeply it means having the scientific and historical knowledge to understand the causal connections that constitute interrelated social locations in their economic, political, ethnic, historical, religious, educational, artistic, and other dimensions. Precisely because of Marx's point about the self-deception involved in the ideologies arising from social locations, the other person's own perspective might not be any more truthful about the realities of the social locations than one's own. Pressing forward to genuine humaneness often requires complicated and difficult inquiry. Whereas learning to love one's own children might be the root from which humaneness grows, learning the realities of people very different from ourselves requires study, and often personal change, so as to be able to accept what we learn about other people and our relations to them.

This chapter has sketched how a contemporary Confucian approach to ritual and humaneness might deal with the issues of the unconscious as they have been introduced by Freud on the one hand and Marx on the other. The operative word in that last sentence is "sketched." No rituals have been devised, and humaneness has been articulated as only an ideal. Nevertheless, the essay gives some direction to a Confucianism that grapples with a global society of conflicting cultures, classes, and interests.

9
The Contemporary Mutual Development of Confucianism and Christianity

THE HONOR OF OPENING this conference dedicated to Julia Ching sets me to two delightful tasks. One is to pay tribute to her pioneering scholarly work in retrieving the past of Confucianism. Her 1976 book, *To Acquire Wisdom: The Way of Wang Yang-ming*, along with Tu Weiming's book of the same year, *Neo-Confucian Thought in Action: Wang Yang-ming's Youth (1472–1509)*, brought Neo-Confucianism into a larger philosophical conversation that has been carried on by Antonio Cua and now many others, most recently Warren Frisina.[1] Herbert Fingarette's 1972 *Confucius: The Secular as Sacred* had opened the philosophical conversation with Confucianism, and Julia Ching interpreted the whole of that tradition during her long career.[2]

The second task of remembering her in this chapter is the one to which she put us: the development of philosophy and theology for the future out of resources that integrate Confucianism and Christianity. Her retrievals of the past were always also prospective, advocating the truth and helpfulness of the Chinese tradition for our own intellectual and spiritual needs. Her work with Hans Kung, especially *Christianity and Chinese Religion*, was explicitly about this task.[3] She was one of the first to point out what most of us now know, that a philosophical approach to the world's problems framed by both the Confucian and Western traditions is far stronger, more enlightened, and readier for creative innovation than an approach by either tradition alone. Undergraduates and journalists understand that each tradition by itself is something of a dead end in this world of competing civilizations, global ecological problems, a global economic system struggling with intensified local cultures, instant Internet worldwide communications, and a new vision of war in which the terrorism of simple technologies flanks the sophisticated might of superpowers. Perhaps only Leibniz in the modern West addressed philosophy prospectively as an agent for understanding and reconciliation while imaginatively embracing the Chinese tradition with an intellectual vigor and curiosity like that called for today. Interestingly, one of the main lessons Leibniz drew from China was that the binary yin/yang system can be used to represent all numbers and also the letters of alphabets so that a total binary system of all representations is possible; that is, Leibniz invented the main idea for computers out of what he learned from China. You can read all about this in the book Julia Ching wrote and edited with her husband, Willard Oxtoby, *Moral Enlightenment: Leibniz and Wolff on China*.[4]

My desire here is to further the project of developing a contemporary philosophy from the twin resources of Confucianism and Western philosophy, especially Christianity. To this end I shall comment on three points: the connection between reformation of the heart and loving the world; the location of the most strategic points for ethical analysis and intervention; and the roles of action and forbearance, or retreat, in the pursuit of peace. Although it should go without saying, it needs to be said that the discussion here does not treat either Confucianism or Western philosophy and Christianity as monolithic; it retrieves and reconstructs positions within each that are controversial with their own traditions.

FROM REFORMATION OF THE INNER HEART TO LOVING THE WORLD

The first point I want to develop is that both Confucianism and the West, especially Christianity, have important strands of thought and practice that connect the reformation of the inner heart with the proper loving of the world. This is the famous point of Wang Yangming in the controversy of his school with that of Zhu Xi. In his reading of *The Great Learning*, Wang argued that making the will sincere and rectifying the mind in some sense precede the task of acquiring knowledge because knowledge will be distorted if the inquiring agent is not set straight. More than many other Confucians and Neo-Confucians, Wang construed the self as an activity so that even knowing is a form of acting well cognitively. Moreover, his doctrine of the continuity of thought and action attacked the distinction between inner life and outer action that was always so tempting to the Confucian tradition. Because the true character of things is to be events shaped by Principle (*li*), in both the afferent action of perceiving and the efferent actions of response, the self as agent whose inner nature is Principle is in potential continuity with all things.⁵ If the clear character of that inner nature of Principle is manifested along the lines of actions, then all the things touched by a person's influence will be loved in the double sense of being appreciated and transformed into a greater manifestation of Principle on their own account. This is how to be "one body with the world" and to "love the people," Wang's interpretation of the phrase from *The Great Learning* that others translated "renovating the people."

Wang differed from other Confucians in his stress on the difficulty of becoming sincere and rectifying the will-mind. Mencius, for instance, had said that the impulses to virtuous action and thought, the "four beginnings," lie innate in all people and only need to be allowed to flourish. If covered over with the corruptions of society, the moral point is to remove the corruptions and they will sprout again like shoots from stumps on a logged over mountain. Wang saw the corruptions of the heart as more difficult. Selfish desires are not mere learned behaviors overlaid on innately good impulses but ways by which the heart-mind's action is fixated on objects and loses touch with its inner principle. Tu Weiming goes so far as to say that the work of overcoming this is like a Kierkegaardian conversion in which the will's commitment to become a sage means to become sincere with rectified mental activity that leads to action that proceeds from true knowledge as its natural extension. This commitment to sagehood is an existential choice that must be repeated and steadied in long practice.⁶ The overall point is that improving one's moral relation to the world depends on first correcting the heart. Once the heart is corrected, the moral attitude and action toward the world is comprehensive but still has the character of the loving heart.

The theme of personal conversion as a precondition for public morality has an important history in the West. In the *Republic* (bk. 7, 518) Plato said that true knowledge is not like pouring information into an empty head but rather like turning the head so that it can see what is there: the foundation for increasing knowledge is a conversion to look in the right direction. This point was greatly intensified in early Christianity (for instance, 1 Corinthians 1–3) with its emphasis on conversion and the development of an existential faith as the precondition for correct understanding. St. Paul was even more insistent than Wang Yangming on the bondage of selfishness within the soul: it led to the contradiction that he did not do the good he wanted to do, and did the evil he wanted to avoid (Romans 7). Paul's solution was to return to the law of God that was innate in him but confused by sin; the way to this was through faith in Christ, for Paul, which allows a restoration of the active effectiveness of God's innate law, in other contexts described as the divine image.

Some parts of the Christian tradition, in accord with various forms of Western dualism, have stressed that the justifying power of Christ is God's action, whereas the process of sanctification or holy living is human action. Other forms of that tradition, however, for instance those following from John Wesley, have emphasized a mutual interpenetration of both divine grace and joint human responsibility, and that in continuity from the innermost parts of converting the heart to the most external of loving political actions. In one sense everything is simply the manifestation of divine creative and re-creative grace working from individual hearts to the perfection of society; in a completely compatible sense everything in that continuum is registered in terms of human response and action.

The relation of inner divine law and effective grace to Neo-Confucian Principle is a sufficient analogue to justify reconstructing both together for a contemporary philosophy of the grounds of moral life. This philosophy needs to say that public policies, moral programs, and movements for justice will be shallow and unsteady without a concomitant conversion of the heart to be in tune with the power of real value. At the same time this philosophy needs to say that conversions of the heart, devotions to meditation, and personal perfection are hypocritical and powerless if they do not issue in action to rectify the world in ways that express love for all concerned.

THE LOCATION OF ETHICAL ANALYSIS AND RECTIFYING POWER

The second point I want to develop is the contribution of the Confucian notion of ritual to ethical analysis and action. Ritual is the other sense of *li*, which Wang Yangming identifies with the first sense, Principle.[7] The Confucian to which I would advert on this point, however, is Xunzi. As I have argued, Xunzi said that the natural endowments of human beings are too underdetermined for civilized life, and that conventions or rituals are needed on top of natural endowments to make possible significant human relations and thus fulfill nature. We would put Xunzi's point in evolutionary perspective by saying that we could not have evolved our complicated human flexibility if we had not at the same time evolved rituals that channel our indeterminate potentials into determinate meaningful relations. The Western way of putting this is that human beings need to learn semiotic behavior in order to function as human beings. Aristotle observed that infants babble in the phonemes of their parents' language, an early learned semiotic behavior.

Pragmatic semiotics is a well-developed theory that provides a ready language for translating the insights of over two thousand years of Confucian reflection on ritual. Both emphasize the point that signs, rituals, and semiotic behavior are what allow human beings to engage reality and one another. Rituals are not artificial stumbling blocks to natural interactions, as Daoists might say; signs are not substitutes for their objects, as European semioticians might say.

Just as language makes it possible to say something to someone else but does not determine what you will say within the structures of the language, so rituals and semiotic systems generally make significant interaction possible but without dictating entirely what that interaction is. Much of moral behavior has to do with specific actions and responses to specific situations; much has to do with long-range policies to sustain institutions or make changes. These are the kinds of moral behavior in which it is not too difficult to assign responsibility to individuals and groups. Nevertheless, specific actions, policies, and programs all take place within a semiotic environment that makes them possible. That is, all presuppose some ritual context that gives their terms meaning and expresses the underlying values and cultural projects. Those ritual contexts themselves have moral freight. Confucius himself inveighed against the corrupt rituals of his time, arguing that they did not allow for peaceful settling of disputes, for faithful family life, for honest public administration, or even for mutual education. He called for improved rituals for his time, not specific policies and programs, but ritual education. He thought the better rituals could be found among those of the ancients.

A serious Confucian contribution to our own time is the analysis of the rituals that underlie our personal, social, intercultural, and international relations. Racism is not a deliberate policy of many North Americans anymore, but it is a ritual in which nearly everyone participates. No one wants to destroy the environment, not even those who prefer to get rich at the environment's expense; nevertheless the ritual basis of our economies includes the degradation of the environment. No religion says women ought to be oppressed or abused, though the ritual practices of many religions do that in fact. We do not have efficient rituals for cosmopolitan interaction among people with different ethnic, gender, class, and cultural backgrounds. We do not have efficient rituals for rich family life in meritocratic cultures where extended families are discontinuous. We do not have efficient rituals for the peaceful resolution of disputes even though we have political agencies such as the United Nations to deal with those.

Contemporary philosophy needs to adopt the Confucian understanding of the pervasiveness and positive importance of rituals and undertake systematic critiques of the rituals of our global societies. Ritual ethical analysis can downplay the more customary but counterproductive Western emphasis on identifying a villain and direct attention to the ritual systems that ought to be changed. Then it can identify the nature of inadequate ritual systems and point out where and how to amend them. Such a project would be a reformation in ethical analysis that might allow for greater realism in light of our seemingly intractable social problems. Meanwhile, the integration of Confucian ritual theory with Western pragmatic categories of semiotics and the habitual foundations of specific actions can tie the Chinese philosophical tradition with the Western in extremely fruitful ways.

PEACE, ACTION, AND RETREAT

My final point about peace, action, and forbearance or retreat is more difficult to formulate than the others because it arises out of current events, not out of comparative scholarship. I have in mind the justifications of preemptive war that have characterized the ideology of the Wahabi Muslim terrorists led by Osama bin Laden and the response of U.S. President George W. Bush and his advisors. The former uses weapons of terrorism, the latter those of sophisticated military technology. Both agree that some identifiable enemy constitutes a real threat to their way of life, that their way of life has something like divine sanction, and that the very existence of a credible threat justifies preemptive action to remove that threat. Both bin Laden and Bush are in contradiction to the mainline traditions in their respective religions regarding the conditions for a just war, according to which preemptive war is not justified. Is there a credible political alternative to this kind of thinking that seems to have the force of necessity in this day in which the threats to prized ways of life are very real and the powers to carry out the threats seem unstoppable without tragic loss of innocent lives?

Neither Confucianism nor the main traditions of Christianity have held to absolute pacifist principles, although both have urged pacifist positions in various contexts. Yet both stand against preemptive war, and might offer alternative models for how to behave.

The first point in this regard concerning Confucianism is the importance of the model of the scholar-official. To be a sage is to be engaged in public life in large or small ways. To be an official is most of all to be ministering to, or protecting and enhancing, the institutions that give the ritual substance of human life. In line with my first point earlier, the inner rectification of heart, mind, and will needs to manifest itself in explicit overt work to improve the world. In line with the second point, one of the most effective places for this is in caring for ritual, that is, institutional, life. This is not alien to Plato's claim that the purpose of philosophy is not to know for its own sake but to guide people in matters of state and family. It is also like John Wesley's characterization of the Christian life of service.

So what happens when affairs are such that one's ministrations are ineffective, when the barbarians come with no regard to negotiation, virtue, or good sense? When the terrorist fanaticism of Wahabi Islam is bent on destroying predatory capitalism and vice versa, and scholar-officials on both sides are blown aside, what can be done by those whose hearts strive to manifest the Principle of Heaven and the Image of God? Plato said that in a seriously unjust world, sometimes a just person can do no better than to hunker down behind a wall until the storm blows over. The Confucian scholar-official, in those circumstances, goes on retreat, retires from office, and attempts an alternate life in a remote spot, recognizing the frustration of not being able to live publicly. In the Chinese tradition, Daoists too go on retreat, but in military fashion, seducing the enemy to extend the lines of supply too far so that the small forces of the Dao can be deployed to overcome the aggressor. The Confucians generally did not take that line of winning through seductive weakness. Rather, the Confucian conviction, at least ideally, has been that forbearance itself is a virtue in face of temptation to violence, preemptively to protect one's own.

The contemporary argument is that without preemptive war, the enemy can destroy one's way of life and will do so, and that therefore preemptive war is necessary. I am not suggesting that either Confucians or mainline Western, especially Christian, thinkers would or should refuse defensive war, although pacifists make that claim. I do suggest, however, that a Confucian-Christian sense of forbearance would decline the option of preemptive war and accept the risks inherent in the threat of the enemy. Permit me to suggest some virtues of this position.

First, if forbearance in the face of real threat were public practice and understood as such, it would remove at least one of the reasons the enemy might engage in counter-preemptive war, namely, fear of one's own intentions. Iraq would have no motive to preemptively use weapons of mass destruction, or terrorism, if it were reasonably sure that no preemptive action would be taken against itself.[8]

Second, forbearance in the face of understandable real threat would demonstrate a public moral commitment to limitation of violence that could give confidence to one's enemies and one's own people that morality, not only force, limits one's use of powers at hand.

Third, forbearance in the face of real threat calls into question the ritualized interactions of threat and counter-threat that prompt both sides to preemptive war. Forbearance breaks the ritual cycle.

Fourth, forbearance in the face of real threat and the possibility of preemptive strikes from one's enemies is the only way to extend inner Principle to the loving of all affected by one's actions, including one's enemies. Christianity and Confucianism are agreed that, in this large political sense, the proper attitude toward enemies is to love them, even when exercising defensive force against their attacks.

The greatest obstacle to forbearance in the face of real threat of a preemptive attack against one's people is that those who depend on you, your children, your institutions, your traditions, and much that you hold dear, can be destroyed because of your refusal to take preemptive action against the enemy first. Thus preemptive war is redefined as defensive war, the argument made by both Bush and bin Laden. The mark of real forbearance is willingness to risk such tragic losses.

This willingness is justified, I believe, on the following ground. To say that preemptive war in fact is defensive war in face of the threat is to say that selfish desires to protect one's own loved ones, possessions, and culture, override the inner Principle to love all under Heaven. It is to reject the rectification of the heart, mind, and will so as to put them in harmony with Principle, the divine law, or the image of God, in favor of an absolute obligation to selfish desires. The Christian theme of divine and human self-sacrifice stands opposed to such selfishness, even when it recognizes the tragedy of putting innocents at risks. So does the Confucian theme of retreat when action cannot be taken without betraying sincerity.

My colleague John Berthrong points out that when war seems inevitable Confucians recognize that the way of the sage is impossible. But rather than the great tragedy of battle with massive loss of life, rulers should first embrace the lesser moral and human tragedy of intrigue and assassination. This low road acknowledges the loss of the moral high ground. Nevertheless, that loss is far more benign than the moral depravity of preemptive battle. Confucians and Christians, at least some of them, have seen through the attempt to disguise the depravity of preemptive war as heroism.

I do not want to gloss over the complexity of attempting to define defensive violence in an age of multiple meanings for every act. But I do want to advocate an aggressive philosophy of conversion of the heart so as to turn action to effective love, of the analysis and amendment of the rituals underlying social interactions, and of public forbearance so that everyone understands that preemptive war by one's enemy or against one's enemy is not necessary and that scholar-officials can minister to institutions that serve the justice of all sides.

10
The Personal and the Impersonal in Conceptions of Divinity

ONE OF THE MOST PERPLEXING phenomena for comparative religion is the diversity with which religions represent what they take to be ultimate. On the surface, this appears to be a problem between religions. The West Asian monotheisms, for instance, represent the ultimate as a god, a singular being who creates the world and interacts with it and with people, as illustrated variously in their common text, the Hebrew Bible. East Asian Daoism and Confucianism, by contrast, represent the ultimate by the Dao, or Heaven, or Principle. South Asian Hinduisms can be sorted into personalistic theisms with one or several gods and also into transpersonal, even transdeterminate, religions such as Advaita Vedanta. Observing this variety, it makes sense to wonder whether the representations of the ultimate are even about the same thing, indeed, whether there is such thing as the ultimate, or several ultimates. Mahayana Buddhism, especially Madhyamaka, would go so far as to say that there is nothing ultimate, and that even to consider that question is to get into ontologizing trouble.

Upon closer inspection, however, the diversity is not so much among the various religions but within them. The West Asian monotheisms all have a strong anti-idolatry streak that militates against personalistic imagery. Moreover, as the conception of the created cosmos expanded to include everything imaginable, the transcendence of the creator became more and more abstract in representation. Jewish Kabalistic thought, Christian philosophical theology from Origen to Thomas Aquinas to Paul Tillich, the Muslim debates between the Asherites and the Mutazilites—all suppose that God is not a Big Guy in the Sky. And yet all related their abstract representations of God to biblical imagery. Thomas Aquinas's simple, unrelatable, pure Act of Esse was conceived as the Father of Jesus Christ whose mother was Mary the Virgin. The functional reality of Christian religious symbolism puts those things together, and the Christian reference to the ultimate cannot be understood without sorting and connecting those personal and impersonal representations.

Similarly, the actual practice of Daoists and Confucians populates the imaginative world with magically powered sages and legendary emperors, heroes, and ancestors. Devotion to superlatives of human action and personality is as powerful in East Asia as any Christian's friendship with Jesus. Mahayana Buddhism, for all its abstracted reference to emptiness and form, to pure Buddha-mind, and indeed to the lack of any own-being in ultimate reality, still fosters the cult of Guanyin. Similarly, the variety of Hinduisms does not sort out by personal versus impersonal representations, but each within itself has both.

POPULAR VERSUS SOPHISTICATED RELIGION HYPOTHESIS

How can this variety internal to each religion be accounted for? The most obvious hypothesis is to distinguish between popular and sophisticated versions within each religion. Plain folks do not bother with the abstract reasoning that drives anthropomorphic representations to greater and greater transcendence. And sophisticated thinkers either distance themselves from folk religion or treat its symbols as merely metaphoric. Surely there is some truth to this hypothesis. It has an analogue in the maturation process whereby children move from childish imagery, often concrete and personalistic, to more abstract representations. Moreover, new converts to a religious path often begin with rather literalistic acceptance of concrete imagery and only slowly, sometimes through several generations, come to appreciate the nuance and play of religious symbols, including those that are abstract and impersonal. Nevertheless, though there is some truth to the popular religion versus sophisticated religion hypothesis, it is not an adequate explanation. In every religion, very sophisticated thinkers who use impersonal representations of the ultimate are also devoted to the ultimate in ways that use highly personal representations. Zhu Xi, whose metaphysics of Principle and Material Force is among the most abstract and sophisticated in the Confucian line, codified family rituals for communing with the dead in ancestral traditions reaching back to the original mandates of Heaven. Thomists believe that the Pure Act of Esse is God the Father, perhaps even the Holy Trinity.

DEVELOPMENT HYPOTHESIS: PRE-AXIAL AGE AND AXIAL AGE

Another hypothesis with much truth is a developmental one. The Axial Age religions of East, South, and West Asia arose in contexts in which gods of nature, particularly sky gods such as Shangdi, Indra, and Yahweh formed the representational orientations of worship and religious conception. Slowly but inexorably in those three main traditions universal conceptions of the world emerged, and human beings were conceived to be in relation to that universal context or its ground or way (I apologize for the fact there is no tradition-neutral language for describing this). But the traditions varied greatly in locating the center of their metaphoric symbolic systems. Some fixed on the early highly personalistic images, and others on later impersonal, even antipersonal images.

So, for instance, the editing of the main part of the Hebrew Bible took place around the time of Jeremiah, in the late seventh century BCE. Jeremiah and his contemporaries Ezekiel and Isaiah had a high view of God as creator of the vast cosmos and Lord of all nations. They also were in close contact with Egyptian and Babylonian, Assyrian, and Persian religions. They were sufficiently distant from the immediate imagery of the two accounts of creation in Genesis, the first rather impersonal and the second very personal, so as to be able to include them both together. This is to say, they adopted personalistic images of varying degrees of concreteness. The book of Job, somewhat later in authorship, is quite clear in using personalistic imagery for God and his heavenly court in explicitly literary ways, all the while making the point that God transcends even moral categories and that humans have no place to stand to categorize God. Christian theologians of the second century of the Common Era employed the abstractions of Greek philosophy to argue that God creates not only the form of the world but its matter as well. The point is that the fixation on personalistic biblical imagery came at a time when there was strong consciousness of the move toward transpersonal if not impersonal imagery.

The case was the opposite in China. The symbolic representations of the Dao, Heaven, and Earth in the classic books of Daoism and Confucianism are rather impersonal. In calling attention to the human in contrast to the ultimate and metaphysical, Confucius broke rather explicitly with the anthropomorphic conceptions of the objects of sacrifice. Only in notions such as that of the mandate of Heaven is there much resonance with the willful Shangdi. Whereas the very idea of propitiary sacrifice supposes something like a personal object of sacrifice, and the mirroring resonance of ordinary parents with the emperor as parent and in turn with Heaven and Earth as parents supposes some notion of ultimate personhood, the rhetorical center of Confucianism and Daoism is resolutely impersonal. Even the notion of personhood in early

Chinese thought does not give much place to consciousness, which is so important in South and West Asian religions.

South Asian religions often do not have a single rhetorical center, like the anthropomorphic in West Asia and the impersonal in East Asia. Rather, they employ several nodes with considerable equanimity, including the Vedic, Upanishadic, sometimes the categories of the orthodox and heterodox philosophic schools, and sometimes devotional materials, for instance in the cults of Shiva and Krishna, down to eighteenth through twentieth-century interactions with the West occasioning new ways of thought. The Vedanta of Ramakrishna is a nineteenth-century phenomenon, distinct in rhetoric and piety from Shankara's or Ramanuja's.

The historical development hypothesis helps to sort the imagery of the ultimate in the main traditions, so that we would expect personalistic imagery in West Asian religions even when the point is being made that God is beyond that, and impersonal imagery in East Asian religions even when waiting upon the mandate of Heaven. But that hypothesis does not explain much. Why did the West Asian religions fix on personalistic imagery even when they had moved to a position when they might have employed impersonal rhetoric? Why did the East Asian religions fix upon the impersonal even when they had to repersonalize it? The answers to these and related questions lie in detailed historical studies that go far beyond the general historical development hypothesis itself.

SEMIOTIC HYPOTHESIS

Another helpful hypothesis might be called a semiotic approach. Its thesis is that concrete imagery, especially personalistic imagery, is closely tied to context, and when it is extended beyond its immediate context, it might become misleading or false. At the other extreme, when thinkers with one rhetorical system meet those with another, they need to find terms for communication that bridge their contexts. The easiest way to do this is with relatively abstract terms, terms that hopefully catch the heart of what each of the communicating rhetorical systems means but without the context-dependent concrete imagery. Thus in the context of Israel's flight from Egypt, Yahweh can be represented concretely and with few qualifications as a great warrior. As the creator of the foundations of the universe in Job, however, Yahweh's warrior qualities are but a distant metaphor. Religious thought tends to theology and philosophy as it develops terms that remain steady in meaning across many contexts, seeking universality of communication. And yet, the devotional lives of individuals are highly contextual. Therefore the same person can use concrete, and perhaps highly personal, devotional images in worship, prayer, and meditation, while also using philosophical abstractions in the debating hall and classroom. Sophisticated religious traditions have lore in practice and thought that keeps straight the contextual nature of concrete personalistic imagery. The Axial Age religions arose at a time when empires were bringing together many local cultures and forcing such questions as whether one's own ancestral storm god is the same or different from one's new trading partner's. The imperial situation in the Han Dynasty, the contemporary empire building in India, and the Roman Empire, fostered what, in its polite moments, we today would call interreligious dialogue, and that produced the great philosophical or theological systems of communicative abstractions. Although this hypothesis throws light upon much of the way religious thinkers think, it does not quite register the passion with which religious representations are held. Religious people believe their ideas are true, and their symbols refer accurately, if with partiality, to the ultimate.

ONTOLOGICAL-ANTHROPOLOGICAL CONTINUUM HYPOTHESIS

The final hypothesis I want to put forward addresses the issue of truth, and it can be called the ontological-anthropological continuum hypothesis. It claims that there is a spectrum from the highly personal to the highly transcendent and impersonal in religious symbolism, and that a profound perception of or engagement with reality lies at each end of the spectrum, each pulling its own way. To take the ontological pole first, the ultimate is engaged as ontologically ultimate, the most real, the encompassing, the ground of things. Because of the variety of different representations of ontological ultimacy, there is no one neutral way to say this. But I suspect that the dialectic behind the ontological ultimate is concerned with contingency and its ground, and often with the possibility of diversity and unity. Some paradigmatic ontological representations are the Dao that cannot be named being the mother of the Dao that can be named, Isvara as creator of the world, Nirguna Brahman as the reality behind or within the illusion of difference, God as Creator, the Neo-Platonic One, the Thomistic Act of Esse, the Scotistic creator whose will makes even the divine nature, Schleiermacher's absolute dependence, Tillich's ground of being. The ontological dialectic of the contingent and its ground lies behind the critique of idolatry in West Asian religions, the distinction between reality and appearance in South Asian religions, and the search for the ultimately harmonizing or centering in East Asian ones. To engage the ultimate ontologically in this way thus pulls representations away from the personalistic, which always seem contingent, toward the more transcendent. Even when the transcendent ground is represented as supreme consciousness, as in Ramanuja's theology for instance, it is a mightily impersonal consciousness.

The other pole of the spectrum I call the anthropological by which I mean how the ultimate is viewed from the standpoint of human need, will, and devotion. The bhakti elements of Hinduism and Buddhism, especially Pure Land, represent the object of worship as personal not because they believe personality is descriptive of that object, but because the worshiper needs to treat the object as personal in order to present himself or herself with the most heartfelt needs. Even in Buddhism, for which there is no ontological object to whom to pray, petitionary prayer is appropriate, for instance to Avaloketeshvara or Guanyin. In East Asian religions the cultivation of proper orientations to things so as to effect harmony and power is often achieved through visualizations of gods and sages; medieval Daoism even makes that a barter relation. In West Asian religions a person needs total purity or honesty, that is, expression of the most heartfelt need and desires, in order to approach God: the primitive address to God is to beg for life, whatever life might mean in the context. Of course in all these traditions there are ritual strains for which the existential inner-heart language I have used is inappropriate. Some argue that this sense of personal interiority is both late and Western. But I suspect the contrary, that it is both primitive and pervasive. The anthropological pole attends to what is most real for persons and their needs, and justifies personifications of the ultimate as the object of religious address and worship without necessarily taking those personifications to be descriptive. A way of saying this in terms of semiotic theory is to note that whereas the ontological pole valorizes symbols that are iconic or descriptive, the anthropological pole valorizes symbols that are indexical or reorienting and personally transformative. Just as the ontological pole pulls symbols down the spectrum toward the impersonal, the anthropological pole pulls symbols down the other way toward the personal.

My intention in these brief remarks has been to muse on the muddle of personal and impersonal symbols for the ultimate that characterizes the main religious traditions that have survived into our time. I have offered several hypotheses, each of which has something to contribute to understanding: The popular versus sophisticated religion hypothesis lifts up a level of religious phenomena especially pertinent to scholars of religion who have to get along with their mothers. The historical development hypothesis articulates some of the relations among personal and impersonal symbols in terms of historical conditions that fix the center of balance in religious tradition's choice of images for the ultimate. The semiotic hypothesis sorts the symbols according to concrete context dependence versus universality of communication and freedom from having to qualify claims by context. The ontological-anthropological spectrum hypothesis shows how the religious imagination is pulled in two different directions by two different ways of engaging the ultimate, each with its claim to a kind of truth. I hope these hypotheses constitute a beginning for inquiry into how the ultimate can be so variously and vigorously symbolized.

11
On Comparison

CROSS-CULTURAL COMPARATIVE THINKING of the sort that has become popular in religious studies, and to a lesser degree in philosophy, and that is exhibited in several of the chapters here, has many models, at least two intentions, and at least one role beyond comparison as such. In this chapter, I shall discuss, first, an array of models of comparison, focusing on comparative theology. The focus is on theology, that is, the religious part of philosophy, because contrasts are sharpest when religions are involved and also because some theologians in several traditions argue that theology should stand alone in principle, not be comparative. When philosophers with broader interests than theology fail to be comparative, it usually is because of ignorance, not because of principled argument. Next, I shall discuss two intentions for comparison, the objective and the normative. Finally, I shall argue that comparative philosophy (including theology) should play a larger role than comparison in developing constructive philosophies appropriate for our time.

MODELS OF COMPARATIVE THEOLOGY

Comparative theologies in this context means theologies within which comparisons of several religions form important and generally positive parts of the theological argument. The *teachings* of comparative theologies include what is learned from interpreting those several religions. What is learned includes both points to be affirmed and points to be denied. More importantly, what is learned includes how elements of each religion are interpreted in light of the comparisons with other religions. Thus each religion's isolated self-understanding (if there be such a thing) is reinterpreted through the comparisons so that each is understood within the comparative theology both internally and externally, as it were. Comparative theologies in this sense differ from theologies that attempt to understand and justify a religious tradition or community on its own terms alone. Stand-alone theologies might simply ignore religions other than their own or might reject attending to them on principle, believing their own teachings to be sufficiently based on one tradition's scripture, creeds, or confessions. Recently some stand-alone theologies have taken the deeply textured practices and language of religious communities to be the sole context necessary for their teachings, treating the communities as "cultural-linguistic" units for whom theology is the explication of their basic grammar.[1]

Within Christianity, comparative theologies are older and likely a more natural sort than stand-alone theologies. St. Paul's theology sought both to ally itself with and distinguish itself from other strands of Second Temple Judaism (of which his Christianity was one). Justin Martyr developed his theology through comparisons, often sympathetic but also often critical, with forms of Judaism and paganism. Origen set his Christian theology in comparative connections with the Greek philosophic world. Augustine's complex theology situated itself with respect to Manichaeism, Ciceronian paganism, and Neo-Platonism, as well as Judaism. Thomas Aquinas elaborated his theology in ever-so-careful comparisons with pagan Aristotelianism and Muslim theology.

Stand-alone theologies first flourished during the Patristic period among those primarily concerned with what they took to be aberrant or heretical forms of Christianity. These theologies resulted in the great creeds of catholic orthodoxy. Perhaps the concern to define Christian theology comparatively diminished because Constantine had declared Christianity the religion of the empire, thus weakening paganism, and Islam had not yet arisen as a vital competitor. The Protestant Reformation saw a resurgence of stand-alone Christian theologies based on scripture and confessions. On the surface this was a negative response to assertions of institutional authority on the part of the Roman Catholic Church. The more powerful dynamic, however, was the democratizing power of basing theology sufficient for Christian salvation on the scriptures that could be read and interpreted by anybody. Although anybody could read the Bible as the age of literacy bloomed, very few Christians were sophisticated in other religions so as to engage them in serious comparison. Much Protestant theology, followed by Roman Catholic theology in the twentieth century, has been so committed to biblical language that to stand-alone theologies, comparative theologies have seemed heterodox on the face of it.[2]

Many factors in the last two centuries—social, economic, political, and military—have brought Christian thinking into vital contact with other religions. Not least among these have been the great missionary efforts of Western Christendom during the modern period. Matteo Ricci's great Confucian-Christian comparative theology at the end of the sixteenth century remains a remarkable achievement even today.[3] Kenneth Cracknell gives a brilliant account of the highly creative comparative mission theologies of Protestant missionaries.[4] The global political situation is highly volatile at the beginning of the twenty-first century, characterized by what Samuel Huntington has called a "clash of civilizations," by which he means religiously defined civilizations.[5] Meanwhile, the development of religious studies as an academic field has fostered much comparative study of religions that is ideally objective at least in the sense of not being controlled by the interests of the scholar's own religious commitments.[6] As a result, theologians cannot claim ignorance of other religions, only lack of study. Moreover, the larger intellectual world has become skeptical of any theology that does not explicitly make its case with reference to its alternatives in other religions as well as its near neighbors in a stand-alone community. In sum, religious communities, Christian and otherwise, do not really stand alone these days; stand-alone theology is desperately artificial in this context, and comparative theologies are the natural mode of critical and normative thinking about theological matters.

Several models for comparative theologies need to be recognized.

First are the social scientific models. These rarely aim to say what is true theologically, only how theological ideas arose and compare with one another. If the social scientific models are not theological strictly speaking (because they do not argue for normative theological teachings), they nevertheless are extremely important resources for comparative theologies. The study of history, beginning with Herodotus, Thucydides, and Ssu-ma Tan, and coming in our own time to global historians such as William McNeill, has provided many comparisons and comparative structures.[7] Arising from global historical studies, scholars such as Jaroslav Krejci have developed historical classificatory and explanatory paradigms.[8] Krejci distinguishes theocentrism (the god-centered view of Mesopotamia), thanatocentrism (the death-centered view of Pharaonic Egypt), anthropocentrism (the man-centered view of classical Greece), psychocentrism (the soul-centered view of India), and cratocentrism (the rule-centered view of China). Christianity reflects an encounter of theocentrism and anthropocentrism; Buddhism emerged from theocentrism and psychocentrism; and so forth. These comparative categories provide large orienting perspectives, but are so broad as to be at very great distance from the singular details of any religion.

Another social scientific model is that of historical comparative theology, as practiced by Randall Collins in his *The Sociology of Philosophies: A Global*

Theory of Intellectual Change.[9] Using a sociological theory of influence and relative importance, Collins traces the genealogies and heritages of the world's great philosophers from all traditions, showing how they so often interacted across traditional boundaries. The power of this approach is in its details. Collins himself treats only philosophies and so misses those theologies within the Christian tradition that are mainly biblical in language and symbols. Nevertheless, his method of analyzing the social production of ideas could very well be expanded to include theological ideas in all senses. Although such a method or model would not produce normative theological conclusions, it is indispensable to the background necessary for comparative theologies today.

Another model for comparative theologies is the derivation of their meanings and relations from some metaphysical scheme. Aristotle invented this model with his classification of pre-Socratic philosophies according to his metaphysical theory of the four causes. Hegel most famously brought world theologies into relation according to his metaphysical theory of the dialectic of Spirit. The Perennial Philosophy has employed a kind of Neo-Platonic metaphysics, to use its most famous Western example, to argue that there are levels of reality, with kinds of spirituality and theological language typical of each level. Most religions exhibit theology on all levels. Huston Smith is the most influential thinker of contemporary Perennial Philosophy and his *The World's Religions* details the kinds of theological comparisons his metaphysics provides.[10] Yet another kind of metaphysical grounding for comparison is the building of a system of classificatory categories so that a grid of possible positions is produced. The truth claim is made for the classificatory grid of possible positions. Plato developed the first great system of this sort with the "hypotheses" in his dialogue *The Parmenides*. Perhaps its most developed form is David A. Dilworth's *Philosophy in World Perspective*, which includes religious thinkers with the philosophers.[11] Dilworth's grid classifies authorial perspectives into the personal, objective, diaphanic (speaking for a higher authority), and disciplinary; ontological focus can be existential, substrative, noumenal, or essential; method can be agonistic, logistic, dialectical, or synoptic; fundamental principles can be creative, elemental, comprehensive, or reflexive. Any philosophy or theology can be understood according to where it stands in each of the categories of the grid. The chief characteristic of all the metaphysical groundings for comparison is that the metaphysical system defines what is important in the theologies, namely, the points that fit the system and how those important things relate according to the structure of the metaphysics. Theologies with points not registered in the metaphysics, or whose own metaphysics has different fundamental relations, are distorted by the metaphysical approach.

Another model of comparative theology is the construction of a fundamentally Christian theology, dealing with the classical loci of the tradition, but drawing on supportive elements in other traditions for the sake of enrichment and pointing out where the other religions differ from or deny Christian doctrine. *Christian Systematic Theology in a World Context* by Ninian Smart and Steven Konstantine is a pioneering venture pursuing this model.[12] Smart in particular was one of the scholarly world's most learned thinkers and brought the richness of comparative religious studies to the task. Yet for all its enrichment of the Christian discussion, this model does not go far to press the question of truth where the traditions are seemingly at odds. Because theology advances beyond the social sciences by taking responsibility for the truth of normative theological claims, comparative theology cannot beg the question by assuming that the Christian agenda and its traditional answers are true.

A related model that addresses this issue is the syncretistic penetration of several religions by mutually inhabiting them, articulating from the inside the sense in which each is true, including the sense in which each defines truth, and integrating them at the level of multiple religious identities. The genius practitioner of this model is Raimundo Panikkar, who is a Roman Catholic priest, a devoted Hindu, and a Buddhist. Through years of study, practice, and initiation into deep levels of each of these traditions, Panikkar has produced a series of books that synthesize deep truths from all three.[13] While this model produces a comparative theology that is normative and responsible for its selections of comparative material, it is highly selective in what to compare and does not deal readily with the many forms of Christianity, Hinduism, and Buddhism that do not fit into the synthesis. The model does not promote vulnerability to correction from comparisons with what might be radically critical.

The ideals of comparative theology turn on the achievement of mutual respect among theologians of the religions. Wilfred Cantwell Smith is famous for saying that a scholar should not trust his understanding of another religion unless a theologically astute practitioner of that religion recognizes himself or herself in the expression of that understanding.[14] Comparative theology goes beyond mere accurate representation of the religions compared, however: it draws out comparisons, says explicitly how the theologies of the religions are similar and different and in what respects, and evaluates the various claims and ways of putting them. A religious tradition thus is likely to be somewhat changed when brought into explicit comparison. It is asked questions arising from the comparative context that might be novel. Its theology is developed so as to engage the other religions comparatively. And most especially its sources and criteria for truth are evaluated in the larger comparative context. So Smith's point about requiring the representatives of the traditions compared to approve the representations of them in the comparison can be extended to explicit collaboration. Collaboration is needed to work through the changes theologies undergo when expanded to fit into comparisons. Collaboration is also helpful, of course, because no one scholar can master enough material to be trustworthy about faithful comparisons of many religions, especially that material derived from participation in religious practice.

Collaborative comparison has a logic of many movements.[15] One movement is the development of comparative categories that do not bias the comparisons for or against any religion. Any comparison is in some "respect": theological positions are compared in some respect or other. The "respect" of comparison is a comparative category. Although all comparative categories have a history in some religious tradition, they can be purified and made vague so as to be able to be specified by the different ways the various religious theologies address the topic. Making a comparative category properly vague and unbiased is a process that includes attempting to classify competing specifications of the category and finding that they do not fit without distortion.[16]

A second movement within the logic of collaborative comparison is the attempt to articulate each of the religious theologies to be compared as ways of specifying the comparative category or respect in which they are to be compared. Like the process of making a comparative category properly vague, the process of articulating each position to be compared in terms of the category moves by tentative hypotheses and corrections. To prevent bias a critical dialectic needs to check candidate articulations of each tradition for distortion within the tradition, and also to see whether the articulations genuinely address the comparative question. This is a point where representatives of the various theologies compared need to be consulted, allowing for the fact that the articulation of their position in terms of the comparative category might be new for them.

A third movement within the logic is to survey the results of articulating all the positions in terms of the vague comparative category. The comparative category is no longer only vague but also variously specified by the positions to be compared. In the complex specified language of the category, comparative hypotheses can then be framed saying how the positions compare: what is similar, what different, what mutually overlapping or extended in different directions, what is singular and incomparable about the positions, and perhaps how positions are simply incommensurate in the respect in which comparison is sought.

These three movements in the logic of collaborative comparison all take place together with the formulations of hypotheses, testing them, revising them, and moving forward. In a given comparative project, the hypotheses can radically shift at first, but settle down into steady temporary conclusions. The search for properly vague unbiased comparative categories settles down after obvious exceptions have caused revisions. The task of articulating the various theological positions with respect to the comparative category settles down after obvious exceptions are met. The comparisons themselves are hypotheses ready for revision but warranted by the fact that the process of testing them by as many means as possible has shown them to hold for the most part. Comparative theology is always fallible and hypothetical, even when it has reached agreement on comparisons that have stood up under every test the collaboration can bring.[17]

Collaborative comparative theologies of course examine the arguments for the theologies compared as well as the conclusions. Some such arguments are verbal and logical. Often the arguments are experiential, historical, contextual, and existential. They have to do with identity and purpose. While collaborative comparative theologies are developed in a religious studies context, those who engage in them have their own "argument" for their theological convictions. Christians engaged in collaborative comparative theologies start with Christian convictions, commitments, and practices. The process of comparison enriches these, and also brings them into judgment as the normative arguments of other religions are articulated and compared with mutual respect. Sometimes the process of comparison leads to changes in the theologian's own theological identity. That is as it should be, because the purpose of theology is to get at the truth about theological topics, not to protect some antecedent theological identity now shown to be biased, misleading, or false. Therefore the best theologies are those most vulnerable to correction and put into a collaborative comparative engagement where their mistakes are found out and corrected. A theology protected against vulnerability might be wrong and the last to know that. A truly vulnerable theology puts itself into a comparative context and makes a case for itself to all who might correct it. That case requires unbiased respect for those from whom it might learn. Comparative theologies can be undertaken by theologians from any of the traditions compared, and their mutual collaboration enhances the steadiness and probity of their conclusions.[18]

OBJECTIVIST COMPARISON

Two fundamental approaches to comparison now dominate the field. For convenience, and with the proviso that the names can be defined through the discussion further on as terms of art, they can be called the "objectivist" and "normative" approaches respectively. The objectivist approach treats the positions to be compared as finished objects, takes up a perspective of distance upon them, and measures its comparative judgments in empirical ways over against the evidence of the positions. The normative approach centers, first, on addressing contemporary philosophical problems and looks to the historical positions as resources for contemporary thinking, bringing them into comparative perspective against the contemporary background. The normative approach thus involves reconstructing the traditions, as any living tradition does in growing to meet new philosophical situations, and does so by bringing them into comparative interaction. Just as a contemporary European philosopher can learn from both Plato and Aristotle in constructing a response to an issue neither Plato nor Aristotle imagined, so a contemporary philosopher in a global public can learn the all the world's traditions to contribute to philosophy for our time.

Obviously the normative approach to comparison needs to embrace the objectivist approach. The hermeneutical movements in philosophy have taught us not to play fast and loose with historical antecedents. We need to be self-conscious about what is carried on and what is left behind in philosophical reconstructions. Objectivist analyses need always to be respected within normative comparison. Less obvious but still true is the fact that the objectivist approach needs to be self-conscious about the norms deriving from contemporary concerns that guide the selection of respects in which comparisons are made. The norms involved in objectivist analyses might be focused on methodological considerations, and yet they nevertheless reflect normative contemporary philosophical reflection and debate. The objectivist approach of course does not obtain its conclusions from comparative analyses within the normative approach. Rather, the considerations within the normative approach for why to reconstruct comparative positions one way rather than another also affect normative considerations about the methods of objectivist comparison.

Contemporary objectivist comparative philosophy generally falls into three main types, or combinations of the types, with a fourth type as a suggestion to be made here. One is what might be called classificatory comparison and derives from the ancient Aristotelian heritage. Aristotle began his *Metaphysics* (in book 1, starting at chapter 3) with a discussion of previous philosophies based on the classificatory system of his theory of four causes. The theory classifying the four kinds of causes itself provided the classificatory system, and the pre-Aristotelian philosophers were interpreted as falling within the classes defined by that system. Richard McKeon revived the Aristotelian classificatory type of comparison in the twentieth century at the University of Chicago. Two of his students deserve special mention with regard to our interest in comparative global philosophy.

Robert S. Brumbaugh was a student of McKeon at the University of Chicago and taught for many decades at Yale University. With Newton P. Stallknecht he published in 1954 *The Compass of Philosophy: An Essay in Intellectual Orientation*, announcing a project that occupied the rest of his career.[19] His claim there was that four types of speculative systems exist: formalisms (like Plato's), philosophies of creation (like Whitehead and existentialism), naturalisms (or vitalisms), and mechanisms or discrete pluralisms (materialisms and sensationalisms). The philosophies discussed were all Western, and noted to be such in contrast to other world philosophies. Later in his career, Brumbaugh developed his categories in increasingly nuanced ways and reflected some on philosophies other than Western. Moreover, in addition to the rather Aristotelian ring of his four types of philosophy he often added a Platonic cross-classification based on the four levels of the Divided Line in the *Republic*: discrete images, concrete process, theoretical entities, and dialectical reality.[20] The types of mechanistic pluralism and philosophies of creation are easily interpretable in terms of the levels of images and concrete process from the Divided Line. The contrast between formalisms and naturalism, however, does not have clear Platonic analogies because the latter means a focus on natural individuals.

The virtue of Brumbaugh's approach is the classificatory system's very great abstractness that allows for specific philosophies to be represented as specifications of one or more of the classes. As a Platonist himself, Brumbaugh was very careful to say what the specifications add to the abstract categories. His ideal, like Plato's in the legendary lost lecture on the Good, was to find mathematical representations of the different classes.

Walter Watson, another student of McKeon, spent most of his career at the State University of New York at Stony Brook. His classificatory system, much more complicated in many ways than Brumbaugh's, is based on what he calls "archic variables," namely the perspectives of the authors, the sense of reality, the methods of analysis, and the types of explanatory principles to be found in a philosophy.[21] He cross classifies this with characterizations of four Western philosophic modes: the sophistic, Democritean, Platonic, and Aristotelian. So, for instance, the archic variable of perspective is personal in sophism, objective in Democritean philosophy, diaphanic in Platonic, and disciplinary in Aristotelian. The yield is sixteen classes for traits of philosophies, and each philosophy can be understood according to whether each of its four archic variables of perspective, reality, method, and principle is sophistic, Democritean, Platonic, or Aristotelian.

Watson does not take his classificatory analysis to be mere rhetorical analysis. Rather it has ontological force. He writes:

> This book presents what I take to be the most significant philosophic discovery of the present [twentieth] century. This is the discovery, first, of the fact of pluralism, that the truth admits of more than one valid formulation, and, secondly, of the reason for this fact in arbitrary or conventional elements inseparable from the nature of thought itself. With this discovery, the very thing that was formerly thought to be a scandal and a disgrace to philosophy, namely, that philosophers do not agree, turns out to be its great virtue, for through it are revealed essential features of all thought, present indeed everywhere, but nowhere so clearly as in philosophy.[22]

Watson's intent is to provide an explanation for why many different systems are true, each in its own way. He holds that philosophical epochs have a cyclic character, starting with fundamental conceptions of reality, followed by concerns for how we know this, and concluded by a preoccupation with the meaningfulness of knowledge, which in turn gives rise to a new orientation to reality. His own work is a study of meaning, but set within the understanding of the cycles that include ontological and epistemological commitments.

Watson's field of examples is Western philosophy and, to a lesser extent, Western literature. His colleague David A. Dilworth, however, explicitly expanded the explanatory field of archic variables and philosophic modes to include philosophies (and also religious systems) from all over the world, especially China (and least from Islamic traditions).[23] Dilworth's own scholarly background is in Japanese philosophy of which he is a distinguished translator and commentator. Reflection on Dilworth's comparative discussions of Chinese and Western philosophers brings great rewards in calling to attention respects of comparison that otherwise might not be noticed.

Indeed, the strength of a comparative approach that begins with a classificatory scheme is that it lifts to attention connections that might not be explicit or even suggested in the philosophies compared, and yet that turn out to be very important in comparative analysis. The weakness of classificatory schemes obviously is that elements of philosophies that are not registered in the schemes get ignored, and positions are jostled and twisted to fit into the scheme's variables. Although Brumbaugh, Watson, and Dilworth are quick to say that their classificatory schemes arise inductively from reflecting on many philosophies, in fact their justification is not in their empirical merit but in dialectical considerations to the effect that the variables they highlight are indeed the important ones. This is to say, contemporary normative philosophy is required to justify the schemes for classifying the positions within various traditions.

A second type of objectivist approach to comparison is the social science causal approach. This type is based on a causal theory of influence and derivation in sociology of knowledge and is represented most brilliantly by Randall Collins in his magisterial *The Sociology of Philosophies: A Global Theory of Intellectual Change*.[24] His causal theory is based on what he calls "interaction rituals" of intellectuals and registers such variables as distinctions between major, secondary, and minor philosophers, the existence and longevity of schools of thought, the influences both of adoption and conflict, the historical conditions of communication, power relations, political loyalties, and guild structures.

Collins's extraordinary erudition allows him to elaborate a complex causal story of Chinese, Indian, and Western philosophies and their interactions. He is not so much interested in what might be true or false in the philosophies, or how they have different truths in senses explained by classificatory schemes, as he is in how philosophers react to one another, how their heritages are changed, and the conditions that affect the longevity and strength of philosophic ideas. Whereas the classificatory type of objective comparison decontextualizes the philosophies, treating them as pure ideas representing archic variables, the sociological causation type notices the content of the philosophic ideas only to establish positions within the changing contexts of philosophies in their histories. *Comparison* itself might seem to be a decontextualized notion of understanding the relations among philosophies. For Collins, the explanation is about more concrete interactions than mere intellectual comparisons. On the other hand, the intellectual comparisons get short shrift in the explanations of the causal interactions.

What is the status of the sociological theory used to tell the story of the interactions of philosophy? Collins derives it by means of a kind of dialectical discussion of recent sociological, historical, and philosophical theories, mostly the sociological theories in the tradition of Durkheim and Goffman. In this respect, its normative status is as good as the arguments in that discussion, a matter of contemporary debate. The theory is used, however, to acknowledge and trace out an enormous amount of data, dealing both with primary texts and with secondary texts and traditions of interpretation. Whatever the profession's ultimate judgment on the sociological theory of intellectual interactions, this theory serves as an extraordinarily useful device for getting many usually unconnected philosophical positions into view at once. The theory of rituals of intellectual interaction does not depend on making the philosophies commensurate in order to compare them, nor on fitting them into a comparative grid that imposes a higher-level commensurateness on them. As Confucians know about ritual, one of its functions is to allow very different and even conflicting people to dance together.

Nothing prevents objectivist comparison from using both the classificatory and sociological causal types. The integration of these approaches, however, remains to be accomplished.

A third type of objectivist comparison is philosophy of culture. The landmark work of this type in the twentieth century is F. S. C. Northrop's *The Meeting of East and West: An Inquiry Concerning World Understanding*.[25] Rather than provide an internal interpretation of any one philosopher, Northrop reflected on whole traditions and derived general characterizations such as that Eastern cultures are dominantly aesthetic and are framed by "concepts by intuition" in contrast with Western culture, which is theoretical and given to "concepts by postulation." Particular philosophers and cultural practices are then discussed within the framework of the general comparative considerations. Chang Chung-yuan represents this approach from the Chinese side.[26] The greatest masters of comparative philosophy of culture, however, and the most influential in the contemporary situation, are Roger T. Ames and the late

David L. Hall in their trilogy *Thinking Through Confucius*, *Anticipating China: Thinking Through the Narratives of Chinese and Western Culture*, and *Thinking from the Han: Self, Truth, and Transcendence in Chinese and Western Culture*.[27] (Their further collaboration in *Democracy of the Dead: Dewey, Confucius, and the Hope for Democracy in China* is not an example of objectivist comparison but rather a brilliant paradigm of normative comparison.)[28]

Hall and Ames greatly extend Northrop's contrast between the aesthetic East and theoretical West. *Thinking Through Confucius* is an interpretation of the *Analects* that develops the nuanced notion of aesthetic order as it would unfold in Chinese thought, in steady philosophical contrast with Western notions that emphasize theoretical, mathematical, or linear conceptions of order. *Anticipating China* is a comparative study of the origins of Chinese and Western cultures (mainly philosophic but also literary) that begins from the contrast between chaos—well tolerated in Chinese culture—and cosmos, the ordered ideal of Western culture. Here and even more in *Thinking from the Han*, Ames and Hall stress the notion that Chinese culture is based on "field and focus" contextuality and correlative thinking whereas Western culture hunts for transcendent absolutes that maintain identity irrespective of context and that function as first principles to explain. They claim that such Western notions as an autonomous self, being, truth, and transcendence have no close analogues in Chinese culture. Although their arguments are based on the analysis of specific texts of philosophers, their conclusions are generalizations about the two cultures conceived as wholes. Hall and Ames employ both categoreal contrasts of the cultures compared, in which they are like the classificatory types of comparison, and narrative developments. The virtue of the narrative developments is that they can tell the story of how the cultural traits they cite evolve and interact through the unfolding or creative development of the separate cultures. This allows them to represent their compared cultures as having integrity through time over against each other. Of course they would admit that some thinkers in China might nurture a love for transcendence and a few Western philosophers have a primarily aesthetic focus. Nevertheless, the dominant characterizations they give of the cultures define the cultural spaces within which Chinese and Western philosophers operate, and these spaces are in different, contrasting, places, they argue.

This last point is the great strength of comparative philosophy of culture: whatever specific philosophers might say within each tradition, the general cultural traits constitute the intellectual medium of assumptions, problematics, and argument forms within which the individuals have to operate. The weakness of this approach also lies here: the characterizations of the culture might not be true of any or many individual philosophers (Hall and Ames make a strong case for their interpretation of Confucius).

From the standpoint of philosophers interested in normative comparison, looking to address contemporary problems with the substance, resources, and imaginative trajectories of the world's philosophic traditions brought to interaction, all three types of objectivist analysis mentioned have a grave difficulty. They all treat the positions, traditions, and cultures compared as if they were dead, objectified, at least "etherized upon a table." This is most true of the classificatory types: a living philosopher has no reason to work at all since a dead philosopher can be found for every possible archic position. All that's left for philosophy is intellectual history and judgments of preference. The sociological causation type allows that a living philosopher can be identified by the influences appropriated or criticized, but such a living philosopher is represented in the analysis only as a confluence of influences. A real living philosopher aims to be an improvement, not merely a result, and the normative considerations about improvement do not register in the social causation analysis. A living philosopher facing the comparisons of philosophy of culture has an even more perplexing position. Perhaps by unlikely chance the philosopher would affirm a position exactly as characterized for one of the compared cultures. But most philosophers today recognize the differences and limitations pointed out in analyses such as Hall and Ames's and attempt to develop conceptual means to affirm both sides. Does this mean that such a living philosopher, though coming from the West, cannot be a Western philosopher because that would require rejecting or failing to recognize Chinese culture? Does a Chinese philosopher have to be baffled by transcendence and theoretical explanation? No living philosophers would embrace everything claimed for either West or China because those cultures contain contradictions. Living philosophers develop positions adopting and reconstructing, criticizing and rejecting, selective elements from both. Does this mean such living philosophers have transcended to a higher, more inclusive realm? That is doubtful because a living philosophy might be far worse than any number of great philosophies in the Western and Chinese traditions (and Indian, Islamic, and so forth).

In light of this perplexity and serious inconvenience for the self-definition of a living creative philosopher, yet another type of objectivist comparison can be envisioned, which can be called core text and motif analysis. A core text such as Confucius's *Analects* or a motif such as the yin/yang distinction that has no locus classicus is to be understood in a complex way through its history. Every Chinese philosopher treats those core texts and motifs in some way or other. Some great philosophers develop new core texts or motifs in their treatments. To trace the historical developments and branchings of responses to core texts and motifs is to arrive at an objectivist comparison based on history, and thus to be ready to employ the causal insights of sociological causal comparisons. Because every philosophic response to a core text and motif is a determinate differential one, classificatory schemes articulating the alternatives available to the responding philosopher can be employed. Because core texts and motifs are responded to by philosophers who do not necessarily identify with them as traditional resources, the comparative analysis need not be bogged down with imposed categories labeling traditions such as Confucianism, Daoism, Advaita Vedanta, Mutazalite, Platonic, or Aristotelian philosophies. Questions of the "essence" of such traditions can be avoided, and the issue of whether these labels are impositions of the imperialist Western traditions can be transformed into an empirical question. According to comparative core text and motif analysis, the conceptual relations among philosophic positions can be expressed in terms of a complicated history, noting continuities as well as irrelevancies and incommensurabilities.

Another advantage of the core text and motifs type of objectivist comparison is that it suggests that a living philosopher can make a reconstructive retrieval of just about any position in the history that suggests itself, because that is exactly what the philosophers in that history did. Core text and motif analysis invites normative comparison as a further move.

NORMATIVE COMPARISON

The normative approach to comparison is undertaken by living philosophers primarily concerned to make normative responses to issues in the contemporary philosophical situation. As remarked earlier, hermeneutical honesty requires normative thinkers to attend to the best possible objective knowledge, being aware of the contemporary normative considerations that have gone into the objectivist methodologies. Nevertheless, the normative approach to comparison introduces a new element of comparison.

In *Democracy of the Dead*, Ames and Hall ask how democracy and human rights might be possible for contemporary China, in light of the fact that those notions, according to them, are absent or submerged in that tradition. Yet world affairs now are pressing China to enter the global cultural economy in which democracy and human rights are tickets of admission. Hall and Ames suggest that the Confucian heritage of China be reinterpreted in terms of the pragmatic social philosophy of John Dewey, and that Deweyan pragmatism, which can so well represent Western cultural values, itself be supplemented with a Confucian rendering. Without for a moment implying that Confucianism and pragmatism are the same, or even much alike, they argue that each can be given a natural extension that meets the other. The resulting comparative connection, they argue, provides important guidance for the development of contemporary Chinese political thinking that both sustains serious connections with the Chinese past and engages Western political thought and practice on its own terms.

What Hall and Ames have done by way of normative comparison in politics, thinkers such as Antonio Cua and Tu Weiming have done in ethics, interpreting classical Chinese sources in terms of their value for the contemporary ethical discussion that is also shaped by Western concerns.[29] Xinyan Jiang's edited volume, *The Examined Life: Chinese Perspectives: Essays on Chinese Ethical Traditions*, brings to attention a new generation of mainly Chinese philosophers in America engaged in serious normative comparison, using Chinese traditions to solve problems where Western modes of philosophy are limited.[30]

Cheng Chungying and Wu Kuangming have developed comprehensive contemporary philosophies based on normative comparisons. Cheng's work ranges freely through Western philosophies from Plato and Aristotle to Heidegger and Whitehead, and through both Confucian and Daoist philosophies in China, appealing most to a reconstructive interpretation of the *Yijing*.[31] His system uses both Western and Chinese terms, but glosses both in comparative discussions of representatives of each tradition. He freely invents neologisms to say what cannot unequivocally be said in either tradition. Although Cheng is a scholar of the texts, the burden of his argument is to stretch the ideas to contemporary relevance.

Whereas Cheng Chungying is fundamentally a Confucian educated at Harvard with a PhD on the logic of Charles Sanders Peirce written with Willard Quine, Wu Kuangming is fundamentally a Daoist educated at Yale in Kant and existentialism under George Schrader and John E. Smith. After studies of Zhuangzi aimed to make him a "world philosopher" for the contemporary scene, Wu has written a massive three-volume system collectively called *A Cultural Hermeneutic*.[32] His subtlety in moving back and forth between the problematic of Western hermeneutics and the deconstructions of that in certain strains of Chinese philosophy is breathtaking. Ironically, he is dissatisfied with the system-builders in Western philosophy, preferring the indirectness of Zhuangzi. But his is the most comprehensive and detailed system yet produced by a Chinese thinker based on normative comparisons.

Just as much as in published works, the normative approach to comparison is embodied in ongoing conversations. There have been a series of conferences in Hong Kong at the Chinese University and in Taiwan bringing together Chinese and Western philosophers, rarely to present merely scholarly papers but to address contemporary problems from the standpoint of the meeting of the traditions. An ongoing Confucian-Christian Dialogue begun in the 1980s has produced many spin-off conversations. Tu Weiming's leadership of the Harvard Yenching Institute has given rise to a conversation group of Boston Confucians that reaches scholars from all over the world. Tu's primary interest is in creating a global conversation shaped by Confucian sensibilities of humaneness that addresses the strengths and limitations of the European Enlightenment project for world culture.[33]

To argue that any viable contemporary philosophy dealing with the nature of a desirable society, the meaning of human life, the nature of existence, or the problems of ecology and distributive justice, could fail to rest upon a comparative base is impossible. Of course the argument that it is possible is made by some persons without the *paideia* for thinking within a global philosophic public, but without viability: to make a case for a philosophic position is to make it to all those with an interest in the outcome, and the global array of philosophies has a global set of interests. We must also admit that few if any people do have the *paideia* today for addressing a genuine global philosophic public. I have spoken bravely here but have limited my comparative discussions to Chinese-Western issues. Who can handle those as well as the Indian and Islamic issues of comparison? Nevertheless, the need for a global public creates the ideal and that ideal drives comparative philosophy.

Objectivist and normative comparative approaches are different, though interrelated. They need each other.

BEYOND COMPARATIVE TO INTEGRATIVE PHILOSOPHY

Vital and creative philosophy today needs to operate within a public that integrates reflections from as many of the world's philosophic traditions as possible. To support this thesis I shall supplement the remarks in the previous section about an appropriate philosophic public for vital philosophy. Then I shall comment on some of the kinds of comparative philosophy that are helpful for the integration of the world's philosophic traditions into a public. Finally, I shall suggest a two-tiered agenda for integrative philosophy.

What Is a Philosophic Public?

A voluntarist answer is that a philosophy's public is anyone the philosopher chooses to address, and this can be quite narrow as in some program philosophies.[34] The advantage of a program philosophy is that everyone understands the terms and advances within the parameters of the program; perhaps it is a little like a scientific experiment to see how far the programmatic ideas go. But such a public is not really public: it is a private conversation.

A traditionalist answer is that a philosophy's public consists of those who accept the cultural premises with which it is framed, the styles of argument characteristic of the tradition, and that tradition's self-understanding of what its philosophy is trying to prove. A tradition, of course, moves through many different positions, but it has an unfolding story that gives contemporary bearers of the tradition their identity. Western philosophy, for instance, is self-conscious about its beginnings with the Socratic movement in ancient Greece (for all the diversity in that movement), its relations to religion in late antiquity and the medieval period, and its Enlightenment heritage of epistemological skepticism, foundationalism, complex relations with science, romantic reactions, and now postmodernism. Chinese philosophy in a similar way defines itself in terms of the core texts and motifs of Daoist and Confucian classics, the struggles with Sinicizing Indian Buddhism, the recovery of Neo-Confucianism, and now a reconstruction of that East Asian tradition in relation to Western thought. The South Asian tradition in its orthodox schools variously affirm the authority of the Vedas while the unorthodox schools finesse them, and the integral South Asian tradition takes its identity from the interplay of these. The Islamic tradition takes a different rise from Plato, Aristotle, and Neo-Platonism than the Europeans took, and developed its philosophic tradition in dialectical relation to Judaism, Christianity, Zoroastrianism, the Hinduisms of the Moghul Empire in India, and the complex forms of Buddhism in Southeast Asia. Although many occasions of contact among these traditions have occurred, their separate identities as traditions have been emphasized in the last two centuries in reaction to imperialism. Representing the imperial winning culture, Western philosophy established itself from Harvard to Hong Kong in the curriculum of the modern university. The other philosophies in reaction have attempted during the last two centuries to define themselves over against Western philosophy. Representatives of each of these world traditions have been able to say that "real" philosophy is the one that accepts "our" cultural assumptions, "our" ways of argument, and "our" interpretation of the horizons that give meaning to philosophy.

The problem with the traditionalist answer is that the philosophic concerns that come from alien cultural premises, different styles of argument, and different interpretations of what is at stake are precisely the ones from which it is most important to learn. They are most ready to illuminate unacknowledged presuppositions, blind spots in argumentation, and disorientation concerning what is at stake. So philosophers have a great need to open their positions to thinkers from other cultures and invite them to come into one's argumentation. Only a philosophy that is deliberately vulnerable to correction is likely to get very far. A philosophy that is heavily entrenched within a set of cultural premises about the nature of philosophy, a certain conception of rationality and argument, and a rigid interpretation of the horizons of its significance is fragile. The best philosophy is the one that is most vulnerable to correction and that has amended and steadied itself through as many corrective examinations as possible. The real public for a philosophy is the set of perspectives that might correct it.

So I would argue that the philosophic public today consists of anyone with an interest in the outcome of the argument and the willingness to work to understand it. This is a global public. People from any philosophic culture are in one's public, if they have an interest and devotion to the necessary work.

Now it might be thought that willingness to work to understand one's argument means accepting the cultural premises with which it is framed, the style of argument, even the argument's self-understanding of what it is trying to prove. But that is not so. Someone from a different philosophic culture might challenge cultural premises, styles of rationality, and even the understanding of the enterprise of philosophy. These are precisely the challenges that make philosophy live. Otherwise, philosophy becomes repetitive, preoccupied with authenticity to its tradition, while the society's need for wisdom gets palmed off on disciplines and groups less able to respond with deep resources.

The global public for philosophy should not be defined only negatively, as if one needs to be ready to defend oneself against alien traditions. The positive definition is that those other traditions should be sought out for the critical insights they might have. Each philosophic tradition needs to build bridges to the others to engage the others in critical dialogue. Here is where comparative philosophy is an indispensable tool.

Comparative Philosophy

Comparative philosophy, of course, is not new. Aristotle began the *Metaphysics* with a classification of philosophies known to him. The six orthodox schools of Indian philosophy were attempts to reconstitute a Vedic-Hindu tradition in the face of Buddhist challenges, and in explicit dialogue with Buddhisms of several sorts. The ancient Chinese philosophers compared one another's perspectives, and the argument can be made that the distinction between philosophic Confucianism and Daoism was not formally important until drawn in the ninth century to set Chinese philosophies over against foreign Buddhist ones.[35] Comparative philosophy is always at work where dialogue takes place between philosophic positions that do not share cultural assumptions, styles of rationality, and interpretations of the meaning of philosophy.

The first thing to note about a comparison is that it always involves a "theory" that holds the things to be compared in view together. Postmodernists and others have long pointed out that the "theory" involved in most cross-cultural intellectual comparisons is not the explicit theory stated but rather a higher level perspective, usually that of Western culture. So, Western philosophy (or religion) defines the categories that we take to be important respects in which things are to be compared. This already biases what counts as philosophy (or religious ideas—outside the West these are not easily distinguished). Some critics point out that any theory is logocentric—that's what a theory is, a logos of what gets registered and related to what. If a theory is logocentric, it marginalizes the philosophies that do not get registered, and therefore should be avoided. Do not compare at all, these critics imply, only juxtapose the different philosophies; let each tell its story without saying how they compare.[36]

Juxtaposition might be necessary at the beginning stages of building a global philosophic public because some philosophers might not realize that there are many modes of philosophy other than their own. But juxtaposition does not get very far. To overcome the criticism that all comparison reflects a logocentric and therefore marginalizing theory, we can recall a lesson from Charles Peirce.

In his delightful essay, discussed earlier, about the logic of theories, called "A Neglected Argument for the Reality of God," Peirce pointed out that the development and testing of a theory have several stages, not all of which are deductive in Aristotle's sense of following according to a rule (e.g., *modus ponens*).[37] The first stage he called abduction or retroduction, and it is a guess at a theoretical idea that might solve the problem at hand; in a comparison, it would be guessing at the respect in which to compare the things at hand. Then this guess, which might be quite fanciful, needs to be elaborated in theoretical terms, well-formed formulas. Neither of these first two moves proceeds according to a rule, but we seem to have evolved pretty good instincts for making progress quickly. The third step is to deduce out predictive consequences from the theory that can then be tested in experience, a kind of reasoning that does follow from rules. Up to this point, most philosophers of science would have followed Peirce and now would have looked to seeing whether the experiential or experimental predictions hold. But Peirce makes a bold unexpected move. He points out that the theoretical categories themselves might have all sorts of bias and that they in turn need to be examined as to whether they distort the experience they are supposed to categorize. Only after they have been demonstrated to be nondistorting (or their distortions understood and controlled for) should the testing of the theory proceed by examining how much experience supports the theory and how much it does not. So a crucial part of theoretical development is to take the side of the phenomena, as it were, to see whether they are registered appropriately in the theoretical categories that classify them. To put the point another way, in the process of formulating comparative hypotheses, it is necessary to install a dialectical check that asks whether the well-formed formulas of the hypothesis in fact resonate with the ideas to be compared. That they can express the ideas in their own terms is not doubted. But that is the problem. The question is whether they do so with bias, and whether that bias can be controlled for.

Of course no completely neutral standpoint exists for saying what the phenomena are before relating them to theoretical comparative categories. But we dare not let the comparative theory say what the ideas have to mean in order to count in the comparison, for that marginalizes what might be the most important elements. So a checklist of sorts needs to be developed to get a new perspective on whether and how the theoretical categories register the ideas to be compared. In the natural sciences, this is the point where theories of instrumentation are very important. In comparing philosophic ideas from different cultures, the following checklist is helpful:

1. Examine the ideas to be compared in their own terms, in their classic texts. This lets the ideas to be compared speak for themselves, a kind of "intrinsic" analysis. But we cannot take them at face value, as the various hermeneutics of suspicion have taught us.
2. Examine how each idea in its cultural context or heritage takes up a perspective on other ideas and practices in its context. This "perspectival" analysis is not to get at the perspective of the comparativist but at the perspective the idea has on its own culture. Here is where ideas that look very similar in expression from different cultures might be shown to be very different indeed, the similarity being an illusion.
3. Examine how each idea to be compared can be understood in the terms of as many explanatory theories as practicable, not including the comparative theory to be applied. Here is the point at which reductionist explanations, such as in the social sciences and hermeneutics of suspicion, have their day, showing their power and limitations.
4. Examine how each idea has practical consequences when lived with or believed in various contexts, both within its culture of origin and in others. One has to be careful of too hasty a pragmatism; nevertheless, the pragmatic point has its moment. If the comparative theory cannot register what an idea means in practice, it is not fit to classify the idea.
5. Cultivate a sense of what is singular about the ideas to be compared, those things that inevitably get lost in comparisons and juxtapositions. This point is explicitly noncomparative, but it works to increase sensitivity to bias.

The heuristic device of such a checklist serves as a kind of phenomenological counterweight to the theoretical unfolding of comparative hypotheses. Of course there is no guarantee that all biases have been identified and controlled for. But attention to the question whether the theoretical terms of the comparison bias the things compared can be focused in some detail if such a checklist is observed.

The most important thing to notice about comparisons is that they are hypotheses. If the comparative work has been done well, they are well-grounded hypotheses and can be taken for granted. Nevertheless, if the public within which the comparisons are made includes those whose traditions include the ideas compared, the comparative hypotheses are vulnerable to valuable criticism. Comparative hypotheses are best justified when they have been made vulnerable to correction and subjected to as many challenges as possible.

Philosophic ideas are not at all easy to compare because each has its own contested provenance. How can we compare Plato's theory of forms with the Neo-Confucian conception of Principle or *li* if Platonists do not agree about the theory of forms and Confucians dispute the meaning of *li*? In each tradition, contests exist between what the ideas have meant in the past and how they might be reconstructed to address issues of the day. This is part of a living philosophic tradition. So the point of comparison for the sake of integrative philosophy is not just intellectual history but the creation of a conversation within which all the parties share in the struggle to develop old ideas into new ones, each appreciative of the heritages of the others as well as the creative challenges. Comparative hypotheses, then, are both backward looking, as in comparative intellectual history, and forward looking as in the work of creative reconstruction for contemporary purposes.

A Two-Tiered Agenda for Integrative Philosophy

Problems face philosophers today for which only woefully inadequate traditional resources exist. These are moral or cultural problems with great urgency, what William James would have called "forced options."

For instance, because of advances in economics and other social sciences, we now can seriously entertain questions about the nature of *global* distributive justice. When Thomas Aquinas thought about distributive justice he had in mind, say, France, with its king, or at most the Holy Roman Empire with its titular monarch, not a global situation with no one government or even a set of competing governments that govern in the same sense: Somalia, Japan, Argentina, France, and the European Common Market need to be conceived together to understand distributive justice. Knowing something new and rich about the causal properties of a global economy presents urgent demands to understand global distributive justice. No philosophic tradition has thought in this context before, however much it might have anticipations.

Advances in biological and chemical sciences have taught us that the Earth is an ecosystem in such a way that no philosophic or religious traditions developed so far can say clearly what it means to "be at home" on the planet. Human activities can radically change the environment in a short time, and none of our old models of "how to inhabit the Earth" gives guidance equal to the scientific knowledge we have or the technological power. The widespread use of the Internet is quickly undermining suppositions in all philosophic cultures about differences between elite and popular thinking and communication. In these and many areas, imaginative philosophic thought is greatly needed and no cultural tradition has the answers. I need not belabor the point that these philosophical problematics are the proper topics of the global philosophical conversation, not especially apt for one tradition over another. This is the first tier of the philosophic agenda: philosophy for practical global life, respectful of all peoples with their philosophic traditions and going beyond all.

The second tier is more subtle to state but should not be unexpected. Practical problems such as those just mentioned were the stimulus of the invention of philosophy in the ancient cultures: problems of war and peace in China, of new religions that destroyed cultural authority in India, of sophistic critiques of the Greek civilization's values in Plato's time. In order to respond to those practical problems, all the world civilizations developed philosophies that ask the grand questions: What does it mean to exist, to have value, to be obliged, to know beauty, to have virtues? What is reality versus illusion, harmony versus disorder, truth versus advantage? How should we understand friendship and families, religion, education, politics, law, and justice? Each tradition has different core texts and motifs for these ideas, and no neutral way of expressing the questions exists. But the questions function in all the traditions. Our own practical problems necessarily force contemporary philosophers, however integrative, to reraise those classic questions. The language for reraising them cannot be merely the reassertion of some tradition's philosophic heritage. The language has to arise out of a vigorous global public within which serious comparison of philosophic ideas has advanced to the point where each tradition provides helpful conversation partners to the others. We should never hope for a nonproblematic global language for philosophy. We do not even expect Platonists to speak like Aristotelians, or Daoists like Confucians, or Vishistadvaita Vedantins like Madhyamaka Buddhists. But we can hope that all the world's traditions can argue with one another fruitfully, as each of those pairs has. Each philosopher in such a world conversation thus has a constructive project shaping his or her contribution.

12

Contributions of Chinese Philosophy: A Summary Discussion

I MEAN HERE TO SUMMARIZE some of the main ideas from Chinese philosophy that I have previously argued are important for the contemporary conversation. This is the same as saying where Chinese philosophy plays a large part in my own thinking as a Western-trained philosopher functioning in a world-philosophy context. My presentation here is not primarily expository, but reconstructive.

THE HAPPY PORTABILITY OF CHINESE PHILOSOPHY

No Western philosopher doubts that one can be a Platonist or Aristotelian without being an ancient Greek, or even a modern Greek. Indeed, the history of Platonism and Aristotelianism is to be understood in large part by tracing how its core texts and fundamental motifs of thought were variously interpreted and indigenized to the cultures of Islam, medieval Europe, modern Western Europe, and now Britain and America. Averroes, Aquinas, Spinoza, Hegel, and Richard McKeon are all Aristotelians in variant senses of that patrimony, and no one would expect that a contemporary Aristotelian would have to agree with any of them, or with Aristotle, in exact detail: contemporary Aristotelianism would be a new interpretation of the contemporary world of philosophical problems from the resources supplied by the Aristotelian tradition.

But many thinkers, East Asian as well as Western, have thought that Chinese philosophy is so intimately related to East Asian cultures as to be portable into the philosophic context of Western cultures only with bad faith. Daoism, interpreted in a superficial mystical way, might pass over easily, but its underlying assumption of the oneness of the cosmos is unique to the East Asian sensibility, many think. Confucianism is too dependent on East Asian family structures and a unified imperial model of human society to be able to address problems in the Western context in which family and social assumptions are so different.

Contrary to this, I argue that the classic ancient thinkers within the traditions we now identify as Confucianism and Daoism thought and wrote in serious, conscious dialectical tension with their culture. In the period of the Warring States their thought ran against the grain of the prevailing assumptions about family and social life, and about the cosmos and what is important within it. For authority they did not appeal to the common sense of their time but to the legendary sage emperors and culture heroes. They took their ideals of virtue, proper behavior, attunement to the real natures of things, spontaneity, and whatever fulfills the trinity of Heaven, Earth, and the Human to be countercultural. Their philosophical social projects of schools of learning and ritual, on the one hand, and of sagely practice to accomplish one's ends without competition against the grain of the Dao, on the other, they took to be political acts, revolutionary in intent in their social context.

Contemporary problems in the West are very unlike any of those the ancient classic Chinese philosophers envisioned. Because my colleagues, including Tu Weiming and John Berthrong, and I have deliberated about what Confucianism might mean in the context of our late-modern Western city, Boston, we have been called, only half in jest, "Boston Confucians." In contrast to the China of the Warring States period, our Boston is urban, not rural; modern in its social diversification and division of labor, not a peasant economy; meritocratic in its distribution of jobs, wealth, and honors, not hereditary; highly mobile in its family structures, not fixed in stable kinship groups; extremely diverse in its ethnic cultures representing all civilizations of the world, not relatively homogeneous with barbarians on the fringes; democratic in its political ideals, not feudal; highly connected with other parts of the world in its communications and economy and filled with institutions of higher education that draw people from around the globe, not relatively isolated or assuming itself to be the center of things; and modern scientific in its assumptions about the size and nature of the cosmos and about causation, not given to an ancient cosmology or to correlative thinking. No Western thinker doubts that Platonism and Aristotelianism have something to say about the problems of life in Boston's culture. The question is whether Confucianism and Daoism do. In this book I have argued Yes.

The first point to consider is what is meant by the portability of Chinese philosophy to the late-modern, urban, Western conditions of Boston, or of the late modern world more generally. The way to address this question is to ask what ancient core texts of the Chinese tradition and motifs of thought might usefully be studied in connection with Boston's philosophic issues. This is not merely to ask the factual question of what the ancient texts and motifs are and then to sort which of them have contemporary plausibility. It is rather a normative dialectical question, going back and forth between the ancient literature and contemporary issues, interpreting each in terms of the other and coming to conclusions about what are the truly fruitful ways of identifying and addressing contemporary concerns and what are the best texts of antiquity and of the intervening tradition to help with that.

This kind of question about which ancient and traditional texts are fruitful and illuminating is part of the reconstruction of a tradition that occurs in every epoch. The most obvious case in the Chinese tradition is Zhu Xi's selection of the Four Books out of all the other ancient texts to be normative for ancient Confucianism and the exam system for many centuries after. But the Han dynasty debates between the New Writings and the Ancient Writings schools involved the same kind of reconstruction of a tradition so that the tradition could live again, that is, be transported as a vital philosophy, into the conditions of the Han. In the Tang dynasty, Li Ao and Han Yu effected a reconstruction of the Confucian tradition against the threats of Daoism and Buddhism by focusing on *The Great Learning, The Doctrine of the Mean*, and the *I Ching*, which remained singularly important in later Sung Neo-Confucianism, and by insisting that Mencius rather than Xunzi was the correct transmitter of Confucianism. Wang Yangming's criticism of Zhu Xi's editing of *The Great Learning* was another debate about what should be carried down as important in the tradition. Those debates intensified as Chinese philosophy became aware of Western thought in the eighteenth century and later. Of course, when Chinese thought became influential in Korea, Japan, and Vietnam there were very deep intercultural debates about what could be transported of the ancient texts and motifs, and in what form. After the fact no one doubts that Korean or Japanese Confucianism and Daoism are Confucian or Daoist, albeit variants on Confucianism and Daoism in other contexts. Boston can have its Confucians and Daoists too.

The second question is just what should be carried over for philosophy in Boston. For the sake of brevity I shall sketch a hypothesis for Confucianism alone, although likely the distinction between Confucianism and Daoism that is important in China is not so important in late-modern Boston. My hypothesis is that the portability of Confucianism involves three things: primary scriptures, secondary scriptures, and interpretive contexts.

For the primary scriptures of Boston Confucianism I recommend the Four Books plus the *Xunzi*. Of the Four Books, the *Analects* is important for three main reasons. First, it is the founding text of Confucianism by which all subsequent Confucians identify themselves, albeit differently. Second, the *Analects* provides the major ideas and motifs on which all subsequent Confucian thinkers, including Boston ones, comment and develop in their own ways: humanity, ritual propriety, righteousness, filiality, learning, reciprocity, the importance of developing personal relations that acknowledge differences as well as the equalities of friendship, and a commitment to public life and service. Third, the *Analects* provides a philosophical project for the life of the sage or *chun-tze*, namely intellectual criticism and public leadership, later codified as the life of the scholar-official. In Boston that translates into the life of the public intellectual concerned to build a civic community in the face of much chaos and social disintegration, much as exemplified in the intellectual career of Tu Weiming.

The Doctrine of the Mean is an important primary scripture of Confucianism because it articulates the ancient Confucian model of the self as a polar structure stretching between the inner core of centered readiness to respond to things, that nature given by heaven, and the ten thousand things. People are the same with respect to the unarticulated readiness to respond to things in recognition of their value and worth, but different in respect of their circumstances and the things to which they need to respond. This is a decisively different model of the self from the Western models, and as I shall argue shortly is an improvement. *The Great Learning* is a primary scripture for Confucianism because it details the continuity of excellence and learning from the most interior personal elements to the political and, by extension of being one body with the world, to the cosmos. This provides a powerful alternative to individual versus society distinctions in the West, and distinctions between the human realm and nature. Mencius's book is a primary scripture not only because of its historical importance in Confucianism but because of its theory of the Four Beginnings. That provides an even subtler position than Plato's regarding the innate intuitive but fallible constitution of the mind as responsive to things in their values, according to which they should be deferred to. From the Mencius derives the main theme of *ren* or humanity by which the Confucian tradition can criticize and amend the Western notions of individual and social relations that reach their limit in late-modern society. The *Xunzi* was not on Zhu Xi's list of scriptures but deserves to be in the Boston context because of its subtle theory of ritual as convention.

By the "secondary scriptures" I mean the great writers of the Confucian tradition, for instance, those in Chan's *Source Book* listed in chapter 5 and the great Korean, Japanese, and Vietnamese writers. These are not necessarily important because each has something to contribute to Boston Confucianism, although many do. Rather, they are important for the contemporary understanding of how the Confucian tradition developed and what its options have been. Knowledge of the interpretive contexts of these thinkers, including their

Buddhist and Daoist dialogue partners as well as the historical conditions within which they wrote are also important. The importance is as much to apprehend what is unusual and context changing in the later modern expressions of Confucianism as it is for the proper understanding of the past.

The proof that Confucianism (or Daoism) is worth reconfiguring to address situations such as that in Boston lies only in the fruitful application of it. To indicate what that might be, although of course not to work it out fully, I shall discuss ritual, ethics, and a definition of the self in terms of orientation.

RITUAL, AGAIN

As indicated earlier, Herbert Fingarette brought the Confucian notion of ritual to the attention of Western philosophers as a form of performative meaning. His texts were Confucius's own. But it was Xunzi who developed the notion of ritual propriety in a systematic way. The remarkable connection of Xunzi to the West does not lie in any naturalism in metaphysics or an affinity of his claim that human nature is evil with some Christian notion of original sin. It lies rather in the neat congruence of his notion of ritual propriety with the semiotic theory of Charles Peirce, the founder of pragmatism.

For Peirce, the world is experienced through signs, and his semiotic or sign-theory elaborates how signs *refer*, how they lie defined within *systems of meaning*, and how they are *interpreted*. Interpretation is the activity of engaging the world with our purposes, suffering its pains and enjoying its qualities, all as shaped by signs. The signs themselves have meaning within semiotic systems, which include our culture and languages. Indeed, there are many semiotic systems that we employ, some nested, others overlapping, many dependent on particular circumstances, and not always consistent. What distinguishes Peirce's semiotic from the European tradition associated with Saussure is that, whereas the European theory takes the interpretation of texts as the paradigm case of interpretation, Peirce's theory takes the interpretation of nature or reality as the paradigm. For the European theory, interpretation is primarily a cognitive enterprise. For Peirce, it is the shaping of the very act of living. So whereas British analytic philosophy can believe that philosophy is primarily concerned with words, and the Continental postmodernists can believe that the world itself is all a text, Peirce's pragmatism asserts that all the world is nature and that part of nature is systems of signs shaping human interpretive engagements. Human interpretations are habits that become objectified for consciousness only in circumstances that make us self-reflective.

This connects with Xunzi in the ways discussed earlier. For Xunzi and other Confucians, ritual propriety, *li*, means conventional signs, and rituals lie along a broad spectrum. At the one end of the spectrum are the obvious court rituals and other explicit rites and ceremonies. Moving down the spectrum are matters of etiquette and interpersonal manners, stylized greetings and conventions for behavior in leisure and business, such as table manners. Then there are formalized relationships such as the conventions determining how to treat one's elders, one's friends, and one's associates; there are formalized relationships for how to treat functionaries in the post office, for instance, or for how the police are to treat persons who might be criminals. Within families and friendships, ritual conventions provide the initial frame within which those relationships can be individuated and deepened beyond their formal structures. Further on down the spectrum are social roles that are learned and played at various stages of life. These roles are not only functional to organize social life but crucial for persons forming a sense of their own identity in relation to others and learning how to distinguish between the roles they play and themselves as players, a distinction that is different in different cultural contexts.

Moving down the spectrum lie what I call "institution exercising behavior." Formal social systems such as those of the law or the economy, or political life, can have verbal directions and constitutions; but the systems actually exist only in their exercise, when people act according to them and have the habits to do so. Their exercise is thus the set of social habits people learn and according to which they act. Informal systems such as those of family life, and of friendship, also exist not in their description or in their directions but in their habitual exercise. The social habits that constitute institutions such as family and friendship are learned conventions, first rather general and then particularized.

Down the spectrum past institution-exercising rituals are languages and semiotic systems of gestures and body language, and the explicit signs of communication in public life such as pictures, traffic signs, advertising presentations, and the like. There are, of course, many such systems and I do not mean to suggest that their relations are explained by locating them on this spectrum of rituals. For purposes of the present point, however, by ritual at this place on the spectrum I mean those signs and systems of signs by which human intent can be communicated.

At the far end of the spectrum from rites and court rituals are what I call "penumbral conventions," that is conventions that are learned and that are culturally diverse but that are not used as signs to convey intent. To understand this point we can recall that the human body-mind is extraordinarily flexible and underdetermined by nature. For instance, the human hips are so flexible that a person can stand with the feet aligned in any position along a wide arc from pointing the toes toward each other to pointing away. Yet in order to stand, some convention is necessary to determine an appropriate habitual foot placement. Penumbral conventions apply not only to gross movement but to eye contact, body posture, how close one stands to another, and many other aspects of life. These conventions might become signs within a meaningful semiotic system, as when one deliberately adopts another's style of moving in order to create feelings of affinity, or uses eye contact to convey respect or insult; but penumbral conventions do not have to bear intentional meaning, just give human behavior definition.

Here is where Xunzi is so important. He argued, for instance in his essay on nature discussed in chapter 3 and elsewhere, that Heaven and Earth endow human beings with a basic biological constitution that includes feelings such as desire, aversion, delight, and so forth, sensibilities such as those of the ear, eye, and nose, and also a native capacity to govern or control ourselves. But the basic endowment from nature does not determine that the feelings are responsive to the appropriate objects, and so babies desire things that are dangerous; we can hear, see, and smell, but nature does not tell us what is important to attend to; and how can we exercise control over ourselves if we do not understand our environment and what is good and bad? The human natural endowment requires conventions, the entire spectrum of ritual conventions, in order for the natural human capacities to fulfill themselves together. Human beings cannot be human without the ritual conventions. The classic Confucian motif for this is that the human, meaning the conventions that make up civilization, is required for the fulfillment of Heaven and Earth.

Important as Peirce was for improving upon the European semiotic theory of interpreting texts with his semiotics of engagement with reality, and clear as his analysis was of the reference, meaning, and interpretation of signs, the Confucian tradition stemming from Xunzi is far subtler at laying out the levels of human and social existence at which ritual is required. Therefore, a late-modern Confucian working to civilize Boston will integrate the Confucian theory of ritual with the pragmatic theory of signs for a vastly more subtle way of understanding human reality. As a side effect, this ties the Western tradition of philosophy that feeds into Peirce's pragmatism to the Chinese tradition that relates to ritual, opening connections for investigation that might otherwise not be noticed.

ETHICS, AGAIN

The adoption of the Confucian theory of ritual in connection with pragmatic semiotic theory into the later modern setting has immediate consequences for ethical thinking. Ritual has an important normative dimension, despite its conventionality. Confucians have traditionally emphasized a difference between civilized people and the barbarians. Civilized people enjoy sophisticated rituals that allow sexual reproduction to become rich family life where love and deference are learned and exercised, and people come to be fully human; they have rituals that turn crude requirements for cooperation into participatory public life and government; they have rituals that turn engagements with strangers into friendships. Barbarians are deficient in these rituals, and so have very crude family life, strongman politics, and no deep friendships that surmount suspicion, or so the Confucians thought. Indeed, the trouble with the Warring States period was that China seemed to be slipping into barbarism and needed to reestablish the old civilizing rituals. The rituals, of course, are conventional. It does not matter whether friends bow, shake hands, or hug; there are many styles of rich family life, many alternative conventions for rich public life. What matters is whether there are some adequate rituals in place, and consistently enough organized, that rich civilized life is possible.

Attention to the normative dimension of ritual opens an opportunity for ethical reflection rather new for the West and for late-modern cultures. The question to ask of a particular situation is whether appropriate rituals are in place so that the obviously desirable values are possible, the values of humaneness in human relations, justice and productivity in economic activity, fairness in the law, deep creativity and imagination in the arts, and so forth. If no appropriate rituals are in place, then no matter how much we might want those things, they are impossible because they exist only in the exercise of the rituals that shape them.

The particular rituals that might have been desirable for Warring States China doubtless would be wholly inappropriate for Boston. Boston needs rituals for riding the subway with people from different ethnic groups whose manners, noise, smells, and sense of social distance are different and perhaps offensive to one another. Boston needs rituals for humanizing economic life where people move from job to job. Boston needs rituals for supporting nuclear families and single-parent families that might be far from any extended kinship group. Boston needs rituals for expressing and celebrating the meaning of life in a cosmos far vaster and less personal than that of ancient China. Boston needs rituals for deliberating in public life about the conditions for social existence when the participants in public discourse represent vastly different cultures, often cultures with a history of opposition and oppression. Boston needs rituals for integrating the fast pace of technological change and the rapidly shifting array of information with the institutions and times for deep considered reflection. Boston needs rituals for reconciling hard work in a meritocratic economy with leisure for enjoying life. Confucius, Mencius, and Xunzi had no need for any of these rituals.

Boston Confucian ethics thus has an opportunity for two new tasks. On the one hand, critical analysis of the rituals that now do obtain is a rich source for understanding what is unjust, wicked, or impoverishing about late-modern urban society. Families break down, for instance, because we have no adequate family rituals that relate to the demands of the modern economy. Civic life breaks down in a culturally pluralistic society because we do not have rituals that can maintain adequate tolerance under the strains of social inequalities for interacting respectfully with other cultures of which one does not approve. And so forth. Analysis of the failures of ritual gets at a dimension of problems usually hidden when we look at specific acts, social conditions, and policies.

The other side of the Boston ethical project is to help develop new and more nearly adequate rituals for personal and social life. This is far harder than the critical analytical side. Sometimes rituals can be brought to permeate society through consciousness raising; sometimes through legislation. But most usually, new ritual behaviors are established the old Confucian way, by the modeling of the emperor; in Boston, however, the persuasive models are more likely to be athletes and professors than politicians, with athletes having the greater influence. It should be remembered that rituals for making possible an ethical and civilized society are not limited to social behaviors of the sort illustrated here, but involve a dense nesting of rituals along the spectrum from penumbral conventions through habitual manners to the explicit court rituals by which athletes from competing teams show respect and deference to one another.

By no means is the ritual dimension the whole of ethics. It does not decide the moral value of specific acts, nor does it direct much by way of social or governmental policy. It does not solve contests of geographic hegemony among nations, nor determine how to balance the need for industrial development with the need to respect the environment. The concern for ritual is directed at making personally and socially possible certain civilized levels of living that might be desirable and obligatory. This is by no means a small consideration for contemporary ethics.

ORIENTATION AND THE SELF

The final point by which I mean to illustrate the importance of Chinese philosophy for the contemporary global philosophical conversation has to do with developing an adequate understanding of the self for contemporary society. Traditional Western conceptions are criticized for being too individualistic, which stems from the root metaphor of selves being substances that relate to others only as external other substances, or too inhuman and mechanical as in Marxist scientific materialism. Traditional East Asian conceptions are criticized for subordinating persons as merely instrumental to group welfare, and hence unable to appreciate human rights, or for dissolving persons into flows of nature that miss what is distinctive about human beings. This is not the place to rehearse or assess these criticisms, only to note that they and others suggest that some imagination is needed to reconceive the human self in community with others and nature. What follows is a suggestion for part of that project that derives from both Daoist and Confucian themes but most particularly from the conception in *The Doctrine of the Mean* mentioned earlier, that the self is a structured continuum between a centered readiness to respond and the ten thousand things.

Let us suppose, by hypothesis, that the self is an organism, with a human biological endowment interacting with its environment (to use John Dewey's terminology), that is given human conventional (ritual) shape by the recursive structure by which it harmonizes its orientations. That is a formula that I shall now explain, beginning with the notion of orientation.

Orientation is how a self comports itself or takes up a stance toward some level or dimension of reality. All specific actions take place within the habits formed by our orientations. Xunzi, again in the essay on nature, pointed out that the rotation of the heavens is something about which we can do nothing but admire and contemplate relative to the scale of our own place in the universe. The rotation of the seasons, however, is something to which we orient ourselves by the dense tissue of activities involved in agricultural peasant culture, an orientation learned, often unconsciously, through imitation and direct participation in seasonal activities. In between, Xunzi noted, are irregular anomalies such as floods and droughts, and barbarians suddenly appearing over the hill. Orientation to these irregularities is where good government comes in to plan ahead, offer emergency relief, and muster the defenses. Orientations are much more diverse than that, however. We have orientations to our families, and to each family member, and those orientations change as life progresses. We have orientations generally to our historical and political situation and specifically to our own economic welfare. We have orientations to our workplace and to the opportunities for leisure. Most intimately we have orientations to our own bodies and to our particular careers.

Orientations are made up of learned ritual conventions. Most are picked up unconsciously as we are socialized into our culture's rituals. But some orientations are problematic, as when we cannot get along with our family or find the workplace intolerable for our personal needs. Other times, our culture might not have an orientation that it ought to have. For instance, we are only now becoming aware of the fact that human societies as well as individuals should have been oriented with greater respect to their natural environment. Who knows what else is important for human beings to be oriented toward but of which we are now innocent?

The point of an orientation is to discern the important or humanly relevant nature of its object and to comport human life appropriately toward it. The ritual structure of an orientation includes both the discernment and the comportment. Accurate discernment is itself a problem for finding adequate orientations, and appropriate comportment is another. But the most interesting problem from the standpoint of understanding the self is that the objects of orientation do not fit together well in the ways they are best discerned. We think about the cosmic realities, the rotations of the heavens, in the mathematical language of modern physics and the poetic language of the mystics. We are oriented to daily life in terms of the calendars of our jobs; only a few of us are farmers whose orientation is determined by the rotation of the seasons, whereas most readers of this book are academics for whom the academic semester system determines life's timings. We employ highly determined semiotic systems to take up orientations on our families, yet other systems for orienting to civic duties, and yet others again for orientation to the historic position of our group. Orientations to our own bodies and careers involve different systems from all these. The systems of signs by which we articulate all these different orientations might seem as if they were connectable by a super system. But they are not. Nineteenth-century Western science had the ideal of reducing all those orientations to the language of mathematical science, an ideal that blossomed and faded with the Encyclopedia of Unified Science movement. The attempt to impose any one language or system of signs on all destroys genuine orientation in those areas where the language blocks real discernment. The symbols of mathematical science only obfuscate the project of taking up an orientation on our mortality and the significance of our legacy to family and culture. The correlative thinking codified in the Han dynasty and again in Shao Yung's work was an ancient way of attempting to systematize different representative structures of orientations, no more successful nowadays than mathematical science. We live disjointed, fragmented lives because our orientations are not commensurate.

Or rather, persons inherit partly and partly work out for themselves patterns of harmonization of their orientations. The objects of orientation are often not static things but processes, such as one's growing family, or career, or historical position. So the patterns of harmonization need constantly to be shifting and accommodating changes. Rather than speak of the structure of a self as a fixed pattern of harmonization, it is better to speak of a self as maintaining poise in balancing all together. The poise has a dynamic or fluid content, but is always singular, singular and moving.

Suppose the self, then, is a continuum beginning from the inner center of responsiveness, that is, the intentionality of orientation, functioning specifically to take on orientations in body and mind to the close things of the intimate body, to things and persons of direct contact such as family, friends, and coworkers, and then to social situations, historical places, nature, and the vast cosmos—the ten thousand things each with its own rhythm, *dao*, and discernible grain. The core inner responsiveness, Mencius's topic, might well be the same in us all insofar as it is by itself. But it is never by itself; it is always expressed in the orientations to our particular bodies, and places in the universe, extending as far as our own particular perspective on the heavens. The orientations are all shaped by ritual conventions, Xunzi's topic.

In this conception of the self there is no fixed boundary of the self, as Western philosophy sometimes has supposed there must be. Rather, the boundaries are set in each instance by the nature of the things toward which a person is oriented. We are individual persons in orientation to the family within which we play specific roles relative to others. We are our family, however, insofar as the family plays a role in the larger community. We can say with Zhangzhai that "Heaven is my father and Earth is my mother, and even such a small creature as I finds an intimate place in their midst."[1] But we can also say with Wang Yangming, commenting on *The Great Learning*, that the great person, manifesting the clear character, forms "one body with Heaven, Earth, and the myriad things."[2] It depends on what the orientation is toward.

In the theory of orientations, the boundaries of the self are functions of differing orientations, and the continuity of the self has to do not with an underlying fixed essence or character but with the history of the person's poise efforts, with the ongoing shifting harmonization of the changing things to which the person must take up or correct orientations. How one is oriented, and how one relates that orientation to other orientations, is part of a person's unfolding essence.

But it is only part. Orientations set the conditions for specific actions but do not wholly determine them. People are essentially constituted in part also by the specific things they do and the moral character deriving from them. Life is filled both with specific actions and with the accidents for which no orientation is preparation. Western philosophy has been rather good at defining the self in terms of specific actions and also in terms of the vicissitudes of accident and fate. It has not had good categories, however, for defining those elements of the self that consist in orientations to the ten thousand different things and the processes of harmonizing those orientations. As a consequence it has not been able to articulate well the self's boundaries or many of its kinds of continuity. For this, the themes of orientation and poise that come from the Daoist and Confucian aesthetic, from the Confucian theory of ritual, and from the conception of the self in *The Doctrine of the Mean* are helpful additions. In this form they do not at all interfere with the Western scientific insights into the self that otherwise seem to delegitimate the prescientific Chinese conceptions.

The conclusion to this chapter, indeed to this book, is open-ended to the point of being disconcerting. Surely nothing has been *proved* about the validity of Chinese philosophy when measured in the context of English-speaking philosophers. I have provided some historical points about how Chinese philosophy has become known in the Western philosophical conversation, and have described some projects that are based on appropriating and extending Chinese philosophical ideas. The projects of Hall and Ames, of Tu, of Cheng, and of Wu are not the only ones that might have been mentioned, although that array illustrates the diversity of Chinese philosophy in English. My own philosophical project is a humble, and likely poorly digested, amalgam of Chinese and Western ideas for addressing current needs.

The chief conclusion to draw, I believe, is that a world philosophical conversation has been started within which European and Chinese philosophical traditions are major participants. Looking to the future, however, the learned understanding and appreciation of all the great civilizations' traditions of philosophy will be required of all participants in the world conversation. We are privileged to live at the verge of that intercivilizational discourse.

Notes

PREFACE

1. *Boston Confucianism: Portable Tradition in the Late-Modern World* (Albany, NY: State University of New York Press, 2000).

1. A CONFUCIAN PROGRAM

1. Translated by Wing-tsit Chan in his *Source Book in Chinese Philosophy* (Princeton, NJ: Princeton University Press, 1963), p. 463.

2. This argument about harmonies as having essential and conditional features has been made out in detail in my *God the Creator* (Chicago, IL: University of Chicago Press, 1968; reprint edition with a new introduction, Albany, NY: State University of New York Press, 1992). It is related explicitly to Confucian concerns in my *The Tao and the Daimon* (Albany, NY: State University of New York Press, 1982), chapters 6–9.

3. These Confucian developments in contemporary terms are detailed in my *Recovery of the Measure* (Albany, NY: State University of New York Press, 1989), chapters 5–8.

4. One thinks of the work of John H. Berthrong, for instance, in his *All Under Heaven* (Albany, NY: State University of New York Press, 1994) and *Concerning Creativity: A Comparison of Chu Hsi, Whitehead, and Neville* (Albany, NY: State University of New York Press, 1998).

5. See my *Recovery of the Measure*, especially chapters 9–12.

6. For citing Peirce, see note 5 in chapter 2.

7. I develop this theory of judgment and truth in *Recovery of the Measure*, chapters 1–4, 13–16.

8. For a detailed argument for this conception of theory, see my *Normative Cultures* (Albany, NY: State University of New York Press, 1995), chapters 1–4.

9. See *Normative Cultures*, chapters 5–8.

10. See, for instance, *The Democracy of the Dead: Dewey, Confucius, and the Hope for Democracy in China*, by David L. Hall and Roger T. Ames (LaSalle, IL: Open Court,

1999) and *John Dewey, Confucius, and Global Philosophy*, by Joseph Grange (Albany, NY: State University of New York Press, 2004). My own argument to this effect is in *Boston Confucianism: Portable Tradition in the Late-Modern World* (Albany, NY: State University of New York Press, 2000).

11. The social theory sketched here has been discussed in more detail in my *The Puritan Smile* (Albany, NY: State University of New York Press, 1987).

2. THE SIGNIFICANCE OF CONFUCIAN VALUES

1. The original lecture began with the following words, which contextualize much of what follows: "Honored Colleagues: I am grateful for the invitation to address the topic of the contemporary significance of Confucian values in Korea, one of the major centers of classic Confucian thought. Everyone appreciates the gentle irony that you have turned to me, obviously not an East Asian, to address the topic. The invitation itself makes the point that the contemporary significance of Confucian values is not for the culture of Confucianism alone. I represent the form of Confucianism whose significance is for Boston, my city in the United States, and for Western society more generally. Doubtless, the reason for the invitation lies in the title of my book, *Boston Confucianism: Portable Tradition in the Late-Modern World.*" The lecture was given at a conference in Seoul honoring Yulgok sponsored by Hallym University on February 25, 2005.

2. See John Dewey's *The Public and Its Problems* (New York: Henry Holt, 1927), in *John Dewey: The Later Works, 1925–1953*, vol. 2: 1925–1927, edited by Jo Ann Boydston (Carbondale, IL: Southern Illinois University Press, 1984), pp. 235–372. For a brilliant study of Dewey and Confucianism, see David L. Hall and Roger T. Ames's *The Democracy of the Dead: Dewey, Confucius, and the Hope for Democracy in China* (LaSalle, IL: Open Court, 1999).

3. See chapter 3 for a more detailed analysis of Xunzi's texts and theories.

4. The essay on Nature is chapter 17 in Xunzi's collected works. The standard English translation is John Knoblock's *Xunzi: A Translation and Study of the Complete Works*, vol. 3, bks. 17–32 (Stanford, CA: Stanford University Press, 1994), pp. 3ff. For an intriguing study of the point made on page 00, see Edward J. Machle's *Nature and Heaven in the Xunzi: A Study of the* Tian Lun (Albany, NY: State University of New York Press, 1993).

5. Peirce's discussions of semiotics run throughout his work. See *The Collected Papers of Charles Sanders Peirce*, edited by Charles Hartshorne and Paul Weiss, volumes 1–6 (Cambridge, MA: Harvard University Press, 1931–1935) and volumes 7–8, edited by Arthur W. Burks (Cambridge, MA: Harvard University Press, 1958). Hereafter in this book I shall cite the *Collected Papers of Charles Sanders Peirce* plus the volume and paragraph or page number. I discuss Peirce's overall philosophy in relation to signs in *The Highroad Around Modernism* (Albany, NY: State University of New York Press, 1992), chapter 1.

6. Wang was once directed by the emperor to pacify rebellious tribesmen and did so through education (as well as military control).

7. See David L. Hall's *The Civilization of Experience* (New York, NY: Fordham University Press, 1973) for an analysis of Whitehead's theory of epitomes of civilization.

8. Samuel P. Huntington, *The Clash of Civilizations and the Remaking of World Order* (New York, NY: Simon and Schuster, 1996).

9. Zhu Xi's "Treatise on *Jen*" is in Wing-tsit Chan's *A Source Book of Chinese Philosophy* (Princeton, NJ: Princeton University Press, 1963). "The moral qualities of the mind of Heaven and Earth are four: origination, flourish, advantages, and firmness. And the principle of origination unites and controls them all.... Therefore in the mind of man there are also four moral qualities—namely, *jen*, righteousness, propriety, and wisdom—and *jen* embraces them all," p. 594.

3. RITUAL IN XUNZI

1. I am pleased to thank T. C. Kline III for many helpful suggestions and criticisms of an earlier draft of this article. For a general narrative of the Confucian story by a scholar sympathetic to Xunzi see John H. Berthrong's *Transformations of the Confucian Way* (Boulder, CO: Westview Press/HarperCollins, 1998), especially the introduction and chapter 7.

2. Confucianism that developed through what might be called the Mencian line has indeed become a major player in the global philosophic conversation. Perhaps this is because of the increasing importance of the students of Chinese expatriates in Taiwan in the second half of the twentieth century such as Mou Zhongsan, who carefully related Western philosophy to the Confucian tradition interpreted through Mencius and Zhu Xi/Wang Yangming. I discuss this line of interpretation, compared with a reinterpretation giving Xunzi a central place, in *Boston Confucianism* (Albany, NY: State University of New York Press, 2000), especially chapters 1, 3–5.

3. John Knoblock, *Xunzi: A Translation and Study of the Complete Works*, vol. 1, bks. 1–6 (1988), vol. 2, bks. 7–16 (1990), vol. 3, bks. 17–32 (1994) (Stanford, CA: Stanford University Press). References to Xunzi's writings will be to this edition and by book and chapter; thus the reference to 17.3a in note 8 is to book 17, which is in volume 3, and chapter 3a. See also *Virtue, Nature, and the Moral Agency in the* Xunzi, edited by T. C. Kline III and Philip J. Ivanhoe (New York, NY: Hackett, 2000). An early version of the present chapter is scheduled for production in a follow-up volume edited by Kline. An outstanding monograph on Xunzi that figures in my reflections here is Edward J. Machle's *Nature and Heaven in the Xunzi: A Study of the* Tian Lun (Albany, NY: State University of New York Press, 1993).

4. *Xunzi*, vol. 3, p. 52.

5. Ibid., p. 49.

6. See my *Normative Cultures*, pp. 166ff.; *Boston Confucianism*, pp. 123–125.

7. See his *Nature and Heaven in the Xunzi*, especially pp. 90–104.

8. *Xunzi* 17.3a.

9. Paul Weiss's *Privacy* (Carbondale, IL: Southern Illinois University Press, 1983) is the most thorough and sensitive treatment I know of the learned character of sensation and taste; see especially its introduction and first two chapters.

10. *Xunzi* 17.2a. Xunzi might have been the originator of this idea, although some earlier scholars had dated the Great Learning and the Doctrine of the Mean prior to Xunzi. The idea itself has frequently been likened to Christian ideas of the Trinity, hence the common translation. The notion could just as well be translated as the "triad" of Heaven, Earth, and the Human. Surely differences in the agendas of Confucians and Christians exist regarding the Confucian notions and the Christian Father, Son, and Holy Spirit. By "Earth" Confucians never meant anything as specifically epitomizing and paradigmatic for ways of life as Christians have meant by Jesus. Nevertheless, Confucians have closely related categories for articulating the epitomes of humanity that need to be appropriated and internalized the way Christians talk about attending to the "mind of Christ." Moreover, the metaphysics of more than one primordial principle is something that Confucians and Christians have in common. The term "Trinity" therefore demarcates a common ground regarding a problematic that runs from obvious phenomena to deep metaphysics.

11. *Xunzi* 4.10.

12. *Xunzi* 17.3a.

13. See Terrence W. Deacon's *The Symbolic Species: The Co-Evolution of Language and the Brain* (New York, NY: Norton, 1997) for a somewhat speculative but excellent summary and explanatory theory of the biological evolution of thinking. It is closely related to Peirce's theory of semiotics, to which I shall relate Xunzi's theory later.

14. Peirce was the greatest of the American philosophers, heir to the New England traditions of Transcendentalism, science, and the wilderness experience, and to the dialectic initiated by Emerson of distinguishing the American from the European traditions of thought. Those not acquainted with his thought should see Joseph Brent's *Charles Sanders Peirce: A Life* (Bloomington, IN: Indiana University Press, 1993). The standard edition of Peirce's philosophical writings is cited in chapter 2, note 5. Peirce wrote on semiotics and signs in nearly all of his papers; the greatest concentration is in volume 2 of the *Collected Papers*, especially book II, "Speculative Grammar." The greatest concentration of his discussions of pragmatism is in volume 5; volume 6 focuses on his metaphysics and contains the great paper, "A Neglected Argument for the Reality of God," that combines his best statement of semiotics, theory construction, and pragmatism (and a little theology). A briefer but more available collection of Peirce's philosophical papers is *The Essential Peirce: Selected Philosophical Writings, Volume 1 (1867–1893) and Volume 2 (1893–1913)*, edited by Nathan Houser and others (Bloomington, IN: Indiana University Press, 1992, 1998). These two volumes stress the chronological development of Peirce's ideas about semiotics. A good general introduction to Peirce, stressing his semiotics and metaphysics, is Robert S. Corrington's *An*

Introduction to C. S. Peirce: Philosopher, Semiotician, and Ecstatic Naturalist (Lanham, MD: Rowman and Littlefield, 1993). See also Corrington's *A Semiotic Theory of Theology and Philosophy* (Cambridge, UK: Cambridge University Press, 2000). For more specialized studies see Vincent Colapietro's *Peirce's Approach to the Self: A Semiotic Perspective on Human Subjectivity* (Albany, NY: State University of New York Press, 1989). On the metaphysical connection of thought and action, see Michael L. Raposa's *Peirce's Philosophy of Religion* (Bloomington, IN: Indiana University Press, 1989). My own integrated interpretation of Peirce is stated briefly in *The Highroad Around Modernism* (Albany, NY: State University of New York Press, 1992), chapter 1.

15. On the relation of Peirce's semiotics to that of Saussure and Husserl, see Jacques Derrida's *Of Grammatology*, translated by Gayatri Chakravorty Spivak (Baltimore, MD: The Johns Hopkins University Press, 1976), pp. 44–52. Derrida consistently misunderstands Peirce's emphasis on science and the engagement with nature, and reduces his semiotics to what registers in the European tradition. Umberto Eco's *A Theory of Semiotics* (Bloomington, IN: Indiana University Press, 1979) is better, discussing Peirce throughout; Eco distinguishes between codes and sign production, noting Peirce's emphasis on the process of forming and deforming signs, but still downplaying the interaction with natural reality that shapes the process.

16. *Xunzi* 19.5b, 9a.

17. Do *not* see *John Dewey: Lectures in China, 1919–1920*, translated and edited by Robert W. Clopton and Tsuin-Chen Ou (Honolulu, HI: The University Press of Hawaii, 1973), which shows Dewey at his scientistic worst. But *do* see *The Democracy of the Dead: Dewey, Confucius, and the Hope for Democracy in China*, by Roger T. Ames and David L. Hall (LaSalle, IL: Open Court, 1999), which brilliantly relates Dewey's thought to the themes of continuities of thought and action, and of individual and communal experience, in Confucianism.

18. *Xunzi* 19.4b.

19. See *Thinking Through Confucius*, by Roger T. Ames and David L. Hall (Albany, NY: State University of New York Press, 1987), for a thorough discussion of correlative thinking.

20. For Xunzi on the rectification of names, see *Xunzi* 22.

21. See Chad Hansen, *A Daoist Theory of Chinese Thought: A Philosophical Interpretation* (New York, NY: Oxford University Press, 1992). The proper employment of Peirce's distinction between iconic and indexical reference is a vast help in clarifying much fustian confusion about Chinese aesthetic sensitivity versus Western propensities for scientific description. Although the claim that the East is sensitive and the West utilitarian is an old cliché, something like that point has been developed with extraordinary subtlety by the late David L. Hall and his Sinologically expert colleague, Roger T. Ames. See the adroit discussion in Hall and Ames's *Thinking Through Confucius*, especially chapter 3. See also their contrast between Chinese and Western cultures in *Anticipating China* (Albany, NY: State University of New York Press, 1993).

22. See John Searle's *Speech Acts* (Cambridge, UK: Cambridge University Press, 1969).

23. Wang Yangming is the representative of Confucianism most noted for stressing the continuity of thought and action, though the theme is expressed one way or another in most Confucians. It is no accident that Antonio Cua, who wrote the fine study *The Unity of Knowledge and Action: A Study in Wang Yang-ming's Moral Psychology* (Honolulu, HI: The University Press of Hawaii, 1982) is also the author of *Ethical Argumentation: A Study in Hsun Tzu's Moral Epistemology* (Honolulu, HI: The University Press of Hawaii, 1985). See also his fine *Moral Vision and Tradition: Essays in Chinese Ethics* (Washington, DC: The Catholic University of America Press, 1998) for his reading of the breadth of the Chinese tradition, including Daoist sources. Other basic studies of Wang Yangming stressing the continuity of knowledge and action are Julia Ching's *To Acquire Wisdom: The Way of Wang Yang-ming* (New York, NY: Columbia University Press, 1976) and Tu Weiming's *Neo-Confucian Thought in Action: Wang Yang-ming's Youth (1472–1509)* (Berkeley, CA: University of California Press, 1976). See also Philip J. Ivanhoe's *Ethics in the Confucian Tradition* (Atlanta, GA: Scholars Press, 1990; reprint edition, Hackett) and *Confucian Moral Self Cultivation* (New York, NY: Peter Lang, 1993), chapter 3. True, Wang and his tradition identified with Mencius rather than Xunzi. So the anachronistic reading of "continuity of thought and action" from its slogan status with Wang to Xunzi is doubly precarious. It surely is anachronistic to transfer it from its sixteenth-century slogan status to pre-Han antiquity. But it applies to Xunzi just as well. He cannot be read out of the Confucian camp on this issue!

24. *Xunzi* 19.11. See also book 20.

25. *Xunzi* 18.1.

26. *Xunzi* 19.1a.

27. *Xunzi* 20.1.

28. *Xunzi* 23.

29. *Xunzi* 4.10.

30. *Xunzi* 1a.

31. He argued this in the Republic, especially books 2–4, in distinguishing the functions of the spirited (aggressive) from the appetitive and rational parts of soul. Nietzsche picked up the theme in the second essay of *The Genealogy of Morals*.

32. Tu Weiming's *Centrality and Commonality: An Essay on Confucian Religiousness* (revised and enlarged edition; Albany, NY: State University of New York Press, 1989) is a fine study of filiality as the central virtue for creating a fiduciary community, explicating the text of the *Chongyong*. Tu interprets filiality as the learning of *ren*, humaneness. Tu's own book, however, can be interpreted as the learning of family rituals—sign-shaped behaviors—relating parents, children, siblings, friends, figures and institutions of public life, and the emperor so that *ren* is possible and itself learned for expression in civilized relations. This is the interpretive take on Tu's North-of-the-Charles Boston Confucianism from South of the Charles; see his foreword to my *Boston Confucianism* (Albany, NY: State University of New York Press, 2000), pp. xvi–xix.

33. *Xunzi* 20, especially 4–5.

34. See the analogous points made by Joel Kupperman and David Wong in their essays, "Xunzi: Morality as Psychological Constraint" and "Xunzi and Zhuangzi," respectively, Kline and Ivanhoe, *Moral Agency in the* Xunzi.

35. *Xunzi* 23, 1b. Knoblock follows the traditional translation from Burton Watson and Wing-tsit Chan, for instance of *e* as "evil," in the phrase, "human nature is evil." The English word *evil* has connotations of culpable wickedness that are not entirely appropriate for Xunzi's meaning. Xunzi means something more like human nature being unformed (like unstraightened wood) and disconnected, so that it does bad, selfish things and misses doing the good it could. I have followed Edward Machle's (*Nature and Heaven in the* Xunzi) stress on ritual as providing the connections that allow human nature to be formed and properly engaged. See my defense of Xunzi relative to Mencius in discussing Tu Weiming's position, in *Boston Confucianism*, pp. 102ff.

36. This hypothesis generalizes the thesis of Rene Girard about sacrifice and social guilt. See his *Violence and the Sacred*, translated by Patrick Gregory (Baltimore, MD: The Johns Hopkins University Press, 1977) and *The Scapegoat*, translated by Yvonne Freccero (Baltimore, MD: The Johns Hopkins University Press, 1986). Whereas Girard writes mainly of socially constructed guilt, my hypothesis locates the beginning of guilt in biological evolution, in the biopsychic dance. I have explored it at greater length in the discussion of Levitical and New Testament atonement theories in *Symbols of Jesus: A Christology of Symbolic Engagement* (Cambridge, UK: Cambridge University Press, 2001).

37. *Xunzi* 9.15.

38. *Xunzi* 18.5c; see Knoblock's notes to this discussion of sacrifice.

39. See Knoblock, volume 2, p. 6.

40. On ritual as the external expression of internal humaneness, interpreted in terms of Mencius over against Xunzi, see Tu Weiming's *Humanity and Self-Cultivation: Essays in Confucian Thought* (reprint edition; Boston, MA: Cheng and Tsui, 1998), pp. 5–34. I have responded to his argument on Xunzi's behalf in *Boston Confucianism*, pp. 92–96.

41. *Xunzi* 9.3–5.

42. *Xunzi* 9.7–15.

43. The quoted phrase is from T. C. Kline III, who also comments: "Xunzi doesn't believe that Heaven cares one way or the other about human beings. He has taken on the Daoist impersonal vision of a Heaven that treats all 'like straw dogs'." Xunzi is more consistent than many Confucians in depersonalizing the high god Shangdi into mere Heaven; many Confucians find a highly personal "mandate" in Heaven.

4. DAOIST RELATIVISM, ETHICAL CHOICE, AND NORMATIVE MEASURE

1. For the ancient roots of Daoism, see Norman Girardot's *Myth and Meaning in Early Taoism* (Berkeley, CA: University of California Press, 1983). In some respects the later "medieval" Daoism with its shamanist connections had more in common with the ancient roots than with the classical "philosophic" texts whose intellectual neighbors

are the classical Confucian writings and those of other philosophical schools. My colleague, Livia Kohn, is careful to interpret the later medieval religious writings as having their own integrity, especially in practical matters such as the development of the spiritual adept, but also as building on the Daoist classic philosophic texts. See her *Taoist Mystical Philosophy: The Scripture of the Western Ascension* (Albany, NY: State University of New York Press, 1991) and *Early Chinese Mysticism: Philosophy and Soteriology in the Taoist Tradition* (Princeton, NJ: Princeton University Press, 1992). See also her anthology, *The Taoist Experience* (Albany, NY: State University of New York Press, 1993) for her editorial philosophy of what counts as Daoism.

2. See the discussion of Wu Kuangming in chapter 5. David Hall also is discussed there and elsewhere in this book, but mainly in conjunction with his work with Roger T. Ames in interpreting Confucianism. The slant that Hall brings to that interpretation is an aesthetic orientation that he says is more fully developed in classical Daoism. See his early books, *The Uncertain Phoenix* (New York, NY: Fordham University Press, 1982) and *The Eros of Irony* (Albany, NY: State University of New York Press, 1982), for his interpretation and espousal of Daoism. Ames and Hall together translated the *Daodejing* with an elaborate commentary that treats it as philosophy, albeit with recognition of the recently discovered more ancient texts and in full knowledge of the divergent path of institutional Daoism; see their *Dao De Jing: Making This Life Significant: A Philosophical Translation Featuring the Recently Discovered Bamboo Texts* (New York, NY: Ballantine Books, 2003). As a practitioner of *taijiquan*, I myself have affinities for both lines of Daoist development, combining the philosophical with the project of personal training. The sense of Daoist training I embrace is fully consistent with, and often a part of, Confucian spiritual life. Others relate *taiji* practice directly to the medical tradition of institutionalized Daoism, complete with its supernatural emphasis on the talismanic significance of the numerology in the *taiji* forms.

3. See his *Tao: A New Way of Thinking: A Translation of the* Tao Te Ching *with an Introduction and Commentaries* (New York, NY: Harper and Row, 1975) and *Creativity and Taoism: A Study of Chinese Philosophy, Art, and Poetry* (New York, NY: Harper and Row, 1963).

4. This ideal of grooving on the Dao in philosophical Daoism is quite distinct from religious Daoism, which represents nature in the wild as so dangerous as to require magical and talismanic protections, and as preferable to the strictures of civilized society only because civilization poisons our few powers to flourish in nature.

5. This is paradoxical, of course, in light of *Daodejing*, chapters 18–20, condemning distinctions of the ideal from the actual and efforts at reform. As of this writing the latest word on the relation of the *Daodejing* to the *Zhuangzi* is Wenyu Xie's "Approaching the Dao: From Lao Zi to Zhuang Zi," *Journal of Chinese Philosophy* 27:4 (December 2000), 469–488. The interest of my chapter here is on neither the historical nor the doctrinal relations between those texts but on their potential function as resources for defining a contemporary Daoism in a pluralistic philosophical situation. I differ from Professor Xie in my philosophical reading of the *Daodejing* because I start with the first chapter that distinguishes the unnameable from the nameable Dao instead of chapter 25 that seems to conflate those. The order of chapters I follow, for

the sake of discussion, is the traditional old (but later) one, not the new version based on the recent discovery of a text more ancient than the traditional one.

6. See Robert Allinson's *Chuang-Tzu for Spiritual Transformation: An Analysis of the Inner Chapters* (Albany, NY: State University of New York Press, 1989), chapter 8, for an analysis of types of relativism ascribed to *Zhuangzi* and that also can be ascribed to the *Daodejing*. The chapters of the *Daodejing* cited in the previous note seem to deny the distinction between ideals and actual states of affairs, making all expressions relative. See also Xie, "Approaching the Dao," on relativism, pp. 479ff.

7. A. C. Graham analyzes ancient Daoism and related schools as the "discovery of the subjective," *Disputers of the Tao* (LaSalle, IL: Open Court, 1989), pp. 95ff. His category of subjectivism, of course, is Western. I have analyzed the European fact-value distinction relative to the emergence of modern science in *Reconstruction of Thinking* (Albany, NY: State University of New York Press, 1981), part 1.

8. One of the most original and brilliant Daoist thinkers of our time, David L. Hall—see his *The Uncertain Phoenix* and *Eros and Irony*—has great admiration for Richard J. Rorty who interprets objective value as requiring foundationalism and advocates regarding argument as persuasive conversation, a form of relativism. See Hall's *Richard Rorty: Prophet and Poet of the New Pragmatism* (Albany, NY: State University of New York Press, 1994). Neither Hall nor Rorty is a real relativist, however, both advocating strong programs of social and intellectual change. See Hall's book co-authored with Roger T. Ames *The Democracy of the Dead: Dewey, Confucius, and the Hope for Democracy in China* (LaSalle, IL: Open Court, 1999) and Rorty's *Achieving Our Country* (Cambridge, MA: Harvard University Press, 1998).

9. Translation of Wing-tsit Chan in his *Source Book of Chinese Philosophy* (Princeton, NJ: Princeton University Press, 1963), p. 139.

10. The neatest expression of Peirce's theory of hypothesis is in his often reprinted essay "A Neglected Argument for the Reality of God," say, in *The Collected Papers of Charles Sanders Peirce*, volume 6. See Whitehead's explanation of metaphysics in chapter 1 of *Process and Reality* (corrected edition; New York, NY: Free Press, 1979), corrected by Donald Sherburne and David Griffin. I analyze their positions and detail this conception of metaphysics as hypothesis in *The Highroad Around Modernism* (Albany, NY: State University of New York Press), part 1.

11. See Wangbi's *Commentary on the* Lao Tzu, translated by Ariane Rump in collaboration with Wing-tsit Chan (Honolulu, HI: The University Press of Hawaii/Society for Asian and Comparative Philosophy, 1979), p. 1. This book has Wangbi's whole commentary. See also Chan's *Source Book*, p. 321.

12. On the treatment of ancient texts as core motifs encompassed in outmoded metaphysical theories, needing to be reconnected with metaphysics adequate for the contemporary world, see my *Boston Confucianism*, especially chapters 3, 4, and 6.

13. Stephen W. Hawking, *A Brief History of Time: From the Big Bang to Black Holes* (London, UK: Bantam, 1988), p. 174.

14. On the use of causal language, see "The Notion of Creation in Chinese Thought," chapter 7 in my *The Tao and the Daimon* (Albany, NY: State University of New York Press, 1982).

15. The theory is argued beyond patience in most of my books, most extensively in *God the Creator* (Chicago, IL: University of Chicago Press, 1968; new edition State University of New York Press, 1992) and most closely connected with issues of time and eternity, important in the present chapter, in *Eternity and Time's Flow* (Albany, NY: State University of New York Press, 1993).

16. The nuances of ontological creativity within temporal novelty are best explored within the complex school of twentieth-century process philosophy, deriving from Whitehead; see his *Process and Reality*.

17. See their chapter, "Ultimate Reality: Chinese Religion," in *Ultimate Realities*, edited by Robert Cummings Neville (Albany, NY: State University of New York Press, 2001), pp. 18–19.

18. On the Daoist adept, see the Kohn and Miller article just quoted and also their "Truth in Chinese Religion" in *Religious Truth* and Kohn's "Chinese Religion" in *The Human Condition*, both volumes edited by Robert Cummings Neville (Albany, NY: State University of New York Press, 2001).

19. Chang Chung-yuan, *Creativity and Taoism: A Study of Chinese Philosophy, Art, and Poetry* (New York, NY: Julian Press, 1963).

20. See my *Reconstruction of Thinking*, part 2.

21. *Eros and Irony*, p. 25.

22. A Christian metaphor also can register this, namely the Logos defining determinate realities pulsing with the Holy Spirit that breaks beyond given determinations to new ones. See my explication of this in *Symbols of Jesus: A Christology of Symbolic Engagement* (Cambridge, UK: Cambridge University Press, 2001), chapter 1.

23. Whitehead's metaphysics makes this Daoist point neatly as expressed in his *Adventures of Ideas* (New York, NY: Macmillan, 1933). The adventure in the title is precisely this breaking of order in the quest of new order, and the list of virtues, including zest, in the final part of the book is evocative of Daoist themes.

24. See Grange's *The City*, chapters 3–4 and passim. I have discussed normative measure in *The Cosmology of Freedom* (New Haven, CT: Yale University Press, 1974; new edition Albany, NY: State University of New York Press, 1995), chapter 3.

25. See *Process and Reality*, part 5. My criticism of this idea, based on paradoxes of totality, is in *The Highroad Around Modernism*, chapter 5.

26. Close friends for over thirty years, the late David Hall and I have long wondered why we are so close but opposite. I think he's the Daoist and I the Confucian.

5. CHINESE INFLUENCES IN ENGLISH-SPEAKING PHILOSOPHY

1. Academic philosophy in the United States and Great Britain has frequently, if not always, come to define itself as a special science among other sciences within the

university and has thus drifted toward methods of self-definition and legitimation that distinguish it from other ways and topics of thought that once broadly fell under philosophy; see the various essays in *The Recovery of Philosophy in America: Essays in Honor of John Edwin Smith*, edited by Thomas P. Kasulis and Robert C. Neville (Albany, NY: State University of New York Press, 1997), especially those of George Lucas Jr. and George Allan. Rather than taking the public for philosophical discourse to be defined disciplinarily, many thinkers now are deriving the definition from the scope of the problems that traditionally have fallen under philosophy, in the West and China as well as elsewhere. Sometimes dismissed by academic philosophers, these "public intellectuals" are quite clear that all the world's philosophic traditions are part of the dialogue. This point of view regarding "public intellectuals" is paradigmatically embodied in Confucianism and those influenced by it. See Tu Weiming's *Way, Learning, and Politics: Essays on the Confucian Intellectual* (Singapore: Institute of East Asian Philosophies, 1989). On the importance of taking into account the philosophical traditions of the world's civilizations, see Samuel P. Huntington's *The Clash of Civilizations and the Remaking of World Order* (New York, NY: Simon and Schuster, 1996).

2. For a wonderful account and translations of the texts into English, see Julia Ching and Willard G. Oxtoby's *Moral Enlightenment: Leibniz and Wolff on China* (Nettetal, Netherlands: Steyler Verlag, 1992).

3. See Needham's *Science and Civilization in China*, volume 2 (Cambridge, UK: Cambridge University Press, 1956), pp. 291–293.

4. Wing-tsit Chan, *A Source Book in Chinese Philosophy* (Princeton, NJ: Princeton University Press, 1963).

5. Wing-tsit Chan, *Chu Hsi: New Studies* (Honolulu, HI: University of Hawaii Press, 1989). Percy Bruce's work is *Chu Hsi and His Masters: An Introduction to Chu His and the Sung School of Chinese Philosophy* (London, UK: Probsthain, 1923).

6. Wing-tsit Chan, *Reflections on Things at Hand: The Neo-Confucian Anthology Compiled by Chu Hsi and Lu Tsu Ch'ien* (New York, NY: Columbia University Press, 1967) and *Instructions for Practical Living and Other Neo-Confucian Writings by Wang Yang-Ming* (New York, NY: Columbia University Press, 1963). Even more recent translations of parts of Chu Hsi's work have appeared, such as Daniel K. Gardner's *Learning to Be a Sage: Conversations of Master Chu, Arranged Topically* (Berkeley, CA: University of California Press, 1990).

7. See Hoyt Cleveland Tillman's *Confucian Discourse and Chu Hsi's Ascendency* (Honolulu, HI: University of Hawaii Press, 1992).

8. William Theodore de Bary, *Sources of Chinese Tradition*, two volumes, with Wing-tsit Chan and Burton Watson (New York, NY: Columbia University Press, 1960), *Self and Society in Ming Thought* (New York, NY: Columbia University Press, 1970), and *The Unfolding of Neo-Confucianism* (New York, NY: Columbia University Press, 1970).

9. William Theodore de Bary, *The Liberal Tradition in China* (Hong Kong: The Chinese University Press, 1983).

10. Herrlee G. Creel, *What Is Taoism?* (Chicago, IL: University of Chicago Press, 1970). Wu Kuangming, *Chuang Tzu: World Philosopher at Play* (Chico, CA: Scholars Press, 1982) and *The Butterfly as Companion: Meditations on the First Three Chapters of the* Chuang Tzu (Albany, NY: State University of New York Press, 1990).

11. Norman Girardot, *Myth and Meaning in Early Taoism: The Theme of Chaos* (hun-tun) (Berkeley, CA: University of California Press, 1983). Isabelle Robinet, *Taoist Meditation: The Mao-Shan Tradition of Great Purity*, translated from the French edition of 1979 by Julian F. Pas and Norman J. Girardot (Albany, NY: State University of New York Press, 1993). John Lagerwey, *Taoist Ritual in Chinese Society and History* (New York, NY: Macmillan, 1987). Livia Kohn, *Taoist Meditation and Longevity Techniques*, edited in cooperation with Yosinobu Sakade (Ann Arbor, MI: Center for Chinese Studies, 1989), *Taoist Mystical Philosophy: The Scripture of Western Ascension* (Albany, NY: State University of New York Press, 1991), *Early Chinese Mysticism: Philosophy and Soteriology in Taoist Tradition* (Princeton, NJ: Princeton University Press, 1992), and *The Taoist Experience: An Anthology* (Albany, NY: State University of New York Press, 1993).

12. Herbert Fingarette, *Confucius: The Secular as Sacred* (New York, NY: Harper and Row, 1972).

13. David S. Nivison, *The Ways of Confucianism: Investigations in Chinese Philosophy*, edited with an introduction by Bryan W. Van Norden (LaSalle, IL: Open Court, 1996).

14. Antonio S. Cua, *Dimensions of Moral Creativity: Paradigms, Principles, and Ideals* (State College, PA: Pennsylvania State University Press, 1978).

15. Antonio S. Cua, *The Unity of Knowledge and Action: A Study of Wang Yang-ming's Moral Psychology* (Honolulu, HI: The University of Hawaii Press, 1982).

16. Antonio S. Cua, *Ethical Argumentation: A Study in Hsun Tzu's Moral Epistemology* (Honolulu, HI: University of Hawaii Press, 1985).

17. Philip J. Ivanhoe, *Confucian Moral Self Cultivation* (New York, NY: Peter Lang, 1993).

18. Philip J. Ivanhoe, *Ethics in the Confucian Tradition: The Thought of Mencius and Wang Yang-ming* (Atlanta, GA: Scholars Press, 1990).

19. Lee H. Yearley, *Mencius and Aquinas: Theories of Virtue and Conceptions of Courage* (Albany, NY: State University of New York Press, 1990).

20. Chang Chung-yuan, *Tao: A New Way of Thinking: A Translation of the* Tao Te Ching *with an Introduction and Commentaries* (New York, NY: Harper and Row, 1975).

21. Chang Chung-yuan, *Creativity and Taoism: A Study of Chinese Philosophy, Art, and Poetry* (New York, NY: Harper and Row, 1963).

22. Roger T. Ames and David L. Hall, *Thinking Through Confucius* (Albany, NY: State University of New York Press, 1987), *Anticipating China: Thinking Through the Narratives of Chinese and Western Culture* (Albany, NY: State University of New York

Press, 1995), and *Thinking from the Han: Self, Truth, and Transcendence in Chinese and Western Culture* (Albany, NY: State University of New York Press, 1998).

23. Roger T. Ames, *The Art of Rulership: Studies in Ancient Chinese Political Thought* (Honolulu, HI: Hawaii University Press, 1983) and *Sun-tsu: The Art of Warfare: The First English Translation Incorporating the Recently Discovered Yin-Ch'ueh-Shan Texts*, with an introduction and commentary (New York, NY: Ballantine, 1993).

24. David L. Hall, *The Civilization of Experience: A Whiteheadian Theory of Culture* (New York, NY: Fordham University Press, 1973), *The Uncertain Phoenix: Adventures Toward a Post-Cultural Sensibility* (New York, NY: Fordham University Press, 1982), and *Eros and Irony: A Prelude to Philosophical Anarchism* (Albany, NY: State University of New York Press, 1982).

25. David L. Hall, *Richard Rorty: Prophet and Poet of the New Pragmatism* (Albany, NY: State University of New York Press, 1994).

26. Wu Kuangming, *On Chinese Body Thinking: A Cultural Hermeneutic* (Leiden, Netherlands: Brill, 1997).

27. Tu Weiming, *Neo-Confucian Thought in Action: Wang Yang-ming's Youth (1472–1509)* (Berkeley, CA: University of California Press, 1976).

28. Tu Weiming, *Centrality and Commonality: An Essay on Confucian Religiousness*, revised and enlarged edition of *Centrality and Commonality: An Essay on Chung-yung* (1976), (Albany, NY: State University of New York Press, 1989).

29. Tu Weiming, *Humanity and Self-Cultivation: Essays in Confucian Thought* (Berkeley, CA: Asian Humanities Press, 1979) and *Confucian Thought: Selfhood as Creative Transformation* (Albany, NY: State University of New York Press, 1985).

30. Tu Weiming, "The Living Tree: The Changing Meaning of Being Chinese Today," edited issue of *Daedalus* 120:2 (Spring 1991) and "China in Transformation," edited issue of *Daedalus* 122:3 (Spring 1993).

31. Cheng Chungying, *Tai Chen's Inquiry into Goodness: A Translation of the Yuan Shan, with an Introductory Essay* (Honolulu, HI: East-West Center Press, 1971).

32. Cheng Chungying, *New Dimensions of Confucian and Neo-Confucian Philosophy* (Albany, NY: State University of New York Press, 1991).

33. Wu Kuangming, *Chuang Tzu: World Philosopher at Play* (Chico, CA: Scholars Press, 1982).

34. Wu Kuangming, *The Butterfly as Companion: Meditations on the First Three Chapters of the Chuang Tzu*. (Albany, NY: State University of New York Press, 1990).

35. Wu Kuangming, *On Chinese Body Thinking: A Cultural Hermeneutic* (Leiden, Netherlands: Brill, 1997) and *On the "Logic" of Togetherness: A Cultural Hermeneutic* (Leiden, Netherlands: Brill, 1998).

36. Chad Hansen, *Language and Logic in Ancient China* (Ann Arbor, MI: University of Michigan Press, 1983) and *A Daoist Theory of Chinese Thought* (New York, NY: Oxford University Press, 1992).

6. METHODOLOGY, PRACTICES, AND DISCIPLINES IN CHINESE AND WESTERN PHILOSOPHY

1. Lawrence E. Cahoone, *The Ends of Philosophy* (Albany, NY: State University of New York Press, 1995), introduction, chapter 1, and passim.

2. Ibid., chapter 4.

3. For an excellent sympathetic introduction to Greek philosophical schools as religious ways of life, see Pierre Hadot's *Philosophy as a Way of Life: Spiritual Exercises from Socrates to Foucault*, edited with an introduction by Arnold I. Davidson, translated by Michael Chase (Oxford, UK: Blackwell, 1995.) For more comprehensive studies, see *Classical Mediterranean Spirituality*, edited by A. H. Armstrong (New York, NY: Crossroad, 1986), especially the essays by Armstrong, Skemp, Atherton, Long, Pinsent, Dillon, Hadot, Saffrey, Kenney, Beierwaltes, Schroeder, Corrigan, and Manchester. On Christianity as a philosophy see, for instance, Helmut Koester's *History and Literature of Early Christianity* (New York, NY: Walter de Gruyter, 1982), pp. 338ff.

4. Wing-tsit Chan, translator and editor, *A Source Book in Chinese Philosophy* (Princeton, NJ: Princeton University Press, 1963); Sarvepalli Radhakrishnan and Charles A. Moore, editors, *A Sourcebook in Indian Philosophy* (Princeton, NJ: Princeton University Press, 1958).

5. See my *Boston Confucianism* (Albany, NY: State University of New York Press, 2000). The limitation of the discussion of Chinese philosophy to Confucianism derives from the limitation of my own expertise.

6. See his *The Sociology of Philosophies: A Global Theory of Intellectual Change* (Cambridge, MA: Harvard University Press, 1998). He lays out a sociological theory of philosophical creativity and influence and integrates the philosophical traditions of the West with China, India, and the Islamic world.

7. Classic discussions of "analytic philosophy" in its early missionary days are J. O. Urmson's *Philosophical Analysis: Its Development between the Two World Wars* (Oxford, UK: Clarendon Press, 1956) and A. J. Ayer's edited collection *Logical Positivism* (New York, NY: Free Press, 1959) and his *Philosophy in the Twentieth Century* (New York, NY: Random House, 1982).

8. See Peter Strawson, *Individuals: An Essay in Descriptive Metaphysics* (New York, NY: Anchor, 1963).

9. See A. J. Ayer, *Language, Truth and Logic* (London, UK: Golancz, 1936).

10. Ludwig Wittgenstein, *Philosophical Investigations*, translated by G. E. M. Anscombe (New York, NY: Macmillan, 1953).

11. J. L. Austin, *Sense and Sensibilia*, reconstructed from the manuscript notes by G. J. Warnock (New York, NY: Oxford University Press, 1964).

12. John R. Searle, *Speech Acts: An Essay in the Philosophy of Language* (Cambridge, UK: Cambridge University Press, 1969).

13. On the particular philosophical commitments of British empiricism, see John E. Smith's essays "John Dewey: Philosopher of Experience," in his *Reason and God* (New Haven, CT: Yale University Press, 1961), and "Three Types and Two Dogmas of Empiricism," in his *Themes in American Philosophy: Purpose, Experience and Community* (New York, NY: Harper and Row, 1970). For his sustained criticism of the British conception of empiricism, see his small book *Religion and Empiricism* (Milwaukee, WI: Marquette University Press, 1967). On the special theme of ahistorical present consciousness, see George R. Lucas Jr., "Philosophy's Recovery of Its History," in *The Recovery of Philosophy in America: Essays in Honor of John Edwin Smith*, edited by Thomas P. Kasulis and Robert Cummings Neville (Albany, NY: State University of New York Press, 1997).

14. Charles Sanders Peirce, the founder of American pragmatism, believed that nominalism was the root of all philosophical mistakes in European philosophy since the medieval period and himself was a Scotistic realist. See *The Collected Papers of Charles Sanders Peirce*, 1.1ff. See also John F. Boler's *Charles Peirce and Scholastic Realism* (Seattle, WA: University of Washington Press, 1963). Peirce held that the concrete reality and intelligibility of any concrete particular thing derives from its general traits or habits expressed through time; see my general exposition of Peirce's system in *The Highroad Around Modernism*, chapter 1. Heidegger too defined individuality (*Dasein*) in terms of extensive temporal and spatial horizons. Dewey agreed with Peirce about nominalism and stressed the reality of habit, which is never completely contained within any particular expression. Whitehead developed the most elaborate realist metaphysics of the early twentieth century with an account of both realistic process and the eternity of forms; of the four, he is the closest to being a nominalist in the sense that actual things for him are only in the present. Yet Whitehead's conception of conscious experience is that it never is at a moment—a present moment is too short to be conscious of anything—but rather involves the integration across time of a specious present.

15. See, for instance, Syed Nomanul Haq's *Names: Natures and Things* (Boston, MA: Kluwer, 1994), a study of the Neo-Platonic alchemist Jabir ibn Hayyan.

16. For a more elaborate introduction to the idea that modernity, beginning with the European Renaissance, has many streams, only one of which is the Descartes-Kant-modernism/postmodernism line, see my *The Highroad Around Modernism* (Albany, NY: State University of New York Press, 1992).

17. For the texts of the *Discourse on Method* and the *Meditations*, plus extraordinarily fine analyses of them by several writers, especially David Weissman, in Weissman's edited book, *Rene Descartes: Discourse on Method and Meditations on First Philosophy* (New Haven, CT: Yale University Press, 1996). It might be helpful to quote the rules of method, from the *Discourse*, p. 13 in that volume.

> The first of these was to accept nothing as true which I did not clearly recognise to be so: this is to say, carefully to avoid precipitation and prejudice in judgments, and to accept in them nothing more than what was presented to my mind so clearly and distinctly that I could have no occasion to doubt it.

The second was to divide up each of the difficulties which I examined into as many parts as possible, and as seemed requisite in order that it might be resolved in the best manner possible.

The third was to carry on my reflections in due order, commencing with objects that were the most simple and easy to understand, in order to rise little by little, or by degrees, to knowledge of the most complex, assuming an order, even if a fictitious one, among those which do not follow a natural sequence relatively to one another.

The last was in all cases to make enumerations so complete and reviews so general that I should be certain of having omitted nothing. (Haldane and Ross translation)

18. See Wittgenstein's *Tractatus Logico-Philosophicus* (London, UK: Routledge Kegan Paul, 1922), 6.53–6.54, 7.

19. See Edmund Husserl, *The Crisis of European Sciences and Transcendental Phenomenology*, translated with an introduction by David Carr (Evanston, IL: Northwestern University Press, 1970).

20. See G. W. F. Hegel's *Phenomenology of Mind*, translated by J. B. Baillie (second revised edition; London, UK: George Allen and Unwin, 1931), preface.

21. See, for instance, Dugald Stewart's *Elements of the Philosophy of the Human Mind*, two volumes bound in one (Albany, NY: E. and E. Hosford, 1822; vol. 1 originally 1792, vol. 2 1813). Charles Peirce called his philosophy "critical commonsensism"; the "critical" part referred to Kant, interpreted nontranscendentally, and the "commonsensist" part referred to Stewart and Thomas Reid.

22. See Peirce's essays "Questions Concerning Certain Faculties Claimed for Man," "Some Consequences of Four Incapacities," "Pragmatism and Critical Common-Sensism," and "Consequences of Critical Common-Sensism," all in *The Collected Papers of Charles Sanders Peirce*, volume 5. For Dewey, see, for instance, his *Reconstruction in Philosophy* (New York, NY: Henry Holt, 1920).

23. See George Lucas's ingenious discussion of this in connection with Bertrand Russell's claim that Whitehead is muddleheaded and Whitehead's counterclaim that Russell is simpleminded in *The Rehabilitation of Whitehead: An Analytic and Historical Assessment of Process Philosophy* (Albany, NY: State University of New York Press, 1989), pp. 109ff. I myself follow the pragmatic version of the rejection of the doctrine of method and emphasize the vulnerability of all philosophic claims as hypotheses subject to test by argument and experience, including experiment. See, for instance, my *Recovery of the Measure*.

24. See their *Thinking Through Confucius* (Albany, NY: State University of New York Press, 1987), *Anticipating China* (Albany: State University of New York Press, 1995), and *Thinking from the Han* (Albany, NY: State University of New York Press, 1998). But see also their *The Democracy of the Dead* (LaSalle, IL: Open Court, 1999), which argues for the analogy between American pragmatism and Confucianism with regard to public debate and consensus formation.

25. See Robert Eno's *The Confucian Creation of Heaven* (Albany, NY: State University of New York Press, 1990).

26. See Collins, *The Sociology of Philosophies*, pp. 142–146, for explicit comparisons and discussions of the relation of these Greek and Chinese academies to their political situations.

27. For an interesting discussion of Zhu Xi and his political involvements, see Hoyt Cleveland Tillman's *Confucian Discourse and Chu His's Ascendancy* (Honolulu, HI: University of Hawaii Press, 1992).

28. See Samuel P. Huntington, *The Clash of Civilizations and the Remaking of World Order* (New York, NY: Simon and Schuster, 1996).

29. See William Theodore de Bary's *Asian Values and Human Rights* (Cambridge, MA: Harvard University Press, 1998). Compare this with Hall and Ames's *The Democracy of the Dead*.

30. For a comparison of Confucian and Western philosophic views on this, see *Confucianism and Ecology: The Interrelation of Heaven, Earth, and Humans*, edited by Mary Evelyn Tucker and John H. Berthrong (Cambridge, MA: Harvard University Press, 1998).

31. See his *Science and the Modern World* (New York, NY: Macmillan, 1925), chapter 13, "Requisites for Social Progress."

32. See William M. Sullivan, *Work and Integrity: The Crisis and Promise of Professionalism in America* (New York, NY: HarperCollins, 1995). See also his earlier *Reconstructing Public Philosophy* (Berkeley, CA: University of California Press, 1982) on the general topic of public philosophy or philosophy as the work of a public intellectual.

33. For process philosophy on the hypothetical nature of all philosophical claims, see Alfred North Whitehead's *Process and Reality* (corrected edition by Donald Sherburne and David Griffin; New York, NY: Free Press, 1978; original 1929), chapter 1.

34. A. C. Graham, *Disputers of the Tao: Philosophical Argument in Ancient China* (LaSalle, IL: Open Court, 1989).

7. METAPHYSICS FOR CONTEMPORARY CHINESE PHILOSOPHY

1. Philosophy's obligation to "fundamental problems" has nowhere been better treated than by Paul Weiss for whom it was a preoccupation throughout a long career. See his *Reality* (Princeton, NJ: Princeton University Press, 1939), *Being and Other Realities* (LaSalle, IL: Open Court, 1995), or *Surrogates* (Bloomington, IN: Indiana University Press, 2002). Weiss died in 2002 at the age of 101.

2. *The Clash of Civilizations and the Remaking of World Order* is the title of the influential book by Samuel Huntington (New York, NY: Simon and Schuster, 1996).

3. See *The Collected Papers of Charles Sanders Peirce*, 1.616–676.

4. This is a consistent theme, defending the practicality of contemporary metaphysics based on ancient Chinese tradition, in Cheng Chungying's *New Dimensions of*

Confucian and Neo-Confucian Philosophy (Albany, NY: State University of New York Press, 1991).

5. That the metaphysical presuppositions of modern science could not account for how the world is mathematically ordered was the theme of Whitehead's *Science and the Modern World* (New York, NY: Macmillan, 1925).

6. Fritjof Capra, *The Tao of Physics: An Exploration of the Parallels between Modern Physics and Eastern Mysticism* (Berkeley, CA: Shambhala, 1975). A treatment with more scholarly depth is Joseph Needham's *Science and Civilisation in China*, volume 2 (Cambridge, UK: Cambridge University Press, 1956), especially chapter 13; Needham draws parallels between Chinese cosmology and the organicism of Leibniz and Whitehead.

7. The connection of a sharp distinction between facts and values with early modern science, and the influence of that connection on subsequent Western culture and science, is the topic of my *Reconstruction of Thinking*, part 1 (Albany, NY: State University of New York Press, 1981). That book includes a discussion of the Chinese contribution to the overcoming of the fact/value distinction.

8. See his fine essay "Confucianism and Liberalism" in *Dao: A Journal of Comparative Philosophy* 2:1 (December 2002), pp. 1–20.

9. In his "Inquiry on the *Great Learning*," say, in Wing-tsit Chan's *Source Book of Chinese Philosophy* (Princeton, NJ: Princeton University Press, 1963), pp. 659–660.

10. The defense of the historical right of ownership is one of the main theses of Robert Nozick's *Anarchy, State, and Utopia* (New York, NY: Basic Books, 1974).

11. Deference, of course, is central to Confucius's conception of *ren* or humaneness; ritual is more fully elaborated by Xunzi. The pairing of humaneness and ritual propriety was the chief plot of Herbert Fingarette's *Confucius: The Secular as Sacred* (New York, NY: Harper and Row, 1972), which introduced many Western philosophers in the analytic tradition to Confucianism. David L. Hall has "deference" as a term of art in his *The Uncertain Phoenix* (New York, NY: Fordham University Press, 1982) and *Eros and Irony* (Albany, NY: State University of New York Press, 1982).

12. See Warren G. Frisina's *The Unity of Knowledge and Action: Toward a Nonrepresentational Theory of Knowledge* (Albany, NY: State University of New York Press, 2002). My *Reconstruction of Thinking*, *Recovery of the Measure*, and *Normative Cultures* (Albany, NY: State University of New York Press, 1981, 1989, and 1995, respectively) constitute a three-volume Axiology of Thinking, my contribution to this contemporary Chinese metaphysics.

8. THE CONSCIOUS AND UNCONSCIOUS PLACING OF RITUAL AND HUMANITY

1. See Robert Eno's *The Confucian Creation of Heaven: Philosophy and the Defense of Ritual Mastery* (Albany, NY: State University of New York Press, 1990).

2. A good English translation is in Wing-tsit Chan's *Source Book of Chinese Philosophy* (Princeton, NJ: Princeton University Press, 1963), pp. 593–596.

3. See the interesting discussion of translation in the glossary of key terms in their *Daodejing: Making This Life Significant: A Philosophical Translation* (New York, NY: Ballantine Books, 2003).

4. See his *Humanity and Self-Cultivation: Essays in Confucian Thought* (reprint with a new foreword; Boston, MA: Cheng and Tsui, 1998; original edition, 1978), chapter 2. See my discussion of his theory of ritual and humanity in the foreword to his book. The school of Boston Confucianism to which Tu and I belong has two branches. The one north of the Charles River (at Harvard) emphasizes the Mencian tradition, whereas the one south of the Charles (at Boston University) emphasizes Xunzi's tradition on the point of ritual. These differences are only matters of emphasis.

9. THE CONTEMPORARY MUTUAL DEVELOPMENT OF CONFUCIANISM AND CHRISTIANITY

1. Julia Ching, *To Acquire Wisdom: The Way of Wang Yang-ming* (New York, NY: Columbia University Press, 1976). Tu Weiming, *Neo-Confucian Thought in Action: Wang Yang-ming's Youth (1472–1509)* (Berkeley, CA: University of California Press, 1976). See Antonio S. Cua's *The Unity of Knowledge and Action: A Study in Wang Yang-ming's Moral Psychology* (Honolulu, HI: University of Hawaii Press, 1982). See Warren G. Frisina's *The Unity of Knowledge and Action: Toward a Nonrepresentational Theory of Knowledge* (Albany, NY: State University of New York Press, 2002).

2. Herbert Fingarette, *Confucius: The Secular as Sacred* (New York, NY: Harper and Row, 1972).

3. *Christianity and Chinese Religion* (New York, NY: Doubleday, 1989).

4. Julia Ching and Willard G. Oxtoby, *Moral Enlightenment: Leibniz and Wolff on China* (Institut Monumenta Serica; Nettetal, Netherlands: Steyler Verlag, 1992).

5. See Wang's *Inquiry on* The Great Learning in *Instructions for Practical Living and Other Neo-Confucian Writings by Wang Yang-ming*, translated with notes by Wing-tsit Chan (New York, NY: Columbia University Press, 1963), p. 279.

6. See Tu's "Subjectivity and Ontological Reality—An Interpretation of Wang Yang-ming's Mode of Thinking" in *Humanity and Self-Cultivation: Essays in Confucian Thought* (Berkeley, CA: Asian Humanities Press, 1979), chapter 10. I have discussed this interpretation of Wang in *Boston Confucianism* (Albany, NY: State University of New York Press, 2000), chapter 5.

7. Wang, *Instructions for Practical Living*, p. 16.

8. This was written before it was learned that Iraq's possession of weapons of mass destruction and its collusion with Al Qaeda were fabrications of the American government.

11. ON COMPARISON

1. See, for instance, George Lindbeck's *The Nature of Doctrine: Religion and Theology in a Post-liberal Age* (Philadelphia, PA: The Westminster Press, 1984) and Stanley Hauerwas's *With the Grain of the Universe: The Church's Witness and Natural Theology* (Grand Rapids, MI: Brazos Press, 2001).

2. See Hans Frei's analysis and lament for the passing of such biblical theology, *The Eclipse of Biblical Narrative* (New Haven, CT: Yale University Press, 1974).

3. See John D. Young's *Confucianism and Christianity: The First Encounter* (Hong Kong: Hong Kong University Press, 1983) and Jonathan D. Spence's *The Memory Palace of Matteo Ricci* (New York, NY: Viking Penguin, 1984).

4. Kenneth Cracknell, *Justice, Courtesy and Love: Theologians and Missionaries Encountering World Religions, 1846–1914* (London: Epworth Press, 1995).

5. Samuel P. Huntington, *The Clash of Civilizations and the Remaking of World Order* (New York, NY: Simon and Schuster, 1996).

6. See Walter H. Capps's *Religious Studies: The Making of a Discipline* (Minneapolis, MN: Fortress Press, 1995).

7. See William H. McNeill's *The Rise of the West: A History of the Human Community*, with a retrospective essay (Chicago, IL: University of Chicago Press, 1991; original edition, 1963).

8. See his *The Human Predicament: Its Changing Image: A Study in Comparative Religion and History*, assisted by Anna Krejcova (London, UK: St. Martin's Press, 1993).

9. Randall Collins, *The Sociology of Philosophies: A Global Theory of Intellectual Change* (Cambridge, MA: Harvard University Press, 1998).

10. Huston Smith, *The World's Religions: Our Great Wisdom Traditions* (San Francisco, CA: Harper, 1991; a revised edition of *The Religions of Man*, originally published in 1958); Smith is a Methodist. For a non-Christian version of the Perennial Philosophy, see the Muslim scholar Seyyed Hossein Nasr's Gifford Lectures, *Knowledge and the Sacred* (New York, NY: Crossroad, 1981).

11. David A. Dilworth, *Philosophy in World Perspective: A Comparative Hermeneutic of the Major Theories* (New Haven, CT: Yale University Press, 1989). His work is in collaboration with Walter Watson, author of *The Architectonics of Meaning: Foundations of the New Pluralism* (Albany, NY: State University of New York Press, 1985).

12. See Ninian Smart and Steven Konstantine, *Christian Systematic Theology in a World Context* (Minneapolis, MN: Fortress, 1991).

13. See, for instance, Panikkar's *The Silence of God: The Answer of the Buddha*, translated from the Italian by Robert R. Barr (Maryknoll, NY: Orbis, 1989).

14. See Wilfred Cantwell Smith's *Faith and Belief* (Princeton, NJ: Princeton University Press, 1979) and *Towards a World Theology: Faith and the Comparative History of Religion* (Philadelphia, PA: The Westminster Press, 1981).

15. This discussion derives from the work of the Comparative Religious Ideas Project carried out in Boston from 1995 to 2000 and resulting in three published volumes: *The Human Condition, Ultimate Realities,* and *Religious Truth,* all edited by Robert Cummings Neville, director of the project (Albany, NY: State University of New York Press, 2001). In this project were six historians of religion, each expert in some strand or period of one of the six world religions (counting Chinese religions as one) and assisted by a graduate student. In addition were four generalists: a sociologist of religion, a historical comparativist, and two philosophical theologians. The project met as a seminar eight times a year for three years, dealing with the topics of the human condition, ultimate realities, and religious truth respectively. Each fall the historians presented papers on what their tradition had to say about the topic, and each spring those papers were rewritten to take on comparative form. The cumulative critical discussion exercised and refined the logic of collaborative comparison as described here.

16. Vagueness is a technical notion arising from the logic of the pragmatist Charles Sanders Peirce. It is explained in "On Comparing Religious Ideas" by Robert Cummings Neville and Wesley J. Wildman in *The Human Condition,* chapter 1. The logic of comparison is explained in greater detail by the same two authors in another essay with the same name, "On Comparing Religious Ideas," in *Ultimate Realities,* chapter 8. See also John H. Berthrong's "The Idea of Categories in Historical Perspective" in *Ultimate Realities,* chapter 10.

17. This theory of comparison comes from the aforementioned collaborative project. See the essay "How Our Approach to Comparison Relates to Others" by Wesley J. Wildman and Robert Cummings Neville in *Ultimate Realities,* chapter 9, and "On the Nature of Religion: Lessons We Have Learned" by the same authors in *Religious Truth,* chapter 9.

18. For a collaborative comparative study of religious truth as conceived in several traditions and as a claim made within comparative theology, see the essays "Religious Truth in the Six Traditions: A Summary" and "A Contemporary Understanding of Religious Truth," both by Robert Cummings Neville and Wesley J. Wildman in *Religious Truth,* chapters 8 and 9.

19. Robert S. Brumbaugh and Newton P. Stallknecht, *The Compass of Philosophy: An Essay in Intellectual Orientation* (New York, NY: Longmans, Green, 1954). Brumbaugh and Stallknecht are explicit in crediting Stephen Pepper's *World Hypotheses* (Berkeley: University of California Press, 1942) and Richard McKeon's *Freedom and History* (New York: Noonday Press, 1952) as ancestors of their work.

20. See his discussion of the Divided Line in *Platonic Studies of Greek Philosophy: Form, Arts, Gadgets, and Hemlock* (Albany: State University of New York Press, 1989), chapter 3. See also his *Plato on the One* (New Haven: Yale University Press, 1961), which is a study of the *Parmenides,* analyzing the hypotheses in that dialogue according to a grid of classifications and cross-classifications of possible ontological positions. See his *Western Philosophic Systems and Their Cyclic Transformations* (Carbondale, IL: Southern Illinois University Press, 1992) for the latest development of his classificatory system and interpretations of Western philosophies.

21. See his *The Architectonics of Meaning: Foundations of the New Pluralism* (Albany, NY: State University of New York Press, 1985).

22. Ibid., ix.

23. See his *Philosophy in World Perspective: A Comparative Hermeneutic of the Major Theories* (New Haven, CT: Yale University Press, 1989).

24. Randall Collins, *The Sociology of Philosophies: A Global Theory of Intellectual Change* (Cambridge, MA: The Belknap Press of Harvard University Press, 1998).

25. F. S. C. Northrop, *The Meeting of East and West: An Inquiry Concerning World Understanding* (New York, NY: Macmillan, 1946).

26. See his *Creativity and Taoism: A Study of Chinese Philosophy, Art, and Poetry* (New York, NY: Julian Press, 1963; reprint edition New York, NY: Harper and Row, 1970).

27. *Thinking Though Confucius* (Albany, NY: State University of New York Press, 1987), *Anticipating China: Thinking Through the Narratives of Chinese and Western Culture* (Albany, NY: State University of New York Press, 1995), and *Thinking from the Han: Self, Truth, and Transcendence in Chinese and Western Culture* (Albany, NY: State University of New York Press, 1998).

28. See David L. Hall and Roger T. Ames, *Democracy of the Dead: Dewey, Confucius, and the Hope for Democracy in China* (LaSalle, IL: Open Court, 1999).

29. See Antonio Cua's *The Unity of Knowledge and Action: A Study of Wang Yang-ming's Moral Psychology* (Honolulu, HI: The University Press of Hawaii, 1982) and *Ethical Argumentation: A Study of Hsun Tzu's Moral Epistemology* (Honolulu, HI: The University Press of Hawaii, 1985). See also Tu Weiming's *Neo-Confucian Thought in Action: Wang Yang-ming's Youth (1472–1509)* (Berkeley, CA: University of California Press, 1976), *Centrality and Commonality: An Essay on Confucian Religiousness* (revised and enlarged edition; Albany, NY: State University of New York Press, 1989), and *Confucian Thought: Selfhood as Creative Transformation* (Albany, NY: State University of New York Press, 1985).

30. See Xinyan Jiang, editor, *The Examined Life: Chinese Perspectives: Essays on Chinese Ethical Traditions* (Binghamton, NY: Global Publications, 2002).

31. See his *New Dimensions of Confucian and Neo-Confucian Philosophy* (Albany, NY: State University of New York Press, 1991) as well as his critical commentary on my own system, "On Neville's Understanding of Chinese Philosophy: Ontology of *Wu*, Cosmology of *Yi*, Normology of *Li*," in *Understanding Neville*, edited by J. Harley Chapman and Nancy Frankenberry (Albany, NY: State University of New York Press, 1999).

32. For the Daoist studies see Wu's *Chuang Tzu: World Philosopher at Play* (New York, NY: Crossroad, 1982) and *The Butterfly as Companion: Meditations of the First Three Chapters of the* Chuang Tzu (Albany, NY: State University of New York Press, 1990). The volumes in *A Cultural Hermeneutic* are *On Chinese Body Thinking* (Leiden: Brill, 1997), *On the "Logic" of Togetherness* (Leiden: Brill, 1998), and *On Metaphoring* (Leiden: Brill, 2001).

33. See Tu's *Way, Learning, and Politics: Essays on the Confucian Intellectual* (reprint edition; Albany, NY: State University of New York Press, 1993) and the two issues of *Daedalus* he edited, 120:2 (Spring 1991) and 122:2 (Spring 1993). See also his long foreword to my *Boston Confucianism* (Albany, NY: State University of New York Press, 2001) in which he spells out the nature of this community of contemporary thinkers.

34. What I call program philosophies are conversations begun by some genius founder and carried on by disciples through a generation or two, with commentaries limited to those working out the founding ideas. Both continental and analytic philosophy in twentieth century European thought have been prone to enthusiasm for special programs.

35. Han Yu and Li Ao, though not original philosophers, did much to reorient Confucianism as an answer to Buddhism, paving the way for the Neo-Confucian movement. They attacked the quietism of both Buddhism and Daoism.

36. I have presented a formal argument for rebutting the postmodern charge of inevitable bias in theory in my *The Highroad Around Modernism* (Albany, NY: State University of New York Press, 1992), chapter 6.

37. Peirce's "Neglected Argument" essay appears in many anthologies and is in *The Collected Papers of Charles Sanders Peirce*, volume 6. I have analyzed it at length in *The Highroad Around Modernism*, chapter 1, and *Normative Cultures*, part 4.

12. CONTRIBUTIONS OF CHINESE PHILOSOPHY: A SUMMARY DISCUSSION

1. Wing-tsit Chan, *A Source Book in Chinese Philosophy* (Princeton, NY: Princeton University Press, 1963), p. 497.

2. Ibid., p. 660.

Index

Abduction, 145
Abiding in the highest good, 24
Absolute dependence, 125
Absolutes, 53
Abstraction, 96, 122
Abyss, 54
Academic, calendar, 55–57; philosophy, 59
Academies, 179; Chi-hsia, 80; Lanling, 81; Plato's, 81
Act of Esse, 43, 122, 125
Action, 3, 23, 118–20; conjoint, 10
Adept, Daoist, 48, 52, 172
Administration, 117; academic, timing in, 56
Adolescence, 56
Advaita Vedanta, 121, 140
Aesthetics, 48, 76, 98, 160, 167; in Chinese sensibility, 65–66; aesthetic criticism, 86; as defining Eastern culture, 137; in harmony, 97; in judgment, 21; perception, 4
Agency, 99, 115; in creativity, 53
Aggregation, statistical, 46
Aggression, 34–35, 107
Al Qaeda, xv, 181
Alienation, 84
Allan, George, 173
Allinson, Robert, 171
Alphabet, 114
American Century, 15
Ames, Roger, xiii, 61, 64–66, 68, 81, 104, 137–40, 160, 163–64, 167, 170–71, 174–75, 178, 184
Analects, 60, 138–39, 151–52

Analysis, moral, 24
Analytic philosophy, 62–63, 76–77, 80, 89; methodology in, 75–87
Ancestors, 122
Anglo-American analytic philosophy, 86
Animal rights, 94
Anthropocentrism, 129
Anthropological symbolism, 125–26
Anthropomorphism, 123–24
Anti-metaphysical thinking, 91–92
Apartheid, 111
Apophatic theology, 43–44
Appreciation, 20
Aquinas, Thomas, St., 11, 35, 43, 87, 121–22, 125, 128, 147, 149
Argument, in comparison, 133
Aristotelianism, xii–xiii, 62, 76, 87, 128; in Hall and Ames, 66
Aristotle (and Aristotelians), 2, 46, 61, 77, 81, 85, 92, 103, 116, 130, 134–35, 140–41, 143–45, 148–50
Armstrong, A. H., 176
Art, 19–20, 24, 69; modernism in, 79
Artificiality, 41
Asherites, 121
Assessment, 9
Assyrian religion, 123
Astrophysics, 45
Asymmetry, between God and world, 65
Attention, 47
Augustine, 46, 61, 128
Austin, J. L., 77, 176
Authenticity, 23
Authoritarianism, 65
Authority, 36; political, 83

INDEX

Avaloketeshvara, 126; *see also* Guanyin
Averroes, 149
Axial age, vs. pre-axial age religious imagery, 123–24
Axiology, 98
Ayer, A. J., 77, 176

Babylonian religion, 123
Balance, 48; under pressure, 38
Barbarians, 13, 20, 103, 118–19, 155–56
Barr, Robert R., 182
Beat, as rhythm, 50–58; wild, 57
Beauty, 148
Behavior, 32; organized and disorganized, 35–40; vs. matters of the heart, 105; semiotic, 116–17, 168. *See also* Signs
Being, 69; at home, 147; and nonbeing, 2–6, 55
Berkeley, George, 80
Berkeley, University of California at, 60
Berry, Thomas, xi
Berthrong, John H., v, xv–xvi, 120, 150, 163, 165, 179, 183
Best of all possible worlds, 79
Bhakti, 126
Bias, in comparative categories, 132, 145
Bible, 121, 123, 128
Big issue philosophy, 80
Bin Laden, Osama, 118, 120
Biology, 29, 34–35, 57, 147, 169
Biopsychic dance, 33–34, 39, 169
Bo Mou, xiv
Body, 98; -thinking, 71–73; trained in ritual, 28–29
Boler, John F., 177
Boston Confucianism, xii, 14, 76, 108, 150, 155, 176; Schools north and south of the Charles River, xvi, 168, 181
Boston, 164; as context for Confucianism, 150–53; rituals for, 156–57; University, xvi, 181
Boundaries, in philosophy, 80; of self, 160
Brahman, 125
Brent, Joseph, 166

Bruce, J. Percy, 61, 173
Brumbaugh, Robert S., 134–36, 183
Buchler, Justus, 75
Buddha-mind, 122
Buddhism, 3, 18, 54, 60, 69, 71, 80, 82, 87, 104, 126, 131, 143–44, 151, 153, 185; in China, 143; an encounter between theocentrism and psychocentrism, 129; Madhyamaka, 121, 148; Mahayana, 121–26; Pure Land, 126; in Sri Lanka, 22
Bureaucracy and integrity, xvi
Burks, Arthur W., 164
Bush, George W., 118, 120
Butterfly, dreaming, 49

Cahoone, Lawrence E., 75, 84, 176
California, 76
Cambridge University, 60
Capitalism, 15–17, 21, 102, 119
Capps, Walter H., 182
Capra, Fritjof, 93, 180
Carr, David, 178
Carry over, in truth, 8–10
Cassirer, Ernst, 65
Categories, comparative, 22, 132–33; *see also* Comparison
Causation, 69; in interpretation, 29–32; ontological, 46
Center (or *zhong*), 95
Ceremony, 27–28
Certainty, 2, 75–76
Ch'eng Hao, 60
Ch'eng I, 60
Chan, Wing-tsit, 60–61, 71, 76, 152, 163, 171–73, 176, 180, 185
Chang Chung-yuan, 42, 48, 63–65, 137, 174
Chang Tsai, *see* Zhangzhai
Chang Tung-sun, 60
Change, 5–7; in orientations, 159
Chapman, J. Harley, 184
Character, murky even in good people, 24; personal, building, 55–57
Chemistry, 147; in ritual interpretation, 30

Cheng Chungying, xiii, 61, 64, 66–67, 69–77, 141, 160, 175, 179–80
Chicago, University of, 134
China, 114, 140, 148; and West compared in philosophy, 135–42
Chinese language, 20
Chinese philosophy, xi–x, 80–82; as analytical, 75–88; as amalgamated with Western, 161; reconstruction of, 69; summary contributions, 149–61; themes of, 1–12, 15–20, 92–95
Chinese University of Hong Kong, 141
Ching Dynasty, 69
Ching, Julia, xv, 113–14, 168, 173, 181
Chi-tsang, 60
Choice, 46
Chou Tun-I, *see* Zhou Dunyi
Christ, *see* Jesus Christ; mind of, 166
Christianity, xv, 18, 22, 38, 81, 113–26, 128–33, 143, 166; an encounter between theocentrism and anthropocentrism, 129; as a philosophy, 76; *see also* Confucianism, and Christianity
Chu Hsi, *see* Zhu Xi
Chuang-tsu, *see* Zhuangzi
Civil service exams, as philosophy tests, 82
Civil society, 12–13
Civilization, 27, 29–30, 34–35, 57–58, 90; high, 19–23; normative, 40; and ritual, 103–05
Civilizations, clash of, 11, 82, 129, 173, 179; commingling of, 21
Class, economic, 109–10
Classification system, in comparative theologies, 130, 134–36
Clopton, Robert W., 167
Codes, of signs, 167
Cognition, in action, 114–15
Colapietro, Vincent, 167
Collaboration, in comparison, 131–33
Collins, Randall, 76, 129–30, 136–37, 179, 182, 184
Columbia University, 60–61; Seminar on Neo-Confucianism, 61

Commentary, 77
Commerce, 21
Commitment, to sagehood, 115
Communications, 18, 82–83, 114
Communism, 68; *see also* Marxism
Community, 24
Comparative, religion, 121–26; Religious Ideas Project, 183; theology, 127–48, models of, 127–33
Comparison, xv–xvi, 22, 127–48; changes traditions compared, 131; of Chinese and Western philosophies, 75–77; classificatory vs. social scientific, 137; as decontextualized, 137; descriptive, xvi; formalism in, 134; juxtaposition as, 145; mechanisms in, 134; normative, xvi, 133, 140–48; objectivist, 133–40; philosophy of culture in, 137–40; steps in, defined, 131–33
Competition, defining the good life, 17
Complexity, 97
Components, 5–7, 48, 50, 96–98
Comportment, 32
Composition, in understanding, 78–79
Conceptual mapwork, 77
Concreteness, vs. abstractness, 73
Conditions, antecedent, 46
Confessions, in Protestant Reformation, 128
Confucianism (or Confucians), xii, 1–14, 16–25, 27–28, 32, 36–39, 49, 62–63, 66–71, 76, 82, 87, 93–95, 98, 101–20, 122–26, 129, 137, 140–41, 143–44, 147–48, 150–53, 155–61, 165, 167–70, 173; Ching Dynasty, 81; and Christianity, 141–42, 166; and Daoism, 41–43, 54–58; as ethics, xiv, 3; as a philosophy, 76–77; a contemporary program for, 1–14; as a religion, 67; *see also* Neo-Confucianism
Confucius, 1, 3, 7, 13, 21, 36, 38, 68, 81–82, 85, 95, 103, 123, 138–39, 153, 156, 180
Congo, 40
Consciousness, 124–26; false, 108–12; ordinary, 49–50; in Whitehead, 177

Consequentialist analysis, 146
Consistency, in ritual behaviors, 106–07
Constant summaries and reviews, 79
Constantine, 128
Constriction, from ritual, 36–37
Contemporary situation, for philosophy, 1–14
Context, of interpretation, 31–32; for ritual, 117; for symbolism, 124
Contextuality, 138–40
Continental philosophy, 89
Continuity, xiv, 47; of thought and action, 114–15, 168
Continuum, in self, 158
Contrast, of Chinese and Western cultures, 65
Control, of impulse, 37–38
Convention, 17–20, 29–32, 36, 57, 104, 152; as normative, 20–23
Conversation, 68
Conversion, of the heart, 120; in Plato, 115
Cooperation, 32
Copulation, 19
Core text and motifs, 139–40, 143, 148, 151–53
Correction, *see* Vulnerability
Correlative thinking, 31, 65–66, 167
Corrington, Robert S., 166–67
Cosmic reality, 47
Cosmology, 90, 180; in Confucianism, xiii; philosophical, 1–2, 5–7, 14
Cosmos, 121
Courage, 63
Court ritual, 62, 106–07; *see also* Ritual
Cracknell, Kenneth, 182
Cratocentrism, 129
Creation, divine, 5, 46, 121; in Chinese thought, 171
Creative act, ontological, 46–47
Creativity, 24, 96; in comparison, 134; cosmic, 48; divine, 116
Creator (*see also* God), 46, 123
Creel, Herrlee G., 62, 174
Criticism, art, 85

Cua, Antonio, 63, 113, 140–41, 168, 174, 181, 184
Cultural-linguistic theologies, 128
Culture, 24; Confucian, 31; philosophy of, in comparison, 137–40; popular, 29; premises of, 142
Cultures, for philosophy, 144
Curiosity, 85–86
Cycles, of philosophy, 136
Cynicism (the philosophical school), 76

Dahrendorf, Ralf, 82
Dai Zhen, 63, 69
Dance, biopsychic, 30; ritual, 19, 23, 32, 35–39, 72, 95
Dao, 37–38, 123, 125, 159; eternal and temporal, 48–51, 53; grooving on, 170; horizontal and vertical dimensions of, 54–58; as mother, 44, 47; namable and unnameable, 43–44, 47, 55
Daodejing, 41–58, 62, 82, 170–71
Daoism, xiv, 3, 6, 18, 32, 41–58, 62–24, 67–73, 76, 82, 87, 93–94, 117, 119, 121–26, 140–41, 143–44, 148, 150–51, 157, 160, 168–72, 184; and Confucianism, 41–43, 54–58; medieval, 42, 169
Daoists, 37; on committees, legislatures, and in administrations, 51–52; engaged, 57; flighty, 57; lacking principles, 52
Davidson, Arnold I., 176
Daxia Lecture, xiii
Deacon, Terrence W., 166
deBary, William Theodore, 61, 67, 173, 179
Decay, 96–97
Deconstructionism, 11, 50
Deference, 34, 94–95, 103, 106, 180; defined, 94
Democracy, 68, 91; institutions of, 17
Democritus, 135
Dependents, responsibility for, 120
Depravity, 120
Derrida, Jacques, 75, 167
Descartes, Rene, 9, 63, 77, 80, 87, 177

Desire, xiii–xiv, 12, 18, 27, 33–35; chaos of, 39
Determinateness, 4–5, 45–46; of ontologically creative nonbeing, 53–54
Determinism, in causation, 46
Devotion, 126
Devotionalism, 124
Dewey, John, 17, 21–22, 31, 77, 80, 82, 98, 140, 158, 164, 167, 176–77
Dialectic, 2, 125–26, 130
Dialogue, xii–xiii; interreligious, 84, 125; as a philosophic genre, 80
Dilworth, David A., 66, 130, 136, 182
Diplomacy, 103–04
Discernment, 158
Discipline, in philosophy, 80, 85–88
Discourse, intercivilizational, 161
Dislocation, existential, 49
Dissent, 17
Dissolution, 47
Distributive justice, *see* Justice
Divided line, in Plato, 135
Doctrine of the Mean (or *Zhongyong*, or *Chung-yung*), 7, 37, 60, 95, 151–52, 158, 160, 166, 168
Doing and being, 73
Dorm room renovation, 42–43
Dragon-riding, 53–54
Dualism, xii–xiii, 9, 98, 116
Ducking, 52
Durkheim, 137

Earth, 5; as material force (*qi*), 97–98; *see also* Heaven and Earth
East Asian Century, 15
East Asian philosophy, 89
East China Normal University, xiii
Eco, Umberto, 167
Ecology, 43, 83, 98, 103, 142; global, 114
Economics, 11, 20, 82–83, 85, 90, 103–04; defining the good life, 16–17; global, 147
Ecosystem rights, 94
Education, 7, 11, 20, 102; institutions of, 22
Egyptian religion, 123

Elders, 28
Elegance, in harmony, 50
Elitism, 7, 50
Emerson, Ralph Waldo, 65, 166
Emotion, 29, 109; infantile, 107; range of, 18
Emperor, 157
Empire, in Axial Age religions, 125
Empiricism, British, 77, 177
Encyclopedia of Unified Science movement, 159
Energy, 49; and harmonization, 96–98
Engagement, 32, 73, 117
Enlightenment (European), 13, 38, 68, 102, 141
Eno, Robert, 178, 180
Entanglement of world cultures, 82
Environment, 24, 117, 157
Envy, 34
Epictetus, 61
Epicureanism, 76
Epistemology, 10
Error, in Descartes, 78
Essence, 140
Eternity, 6, 172 ; of creative act, 46–47; logic of, 46; *see also* Time
Etherized upon a table, 139
Ethics, xii, xiv, 15–16, 62–64, 70–71, 95, 155–57; analysis and intervention, 114; in Daoism, 5–54; as needing metaphysics, 89–91
Evidence, 9
Evil, 169; in Confucianism, 38–39
Evolution, 12–13, 29, 34; and ritual, 116–17
Excellence, 24
Existence, 2, 45; meaning of, 85, 148; nature of 141–42
Existential location, 5, 48–51; dislocation, 49
Existentialism, in comparison, 134
Expatriates, in Chinese philosophy, 67
Experience, 1–2, 7–10
Experiment, controlled, 78
Explanation of the Diagram of the Great Ultimate, 3, 55

Explanation, 69
Exploitation, 110
Eye contact, 19, 28
Ezekiel, 123

Fabrications, of government, 181
Fact and value, 43, 93–94, 98
Fallibilism, 2, 9, 21
False consciousness, 110
Family, 12–13, 23, 103, 117, 160; in Confucianism, 104–05, 150; rituals, 122; structure, 11
Features, conditional and essential, 3–6, 96–97
Fecundity, ontological 54–55
Feudalism, 10–11
Feuding, 36
Fiduciary community, 69
Field/focus, 105, 138
Field-being, xv
Fight or flight response, 33
Filiality, 24, 152, 168
Fingarette, Herbert, xiv–xv, 23, 62, 113, 153, 174, 180–81
First Corinthians, 115
First-person verification, 77
Fish, happy, 49
Five Agents, 3; elements, 65
Flourish, 24
Flying decayed matter, ducking, a Daoist skill, 51
Fordham University, xi
Form, 5, 48; Plato's theory of, xiii, 147
Foucault, Michel, 64
Foundationalism, 2, 64, 79, 143, 171; non-, 75–76
Four Beginnings, 7, 95, 115–16, 152
Four Books, 27, 151–53
Four Causes, 66, 130, 134
Frankenberry, Nancy, 184
Freccero, Yvonne, 169
Freedom, 99; defining the good life, 17
Frei, Hans, 182
Freud (or Freudianism or Freudians), xiv–xv, 35, 38, 101, 105–09; model of love, 108–09

Freudian slips, 107
Friendship, 19, 24, 152, 156
Frisina, Warren G., 98, 113, 180–81
Fu, Charles Wei-shun, 64
Fuller, Steve, xiv
Fundamentalism, 22
Funerals, 31
Fung Yu-Lan, 60
Future, 46–47; the essential, 96

Gardner, Daniel, K., 174
Generality, metaphysical, 99; of signs, 19
Genesis, 123
Genesis, of signs, 30
Gentle and brave, the, 50
Gesture, 18
Girard, Rene, 169
Girardot, Norman, 62, 169, 174
Goals, 51
God, 5–6, 53, 115, 120; as Big Guy in the Sky, 121–22; creating possibilities, 79; as creator, 125, *see also* Creation, Creativity, Creator; as father, 122; given a nature in creation, 46
Goffman, Irving, 137
Good life, the, xiii–xiv, 15–17
Government, 13, 19–20, 90, 103
Grace, 115–16
Graham, A. C. 65, 87, 171, 179
Grange, Joseph, 50
Great Britain, Chinese philosophy in, 59
Great Learning, The, 23, 46, 60, 114–15, 151–52, 160, 166
Great Robber Chi, 49
Great Satan, 110
Great Ultimate, 3
Greece, 20, 36, 65; philosophy of, 123, 142
Gregory, Patrick, 169
Griffin, David Ray, 171, 179
Ground, infinite, 54
Guanyin, 122, 126; *see also* Avaloketeshvara
Guessing, 9, 145
Guilt, 38–39, 169
Guo Xiang, 42

Index

Habit, 18–19, 109, 158, 177; and ritual, 106–09
Hadot, Pierre, 176
Haecceity, 32
Hall, David L., xiii, 42, 48–49, 61, 64–66, 68, 71–72, 81, 104, 137–40, 160, 163–65, 167, 170–72, 174–75, 178, 180, 184
Han Dynasty philosophy, 82, 125, 151
Han Feizi, 41
Han Yu, 41, 60, 151, 185
Hansen, Chad, 32, 71, 167, 175
Harmony, 3–5, 6–7, 32, 39, 48–51, 65, 95; with Dao, 55–57; and decay, 98; in metaphysics, 96–99; of orientations, 158–61
Hartshorne, Charles, 164
Harvard University, 60, 67, 69, 141, 143, 181
Harvard Yenching Library, 68
Hatred, 34
Hauerwas, Stanley, 182
Haq, Syed Nomanul, 177
Hawaii, University of, 59
Hawking, Stephen, W., 45, 171
Heart, 23, 109; Confucian, 13; reformation of, 114–16
Heart-mind, 115–20
Heaven and Earth, 34, 37–40, 44, 49, 55–57, 92, 95, 104, 123, 155, 160, 165; in Xunzi, 28–29
Heaven (and as Principle, *li*), 5, 97–98, 103, 119–22, 169; *see also* Principle
Heaven, Earth, and the Human, 166
Heavenly endowment, of human nature, 109
Hebrew, 20
Hegel, 72–73, 77–78, 80–81, 130, 149, 178
Heidegger, 44, 63, 70, 77–78, 82, 141, 177
Heresy, 128
Hermeneutics, 69–73, 134
Herodotus, 129
Heroism, disguise of, 120
Hexagrams, 6, 97

Hinduism, 18, 22, 121–22, 126, 121, 143–44
Historiography, 86
History, not inevitable, 53
Ho Yen, 60
Hobbes, Thomas, 11–12, 79
Holy Roman Empire, 147
Honesty, 111, 126
Hong Kong, 67, 143
Hospitality, 28
Houser, Nathan, 166
Hsiung Shih-li, 60
Hsuan-tsang, 60
Hsun-tsu, *see* Xunzi
Huai-nan Tzu, 60
Human, life, 141, meaning and value of, 83, 90; nature, 1–2, 7–10, 157–58, as evil, 169, without ritual, 29–30, in Xunzi, 28–30; relationships, 68; rights, 61–83
Humaneness (*ren, jen*, also translated humanity, love, human-heartedness), xiv–xv, 11, 13, 23–25, 39–40, 62, 67–68, 101–05, 141, 152, 168–69, 180
Humanism, 7, 93
Humanity, 165; *see also* Humaneness
Hume, David, 69, 77, 79–80
Hunt, the, 19
Huntington, Samuel, 21, 82, 129, 165, 173, 179, 182
Husserl, Edmund, 79, 167, 178
Hypocrisy, 116
Hypothesis, xi, 2, 8–10, 21, 86–87; in comparison, 132–33, 146–47; in metaphysics, 91–92

Ibn Hayyan, Jabir, 177
Iconic reference, 31–32; *see* Reference
Identity, Confucian or Daoist, 172; temporal, 105; of theologians in comparative projects, 133
Ideology, 52, 110–11
Idolatry, 121
Illusion, 125
Image, divine, 115, 119

Imagination, 8–10, 22
Immanence and transcendence, 72–73
Imperialism, 15; intellectual, 140; Western, 143
Imposition, of categories, 66
Improvisation, 51
Incommensurability, 140
Indeterminateness, 5
Indexical reference, 31–32, 126
India, 40, 125, 148
Individualism, 152, 157
Individuation, 32, 53; of ritual play, 22–23
Indra, 123
Inertia, 51, 57
Infinitesimal, the, 53; Dao as, 47
Influence, of government and business on academic life, 84
Inquiry, rather than method, 80
Instinct, 12
Institution-exercising behavior, 154
Institutions, 104; ministering to, 118–19
Instructions for Practical Living, 61
Integration, 48; horizontal and vertical, 38–39
Integrative philosophy, as beyond comparison, 142–48
Intelligibility, 177
Intentions, in comparison, 127
Interaction, 21; social, 99
Interiority, xv, 126
Interpretation, 8–10, 14, 29–30, 69, 137, 147
Intervention, 52
Intrinsic analysis, 146
Intuition, 79–80, 91
Invisible hand, 105
Iraq, 40
Ireland, 40
Isaiah, 123
Islam, 2, 16, 18, 22, 38, 81, 87, 106, 110, 121, 128, 139, 142–43, 149; Wahabi, 118–29
Israel, 124
Ivanhoe Philip J., 63, 165, 168–69, 174

James, William, 28, 147
Japan, 76; Confucianism in, 151
Jen, see Humaneness
Jeremiah, 123
Jesus Christ, 31, 115–16, 122, 166
Jiang, Xinyan, 141, 184
Job, 123–24
Journal of Chinese Philosophy, 69
Journalism, vs. scholarship 90
Judaism, 18, 38, 128, 143; Second Temple, 128
Judgment, 8–10
Judiciary, the, 20
Justice, 90, 120; distributive, 83, 94, 98, 142, 147; social, 110
Justification, 116
Justin Martyr, 128

K'ang Yu-wei, 60
Kabalistic Judaism, 121–22
Kang Ouyang, xiv
Kant, xiv, 2, 44, 71, 77–80, 87, 91, 93, 178; contra metaphysics, 89–92
Kasulis, Thomas P., 173
Koester, Helmut, 176
Kierkegaard, Soren, 71, 73, 77, 80, 115
Kinds, 2
Kline, T. C., III, xiv, 165, 169
Knoblock, John, 27–28, 164–65, 169
Knowledge, 69
Kohn, Livia, 47, 62, 170, 172, 174
Konstantine, Steven, 131, 182
Korea, 17, 76; Confucianism in, 151, 164
Krejci, Jaroslav, 129
Krishna, 124
Kung, Hans, xv, 113
Kuo Hsiang, 60
Kupperman, Joel, 169

Lagerway, John, 62, 174
Language, 18, 103, 153; biblical, 128
Lanling academy, 81
Lao-tzu, *see* Laozi
Laozi, see *Daodejing*
Laozi, 60, 62
Laplace, 46

Law, 154
Learning, 152; of ritual and humaneness, 102–05, 111
Legalism (the Chinese school of), 39, 41–42, 60, 82, 87
Leibniz, Gottfried, 2, 46, 59, 77, 79, 114, 173, 180
Li Ao, 41, 60, 151, 185
Li, see Principle
Liberalism, 83, 93
Lieh Tzu, 60
Light, of reason or of nature, 78
Lindbeck, George, 182
Liu Shu-hsien, xiii, xv, 64
Loci, of classical theology in comparison, 130–31
Locke, John, 11–12, 79
Locutions, 32
Logical deduction, 9
Logocentrism, 144
Logos, 172
Love, 23, 115–16; in action, 120; with differences, 13; learning to, 104–05; as *ren/jen*, 104; of the world, 114; *see also* Humaneness
Loving the people, 23–24, 115
Lu Hsiang-shan, 60
Lucas, George, Jr., 173, 177–78
Lyceum, Aristotle's, 81

Machle, Edward J., 28–29, 164–65, 169
Madhyamaka Buddhism, 148
Mandate, of heaven, 169
Manifestation, of eternal in the temporal, 46–47
Manifesting the clear character, 23–24, 160
Marco Polo, 59
Marginalization, 9, 144–45
Marx, Karl, 101–02, 106, 109–12
Marxism, xv, 67, 10–11, 68, 76–77, 87
Mary, the Virgin, 122
Material force (*qi*), 5–7, 92, 97, 122
Materialisms, 134
Mathematics, 45, 159; inapplicable to substance metaphysics, 92–93

Maturation, in religious imagery, 122
McKeon, Richard, 66, 134–35, 149, 183,
McLean, George F., xv
McNeill, William, 129, 182
Meaning, 31–32; systems of, 153
Meditation, 116
Membership, xii, xv
Mencius, xii, xiv, xvi, 1, 7, 10, 23, 34, 37–39, 60, 63, 67, 80–82, 85, 87, 95, 108, 115, 151–52, 156, 159, 165, 168; as irresponsible, 34
Meritocracy, 150
Metaphysics (Aristotle's book), 144
Metaphysics, xii, xiv, 1–5, 13, 64–65, 153, 166; in Chinese philosophy, 89–99; in comparative theologies, 130; in Confucianism, xiii; in Daoism, 43–48; dialectical, 50; hypothetical, 44–45; impossibility of, 2–3; as impractical, 92; incompleteness of, 91–92; Peirce's, 30
Method, 177–78; in Descartes, 78–79; as a philosophical concern, 77–80
Microcosm, 5
Military, 119
Miller, James, 47, 172
Mind, 69; external to, 79
Ming Dynasty, 11, 63
Ministry, 118
Missionaries, 59, 129
Missouri, University of, 71
Modernism, 78–79
Modernity, as a problem for Confucians, 68
Moghul Empire, 143
Moism, 13, 42, 77, 81, 87
Monkeys, 49
Monotheism, 121
Montaigne, 81
Moore, Charles, 76
Moral metaphysics, 70
Morality, 20, 28, 69; in professional engagement, 85; public, 115–20
Mother, Dao as, 44, 47
Motivation, unconscious, 109–12
Mo-tzu, *see* Mozi

Movement, 18
Mozi, 13, 60
Multiculturalism, global, 83
Music, 31, 36
Mutazilites, 121, 140
Mystery, 54–55
Mysticism, 159; Daoist, 54

Naiveté, first and second, xv
Narcissism, 37
Nasr, Seyyed Hossein, 182
Naturalism, 153
Naturalisms, in comparison, 134–35
Naturalness, 95
Nature, xiv; vs. institution building, 55–58; interaction with, 21; interpretation of, 153; romanticism, 54; in Xunzi, 18–19
Nazism, 82
Needham, Joseph, 59–60, 173, 180
Negotiation, 118–19
Neo-Confucianism, 1, 20, 41, 59–61, 77, 81–82, 87, 97, 108, 113, 143, 147–48, 151, 185; Song Dynasty, 69–70; *see also* Confucianism
Neo-Platonism, xii, 44–45, 54, 76, 125, 128, 130, 143; in Islam, 177
New Confucians, 70
Nietzsche, Friedrich, xiv, 38, 65, 75, 168
Nivison, David S., 62, 174
Nominalism, 70, 77, 80
Nonbeing, 44–48, 51; flight to, 54
Non-temporality, 4–5
Non-ultimate, 3
Normative comparison, 140–48
Normative measure, 48–51; as catching the beat, 51; defined, 50
Normativeness, 12–13, 17, 44–45, 50–54; of ritual, 156–57; in theology, 129–30
Norms, for objectivist comparison, 134–35
Northrop, F. S. C., 66, 137, 184
Nothingness, 78
Novelty, 46–47
Nozick, Robert, 180

Objectivism, in comparison, 133–40
Obligation, 9, 94, 148; channeled, 12–13
Occasions, 46
Oil, 110
One body with the world, 7, 91, 93, 104, 115, 160
Ontological creation, 48, 53
Ontological power, 47
Ontological-anthropological continuum, 125–26
Ontology, 46
Openings, in the Dao, 51–58
Oppression, 110
Optimizing choice points, 105
Order, 64–66; aesthetic and logical, 48, 138
Ordinary language philosophy, 77
Organic connection, xii
Organicism, 180
Organism, 96
Organization, of behavior by signs and rituals, 33–35
Orientation, defining the self, 157–61
Origen, 121, 128
Originality, in metaphysics, 91
Orthodoxy, 128
Ou, Tsuin-Chen, 167
Own-being, 122
Oxford University, 60
Oxtoby, Willard, xv, 114, 173, 181

Pacifism, 118–20
Paganism, 128
Paideia, 82, 142
Pain, felt for broken tiles, 93–94
Pakistan, 40
Panikkar, Raimundo, 131, 182
Parmenides, 44
Parochialism, in philosophy, 143
Participation, in rituals, 22–23; social, 99
Particle physics, 45
Particularity, 16
Pas, Julian F., 174
Pascal, 77
Past, 46–47; the essential, 96

Patristics, 128
Pattern, 5–7, 35, 48, 51–52, 97–98; Dao as, 47
Paul, St., 115, 128
Peace, 84, 117–20
Peirce, Charles S., xiii, 8–9, 19, 30–32, 44, 69, 75, 77, 80, 91–92, 98, 141, 145, 153–55, 163–64, 166–67, 171, 177–78, 183, 185
Penumbral conventions, 154
Pepper, Stephen, 183
Perennial Philosophy, 130
Performance, ritual, 32
Performatives, 32
Persian religion, 123
Personal relationships, 152
Personalistic imagery, 123–26
Personality, 35–40, 122
Perspectival analysis, 146
Perspectivalism, 49–50, 78; in value, 48
Perspectives, integrative, 51; letting go, 50
Phenomena, as judge of categories, 145
Phenomenology, 79
Philosophers, 54; bridging, 61–64; contemporary, who use Chinese philosophy, 61, 64–73; interpretive, 61–62
Philosophy, 113–14; academic, 84–85, 172; Chinese, xiv; comparative, xi, 144–48 (*see also* Comparison); Confucian, xii, 29 (*see also* Confucianism); constructive, 148; of culture, 64, 137–40; and other disciplines, 84–85; global, xi, 1, 16, 147, 149–61, 165; not a guild with a method, 85; Indian, xi, 87; integrative, xvi; Jewish, 87; living rather than classified, 139–40; modern European, 77–78; of nature, 70; influence on politics, 81–82; defined by practice, 80–85, 87–88; dull prose in, 77; purpose of, 118; as religion, 81; of religion, xi; of science, 70; social, xii; sociology of, 176; systematic, xii; western, xii, 11
Pinyin, xvi

Plato, 2, 35, 44, 46, 50, 61, 63, 77, 80–81, 85, 92, 98, 103, 115, 118–19, 134–35, 140–41, 143, 147–50, 168, 183; lecture on the Good, 135; model of love of, 108–09
Platonism, xii, 70, 76, 87; Christian, 87
Plotinus, 77
Pluralism, 16–17, 91, 121–26, 156–57
Pointing, in reference, 31–32
Poise, in the self, 98
Politics, 51–52, 65, 82–83; in Daoism, 43
Popular religion, vs. sophisticated, 122
Portability, of Chinese philosophy, 149–53
Positivism, 77–79
Postmodernism, 9, 78, 80, 143, 153
Postulation, concepts by, as defining Western culture, 137
Poverty, 16, 33, 105, 110–11
Power, 126; inertial, 54–58; relations, 11
Practice, 31–32, 76
Pragmatism, xii, 8–10, 16, 19, 30–32, 69, 76–77, 80, 86–87, 116–17, 140, 153–55, 167, 177–78; and Confucianism, 140–41
Pratitya samutpada, 44
Preemptive war, 118–20
Present, 46–47; abstract, 105 essential, 96; past, and future, 50
Pre-Socratics, 130
Pressure, released in ritual, 36–40
Primary process, in the unconscious, 107, 109
Princeton University, 60
Principle (*li*), 5–7, 41, 92, 114–16, 119–22, 147; of Heaven, 119; innate, 115–16; transcendent, xii; *see also* Heaven
Process, xii, 92; philosophy, 6, 76–77, 80; swarming, 54–55
Production, means of, 109–11
Professions, 85
Program philosophy, 185
Property, 94
Prose, in philosophy, 80–81

Protestant Reformation, 128
Psyche, 98
Psychoanalysis, 39
Psychocentrism, 129
Psychology, 85
Public, global, 134, 143–44; intellectual, 67, 82–87, 152; life, 152; for philosophy, 82–83, 87–88, 142–44, 173; and private, 17
Puck, 49
Pulses, of Dao, 49–51, 53
Pythagoreanism, 76

Qi, children as bundles of, 104
Quantum mechanics, 46
Quine, Willard, 141
Qur'an, 16

Racism, 117
Radhakrishnan, S., 76
Rahner, Karl, 44
Ramakrishna, 124
Ramanuja, 124
Rantallion, 74
Raposa, Michael L., 167
Rationalism, 79–80, 102
Realism, 72, 75–76
Reality, as a metaphysical problem, 90
Reason, for existence, 3
Reciprocity, 48, 152
Reconciliation, through philosophy, 114; rituals of, 111
Reconstruction, of traditions in normative comparison, 133–34, 151
Rectification, of names, 31–32, 101–02, 110; of the heart-mind, 115–16
Reductionist analysis, 146
Reference, 31–32, 153; iconic and indexical, 167
Reflections on Things at Hand, 61
Relation, 4–5
Relativism, 171
Relativism, 42–43; Daoist, 48–58
Relevance, 84
Religion, 20–21, 95; Confucianism as, 67; defining the good life, 17–18; for Marx, 110; philosophical schools as, 76; as a problem for philosophy, 83–85
Religious philosophy, xi
Ren (humaneness, love, humanity, human-heartedness), *see* Humaneness
Representationalism, 72
Reptilian brains, 33
Republic (Plato's), 115, 168
Research, 84
Respect, of comparison, 132
Responsibility, 9–10, 12–13, 117
Retreat, as forbearance, 118–20
Rhythm, 96–97; for Confucians, 56–58
Ricci, Matteo, 129
Righteousness, 152
Risk, 119–20
Ritual (*li*), xiii, 7, 10–14, 18–20, 57, 62–63, 68, 91, 94–95, 98–99, 101–05, 116–17, 126, 153–55, 158, 169; analysis, 110; appropriateness of, 31; court and religious, 18, 28; Daoist critique of, 41; ethical analysis of, 156–57; of high civilization, 22–23; as false consciousness, 110; family, 19; and harmony of feelings, 107–08; contemporary importance of, 102; of personal integration, 23; kinds of, 153–54; master, 212–22; mastery, 29, 105–09; normative construction of, 157; origin of, 33; as releasing pressure, 39; propriety, xiv–xv, 11, 62, 152–54,; religious dimension of, 39; of threat and counter-threat, 119–20; theory of, 137; training in, 81; value of, 24; in Xunzi, 27–40
Road rage, 37
Robinet, Isabelle, 62, 174
Roles, 23; in families, 36
Roman Catholicism, 128
Roman Empire, 125
Romans (St. Paul's letter to), 115
Romanticism, 143; in philosophy, 80
Roots and branches, 46
Rorty, Richard, 64, 75, 82, 171
Rules, 51; in argument, 145

Index

Rump, Ariane, 171
Russell, Bertrand, 82, 178
Rwanda, 40

Sacrifice, ritual, 39
Sage kings, 29, 34, 37, 150
Sages, 7, 24, 29–30, 120, 152
Sagehood, 94, 102, 115
Sanskrit, 20
Saussure, Ferdinand de, 30, 153, 167
Schleiermacher, Friedrich, 125
Scholar-official, xvi, 67, 69, 82, 118–20
School of Names, 60
Schrader, George, 141
Science, xiv, 6–7, 20, 45, 54, 65, 70, 84, 91–92, 111, 143, 147, 159–60, 172; for Kant, 79–80; natural, 5–7; natural and social, 7–10; social, 13
Scotistic realism, 177
Scottish common sense philosophy, 80
Scotus, Duns, 125
Scriptures, primary and secondary, 151–53
Searle, John, 62, 77, 167, 176
Seasons, 56; rotation of, 158
Secretary General, of United Nations, 22
Sectarianism, xii
Secularity, 110
Self, xiv, 157–61; in Chinese metaphysics, 95; in Confucianism, 152; -cultivation, xii; deception, 106–11; -integration, 107–09; -sacrifice, 120
Selfishness, 7, 11, 23, 29–30, 34, 107, 109, 115; unlearned, 38
Semiotics, pragmatic, xiii, 8–10, 19, 27–28, 39, 98, 116–17, 153–55, 159, 166; explaining diverse religious symbolism, 124–25
Seng-chao, 60
Sensationalisms, 134
Sense data, 79
Seriousness, 24
Service, public, 152
Sex, 109, 155
Shangdi, 123, 169

Shankara, 124
Shao Yung, 59–60, 159
Shen, Vincent, xv
Sherburne, Donald, 171, 179
Shiva, 124
Signs, 8–10; 29–32, 116–17, 153–55; behavior guided by, 19; in orientation, 159; see also Semiotics
Similarity and difference, in comparison, 132
Simples, 78–79
Simplicity, 97
Sin, 115; original, 38
Sincerity, 23, 108, 115–16, 120
Sincerity (*cheng*), 7, 23, 102, 108, 115–16, 120
Singing master, as ruler, 32
Singularity, in comparative analysis, 146
Sinology, xii, xvi, 63
Sites of comparison, 146
Six orthodox schools, 144
Skepticism, 142–44,
Sky gods, 123
Smart, Ninian, 131, 182
Smith, Adam, 105
Smith, Huston, 130, 182
Smith, John E., 141, 173, 177
Smith, Wilfred Cantwell, 131, 182
Social, character of human life, 10–14; context, for Confucian philosophy, 82; contract theory, 11–14; location, 109–12; science, 83, in comparative theology, 129–30, in objectivist comparison, 136–37; theory, in Confucianism, xiii, 1–2
Society, late-modern, 28
Socrates, 142; philosophy of, 76
Son of Heaven, 39
Song Dynasty, 11; Neo-Confucianism, 6
Sophism, 148
Sophistication, cultural, 8
Soul, in Descartes, 78
South Asia, 143
Southeast Asia, 76
Space-time, 4
Specification, in comparison, 132

Specious present, 46
Speculation, 70–71
Speculative grammar, in Peirce, 166
Speech acts, 32
Speech and silence, in Wittgenstein, 79
Spence, Jonathan D., 182
Spinoza, 2, 77, 79, 81, 149
Spirit, in Hegel, 130
Spivak, Gayatri Chakravorty, 167
Spontaneity, xiv, 5–6, 41, 46–51, 53, 95, 101; in administration, 51; vertical, 55–56
Sports, as ritualized aggression, 107
Ssu-ma Tan, 129
Stallknecht, Newton P., 134, 183
Stanford University, 60, 63
Starting points for knowledge, 77–80
Starvation, 13
State of nature, 12–13
Statesman (Plato's), 50
Statesmen, 57
Status quo, 41
Stewart, Dugald, 178
Stoicism, 76, 81
Stony Brook, State University of New York at, 135–36
Straw dogs, 49
Strawson, Peter, 77, 176
Subjective, the, in Daoism, 171
Substance and function, 53
Subtlety, 4, 47, 50; inattention to, 56–57
Sullivan, William M., 85, 179
Superiority, of Chinese to Western cultural tradition for doing philosophy of culture, 66
Supernaturalism, 29
Swidler, Leonard, xv
Symbolic reference, 31
Symbolism, 122
Symmetry and asymmetry, 65
Syncretism, in comparison, 131
System, 141; in Chinese philosophy, 69–70

T'an Ss-t'ung, 60
Tai Chen, 60
Taijiquan, 170
Taiwan, 67, 141
Taking the long view, 56
Tang dynasty, 151
Teaching, 84
Technology, 70, 114, 147
Temporality, and Dao, 46
Ten thousand things, the, 53, 95, 109, 160
Tension, 38
Terrorism, 118–20
Testing, comparative hypotheses, 132–33
Texts, of Confucianism, 7; vs. nature, in interpretation, 30
Thanatocentrism, 129
Theism, personalistic, 121–26
Themes, Confucian, 1–14
Theocentrism, 129
Theology, xi, 85, 113–14, 124; biblical, 182; Christian, xii, 81; constructive, inclusive of comparison, 128–33; Jewish, 81; normative, 129–30; of other religions, 21–22; as the religious part of philosophy, 127; stand alone, 127–29
Theory, 8–10, 76, 31; in comparison, 144; scientific, 45
Thomism, *see* Aquinas, Thomas, St.
Thucydides, 129
Tillich, Paul, 121
Tillman, Hoyt Cleveland, 61, 173, 179
Time, xiv, 54–58; and eternity, 172
Titarenko, Mikhail L., xv
Ti-yung, 53–55
Togetherness, 97
Tolerance, 53, 83; cultural, 16
Tong, Lik Kuen, 64
Toronto, University of, 60
Totum simul, 46
Traditions, xv–xvi, 1, 76, 90, 142–44; changed by comparison, 131; Chinese and Western, 45; Confucian, 107;
Tranquility, 3
Transcendence, 125–26, 138; in Chinese philosophy, 65–66

Transcendental knowledge, 91
Transcendentalism, 166
Transformation, economic, 16–17
Translation, 42, 60, 62
Transliteration, xvi
Trinity, 122, 166; of Heaven, Earth, and the Human, 56–57; in Xunzi, 29
Truth, xvi, 8–10; multiple formulations of, 135–36; and reconciliation trials, 110–11; religious, 125–26, 183
Tsu-jan, 54
Tu Weiming, xiii, xvi, 61, 64, 66–69, 71, 73, 93–94, 108, 113, 115, 140–41, 150, 160, 168–69, 173, 175, 181, 184–85
Tucker, Mary Evelyn, 179
Tung Chung-tzu, 60

Ultimacy, 47; childish representations of, 122; in comparative perspective, 121–26
Ultimate, of non-being, 3; realities, 172; as personal vs. impersonal, 122–26
Unconscious, the, xv, 101–12; in contradiction to conscious awareness, 107–09
Underdetermination, of human nature, 18, 28–29, 32, 35, 39, 56–57, 116–17, 154
United Nations, 85, 117
United States, Chinese philosophy in, 59
Universal love and social location, 111
Universities, 81, 84
University of Hawaii, 64
University of Texas at El Paso, 64
Upanishads, 124
Urmson, J. O., 176

Vacuity, 54
Vagueness, 45, 53–54, 183; in comparison, 132; in rituals, 32
Value, xii, xvi, 3–5, 7–10, 21, 48–51, 116, 148; achievement of, 51; in Confucianism and Daoism, 93–94; as conventional yet normative, 15–18; eternal, 48; as human projection, 5; perspectival, 48

Values, Confucian, 15–25, 68;
Van Norden, Bryan W., 174
Vedanta, 124; *see also* Advaita Vedanta, Vishistadvaita Vedanta,
Vedas, the, 18, 124, 143–44
Vietnam, Confucianism in, 151
Virtues, 51, 63, 117–19
Vishistadvaita Vedanta, 148
Vitally important topics, 92
Volvo, with velociraptor, 37–38
Vulnerability, xi; to correction, 2, 86–87, 133, 143, 146, 178

Wade-Giles, xvi
Wang Ch'ung, 60
Wang Fu-chih, 60, 81
Wang Yangming, xii, 1, 20, 23, 60–61, 63, 67–69, 82, 93, 98, 114–16, 151, 160, 165, 168, 181
Wangbi, xiv, 42, 44–45, 53, 55, 60, 81, 171; as Confucian or Daoist, 55
War, 19, 56, 84; and peace, 148
Warlords, 103
Warring States period, 150, 156
Warrior, 124
Watson, Burton, 169
Watson, Walter, 66, 135–36, 182
Wealth, 16, 105
Weapons, of mass destruction, 119–20
Weber, Max, 65
Weddings, 28
Weiss, Paul, 164, 166, 179
Weissman, David, 177
Wesley, John, 116, 118
Western, philosophy, 87; traditions, xi, 113; values, 15
Whitehead, Alfred North, 2, 6, 21, 44, 53, 60, 63, 70, 77, 85, 92–93, 96, 98, 134, 141, 171–72, 177–80
Wildman, Wesley J., 183
Will, 126
Will, 18, 126; in understanding, 78
Wind, controlling the, 55
Wisconsin, University of, 60, 71
Wittgenstein, 75, 77, 79, 176, 178
Women, oppression of, 117

Wonder, in philosophy, 85
Wong, David, 169
Work, 11
Worship, 126
Wu Kuangming, 42, 61–64, 66, 71–73, 141, 160, 170, 174–75, 184
Wuji, 46

Xie, Wenyu, 170–72
Xunzi, xii–xiv, xvi, 1, 10–11, 18, 27–41, 56, 60, 63, 81, 85, 87, 98, 103, 108–09, 116–17, 151, 153–56, 158–59, 164–69, 180–81
Xunzi, The, 151–52

Yahweh, 123–24
Yale University, 60, 64, 71, 134
Yang Hsiung, 60
Yearley, Lee H., 63, 174
Yen Yuan, 60

Yijing, 6, 47, 54, 59, 69, 70, 97, 141, 151
Yin and yang, 3, 49, 65, 92, 97, 114, 139
Yin-Yang School, 60
Young, John D., 182
Yugoslavia, 40
Yulgok, xiii

Zhangzhai, 60, 160
Zhongyong, see *Doctrine of the Mean*
Zhou Dunyi (or Chou Tun-I), 1, 3, 42, 55, 60, 68
Zhou Dynasty, 11
Zhu Xi, xiii, 1, 24, 27, 42, 60–61, 63, 82, 87, 104, 114, 122, 151–52, 165, 173, 179
Zhuangzi, The, 43, 48, 62, 170
Zhuangzi, 44, 49, 60, 62, 71–73, 77, 80, 141
Zimbabwe, 40
Zoroastrianism, 143

www.ingramcontent.com/pod-product-compliance
Lightning Source LLC
Chambersburg PA
CBHW020329240426
43665CB00044B/1054